The Wine and Food Society's Guide to

Cheese and Cheese Cookery

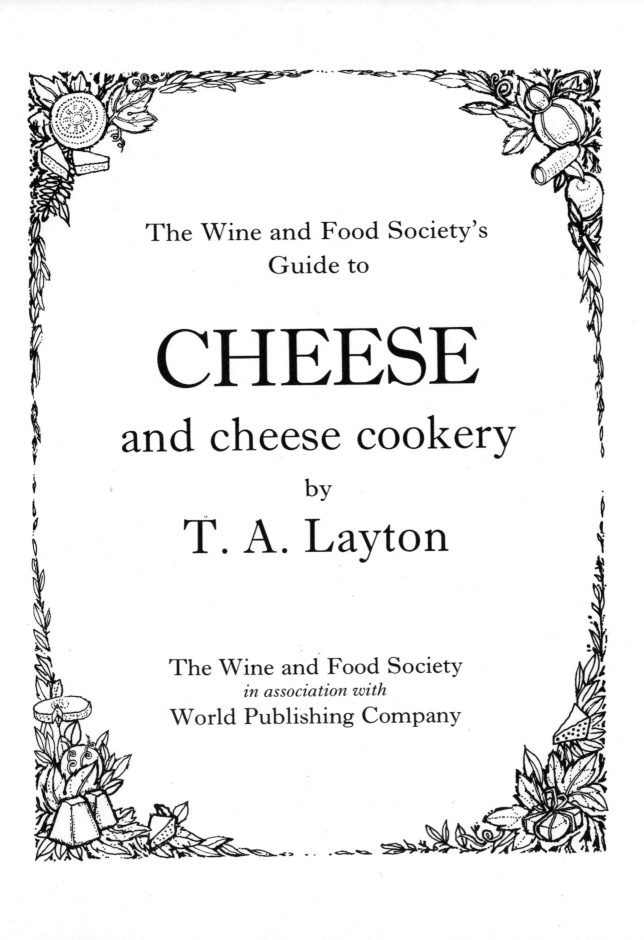

The Wine and Food Society's
Guide to

CHEESE

and cheese cookery

by

T. A. Layton

The Wine and Food Society
in association with
World Publishing Company

A publication of
The Wine and Food Society Limited
in association with
World Publishing Company
2231 West 110th Street, Cleveland, Ohio

Library of Congress Catalog Number 66-22341

This book was designed and produced by
George Rainbird Limited,
2 Hyde Park Place, London, w.2

Phototypeset in Imprint by
Oliver Burridge Filmsetting Limited, Crawley, Sussex,
England

The binding material was supplied by Balamundi Nederland
N.V., Huizen, Holland
Printed and bound in Hungary

House Editors : J. E. M. Hoare and Rosemary Joekes
Designer : Ronald Clark

Contents

List of Color Plates

Acknowledgements

I wish to thank M. Louis Cipolla of the Café Royal, M. René Giordano of the Mayfair Hotel, M. Eugène Kaufeler of the Dorchester Hotel and Geoffrey Sharp Esq., the Garden Restaurant, for the information and help they so generously gave me and also for permitting me to reproduce their recipes.

I am grateful to Mrs D. Mangakis, Mrs Jack Moore, Mrs Alison Wainman and Mrs Jennifer Douglas Webster for permission to include their recipes, and to my old friend Sir Guy Bracewell Smith.

I should also like to acknowledge and thank the following publishers and individuals for permission to quote material from the sources given:

Arco Publications and Major Ellert Forbes, *Recipes of all Nations* by Countess Morphy; Mrs W. A. Bradley, *Aromas and Flavours* by Alice B. Toklas; Cassell & Co. Ltd, *Cassell's Shilling Cookery* edited by A. G. Payne; W. & R. Chambers Ltd, *How to Cook in Casserole Dishes* by Marion H. Neil; Controller of Her Majesty's Stationery Office, *War Office Manual of Military Cooking and Dietary, Part I, 1940*; Country Life Ltd, *Country Recipes of Old England*; Curtis Brown Ltd, *Good Food from Sweden*, by Inga Norberg; Danish Food Centre, London, *Danish Cheese Recipes*; André Deutsch Ltd, *Russian Cookery* by Robin Howe; Gerald Duckworth Ltd, *Cooking and Curing* by Oriana Haynes; Faber & Faber Ltd, *Home Book of Spanish Cookery* by Marina Pereira de Aznar and Nina Froud; Farmers Weekly, *Farmhouse Fare*; Farringtons School, Chislehurst, (in aid of the Freedom from Hunger Fund), *Pot Luck*; Peter Garnett Ltd, Robin Howe and Pauline Espir, *Sultan's Pleasure* by Robin Howe and Pauline Espir; William Heinemann Ltd, *A Guide to Modern Cookery* by Georges Auguste Escoffier; Alfred A. Knopf Inc., *Italian Food* (U.S.A. Edition) by Elizabeth David; Macdonald & Co. Ltd, *Italian Food* (U.K. Edition) Thomas Nelson & Sons Ltd, *Cookery for Every Household* by Florence B. Jack; Oliver & Boyd Ltd, *Moorish Recipes* by John, 4th Marquis of Bute; Random House Inc., *The Complete Book of Cheeses,* Clifton Fadiman's Introduction; Routledge & Kegan Paul Ltd, *Little Dinners How to Serve Them with Elegance and Economy* by Mary Hooper; Spring Books Ltd, *Cooking the Russian Way* by Musia Soper.

The publishers and producers wish to express their gratitude to all those who have supplied technical advice and information and especially to the following for the loan of colour transparencies and illustration material:

The American Dairy Association, Chicago, Illinois; Canada Department of Agriculture, Ottawa; Danish Dairy Office, Aarhus, Denmark; Dutch Dairy Bureau, London; Italian Institute for Foreign Trade, London, Messrs G. Street & Co. Ltd, London, and *Verein zur Forderung des Milchverbrauchs E.V.,* Frankfurt, Germany.

The colour photographs of Messrs Paxton and Whitfield Limited are by Kenneth Swain; the decorations, key drawings and endpapers by Stewart Black.

T. A. LAYTON

Introduction

Many years ago, on a veritable pittance, I started a little wine bar just opposite the British Museum. It got off to a poor start, and so frightened was I of failure that I started serving food. First cold salads, with no success; then hot food at give-away prices, which was a washout; then better food at higher prices. This caught on; the little wine bar and restaurant had quite a vogue for a year or two, and I made money.

The success must be repeated, I felt, so with more capital I found more spacious premises only two hundred yards away up the road and equipped it in comparative luxury. I had been successful specializing in wine; now I felt it was the turn of the food that went with it – cheese. I thought of two famous restaurants in Paris and Brussels which were 'Roasts' instead of the over-worked 'Grills', the Rôtisserie Perigourdine in Paris and the Rôtisserie Ardennaise in Brussels, which I think has tremendous atmosphere. Then I thought of the Cheshire Cheese in Fleet Street, but naturally did not want to be accused of aping any of them. The result was The Cheddar Roast; a very good name, even if I do say so.

Next I turned to the design of the shop and restaurant. I tore out the existing front at great expense and put in a new one of plate glass with a surround of teak. Inside I made a circular counter of one piece of solid teak – wildly extravagant – and organized the restaurant so that no one could get in or out without passing the cheese counter pretty closely.

Then I set off around the shires of England to make discoveries. First, I went Exeter way and got the names of a handful of good wholesalers. I had planned to travel to the north, but at Cambridge I went into an inn for a good lunch and had such a good cut of cheese that I asked the waiter what it was. He didn't know, but sought out the manager who, in a voice made thick by drinking tawny port, told me that he thought it came from a neighbouring village called Cottenham. I would have given up, but it so happened that my car was parked by an old-fashioned grocer's shop and there, in the window, was a fine-looking blue veined cheese called Double Cottenham.

I gave up my trip to Yorkshire, found the village and a local supplier and launched this cheese onto London; I even sold it to several of the big stores.

That, however, was only incidental to offering it in my new restaurant – for which, in the teeth of fierce opposition from every brewer and licensed restaurant in the district, I actually got a licence. The reason they opposed me so vehemently was that at the other restaurant I was trading under a most rare Free Vintners privilege* and, not being clear how it worked, they thought I was up to some hanky-panky.

The day came to open; an inquisitive public turned up to see what was afoot. They had lunch and finished up with the cheese platter. This quite captivated them; I am not surprised because, as they could have anything which was on sale retail, they were partaking of what I knew was the most varied cheese platter that had ever been served in England.

So people talked about it, my reputation as a cheese 'fancier' grew afar and as, of course, this appealed to my vanity, I had to have more and more varieties. I then heard of M. Androuet of the Rue d'Amsterdam in Paris with his cheese restaurant and his fabulous collection; of course, I had to go over and lay on a supply of extra-perishable ones to be brought in by air.

My reputation continued to grow, but the one thing the customers did not do was to buy the cheese to take away; the retail sales side was a disastrous financial failure; for I had overlooked the fact that a van with a driver shooting round London just delivering half pounds of cheese and no other groceries would be murderously expensive. Apart from this the shopping public cannot be bothered to telephone for one item at one shop alone.

Drawing in one's horns is never pleasant, and can hardly ever lead to success, but in this instance it did enable me to carry on for a while longer. Fortunately for me and the restaurant, I cut out the personal deliveries and wholesale buying and concentrated on introducing more varieties of cheese, albeit at a far reduced profit margin. I also developed a technique for better storage of the cheese. My accountants, however, soon proved to me that I was living in a fool's paradise and so the variety had to be cut down; but even so I still boasted the best cheese restaurant in London. So I had my years of cheese fame, and the curious thing is that this has lasted from what was really a failure. That is one of the ironical things of life; one spends thirty

---

*It dates back to Edward III's reign and right to this day, six centuries later, a freeman of the Vintners' Company can sell wine in London without applying to the Justices of the Peace, but only wine, and only under one roof.

years building up an image of oneself as a wine pundit and after all that it is on cheese that the Wine and Food Society ask one to write!

My Cheddar Roast, whose window in Great Russell Street still gives me a twinge to look at, has paid a dividend after all.

CHEESES

There were round cheeses
and green cheeses,
brown cheeses.
Ones with seeds in between cheeses.
There were new cheeses,
blue cheeses.
There were strong cheeses,
long cheeses.
There were cream cheeses
and dream cheeses.
There were even the English stuffy cheeses.
There were the white feathered fluffy cheeses.
There were goat, cow and ewe cheeses;
There were old, very old and new cheeses,
Cheeses with soft rinds and hard rinds,
Cheeses with holes in the middle kinds,
Cheese that could be eaten by cats,
Cheese that could be nibbled by rats,
Some to be eaten with ladles,
Some to be given to babies in their cradles.
There were cheeses from the North.
There were cheeses from the South.
There were dozens of ones which
Melted in the Mouth.
There were cheeses which were abominably smelly,
Fromages de Régime, that is 'good for the belly'.
Cheeses some too good for mortals,
Cheeses to be taken to the portals of heaven
And offered to the gods.

T. A. LAYTON

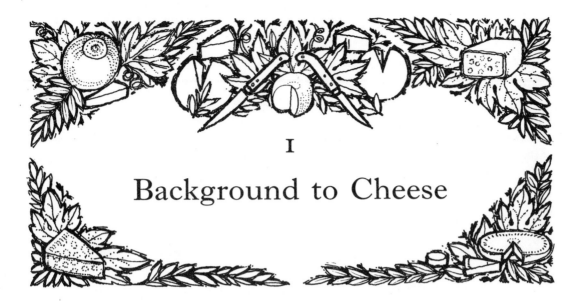

I

Background to Cheese

Mythology tells us that the invention of cheese was ascribed to Aristaeus, the son of Apollo by the nymph Cyrene. The derivation of the word comes from the Latin *caseus* and, in German, Dutch, Irish, Welsh and English before A.D. 1100 it is and was *Käse*, *kaas*, *cais*, *caws* and *cyse* respectively. Later in England it became *cæse* or *cease*, and in the sixteenth and seventeenth centuries *ches*, *chiese* and *schese*.

More interesting, I find, is that the word in Spanish is *queso*, and *queijo* in Portuguese, which obviously means that it has the same Latin root as our English word and yet in the other important countries whose language derives from Latin the word for cheese is quite different.

In France, *fromage* comes from the old French word *formos* which comes from the Latin *formia* and this in turn from the Greek *formos*. This word designated the diminutive rush baskets in which the curdled milk was placed and so took the shape of a little cream cheese.

There are a large number of words which are the same in Spanish, Italian, French and English, and the best example is wine. There are thousands of words which are the same in the three Latin countries yet quite different in Anglo-Saxon, but not all that many are the same in Anglo-Saxon and one Latin country and quite different in the other countries which derive their language from Latin.

Like wine, cheese probably came into being by sheer accident. Persia or Turkey may well have seen its birth when some wandering traveller placed his daily supply of goat's milk into a bag made of some animal's intestines, hoisted himself onto his beast of burden and wandered off. The animal's movement and the hot sun separated the curd from the whey and that accounts for ordinary cheese. The origin of blue veined cheese is, in the same way, complete conjecture, but again legend may well be

13

true. In the craggy, dried-up Causses mountains, where the king of French cheese, Roquefort, is made, they like to tell the following one.

In those far-off days, when brigands were known by some even more ancient name, some shepherds were taking their sheep to graze. Their day's food consisted of a *fromageon*, which is a soft cheese made of sheep's milk and bread. On arrival at the place where they usually rested they placed their frugal meal under a bush and were surprised by marauders who drove the shepherds away and stole their flock. Days later, the men came back with reinforcements to find neither bread nor milk but a greenish mass covered with a blue-green mildew; and so Roquefort was born.

The very earliest references to this food go back nearly six thousand years, and there are quite a few references to it in the Bible. The first is in the book of Samuel, where Saul goes out to fight against the Philistines. Here Jesse tells his son David to take food to his brothers 'and carry these ten cheeses unto the captain of their thousand'. Also in the first book of Samuel we read 'And honey and butter and sheep and cheese of kine for David and for the people that were with him to eat'. There is a reference too in the book of Jonah where the gloomy patient prophet says 'thou hast poured me out as milk and curdled me as cheese'.

Unless one is a Hebrew scholar it is difficult to be dogmatic but I have the feeling, reading between the lines, that the milk of cows was considered somewhat superior to that of others.

I wonder how hard or how soft cheeses were in those very far-off days? One gets the impression that in really distant times they were extremely watery; but if that is the case what would one be doing with a cheese scraper? For there were such things, as witnessed by lines in a play written three centuries before Christ. In this one of the actors says 'Bring a dozen skewers, a meat hook and a small cheese scraper'. This scraper may have been an implement such as a painter uses to scrape paint off furniture, which would indicate a very hard outer rind.

On the other hand, it could have been one of those scrapers the Norwegians use for their curious sweet-sour brown national cheese Gjetost, where a slit in a flat piece of stainless steel enables you to pare off wafer-thin slices which go on to buttered rye bread. If so, that means that the Greeks had achieved a high degree of culinary sophistication, for this odd fudge-like substance needs a deal of blending and boiling.

There were certainly regional cheeses in Roman times, and just as we now have our Cheshire and Lancashire in England, our Livarot from Calvados, our Blue from the Auvergne in France and our Herkimer from Herkimer County, New York State, so in about the first century did Hypata in Thessaly have such a great reputation for fresh cheeses that enterprising middlemen made special journeys there to procure it. Another famous place was the sunny island of Samos, now reputed for its sweet white wine; here the speciality was a sort of hot cheese cake where the cheese was pounded together with honey and spring wheat flour, all cooked up together.

In Rome, all through Nero's, Hadrian's and Caesar's time, cheese was everywhere. Along with dried raisins and olives we learn that cheese was always included in the Roman infantryman's daily ration, and it was also one of the favourite foods of athletes. Apart from being the food of the plebs it was also very much the food of the epicure. It was, we are told, sometimes green in colour, it was smoked and there was a very gastronomic bread occasionally on sale which was seasoned with coriander, aniseed, cheese and oil.

Three other cheese specialities were almost certainly on sale in the streets of the Eternal City, because the Romans liked to have dishes which had derived from ancient Greece. One was a cheese cake called Glycinas, made with sweet white wine and olive oil; Tuniai was another variety of cheese cake, even more popular; and the third was an extraordinary concoction which might have looked like a Burns' Night Haggis, consisting of onions, coriander, raisins, the ever-popular Silphium*, thyme, vinegar and toasted cheese all pounded up with pig's blood.

In the same way as today, cheese was an end-of-the-meal dish and especially one taken to sop up the evidence of heavy drinking. (And, in passing, did they not drink in those great days! Wine at banquets then was supposed to have been drunk mixed with water, but as the meal progressed the master of ceremonies would tend to cut down the proportion of water until the wine was drunk neat. Then there would be a pause and the men would go outside and tickle their throats with a feather – this is all recorded fact – to make themselves sick so they could imbibe again. No wonder cheese – wine's eternal companion – was so popular.)

When I was asked to write this book, the point was particularly made that I should not forget to trace the time or era when cheese ceased to be plain substance and moved into the realms of gastronomy; to write, in fact, about its epicurean evolution. Since the time comes when authors write so much on their chosen subject that they cannot see the cheese for the rind, I took kindly to this direction, at the same time reproaching myself that in the dozens of articles that I have written I had never covered it before.

I have been, apart from my trips to England's shires which I mentioned in the Introduction, to most of the cheese-making districts of France, and my library on the subject is fairly extensive. Why, then, could I find nothing written on this fascinating subject? How, and at what period, did cheese move from kitchen to court or, to be

---

*You cannot get far reading a Roman cookery book without reading about this greatly-prized plant. It yielded up a gum and a resin from which a sauce was made. If my reading of ancient recipes is correct I feel that housewives and cooks dashed it in anywhere.

a little arch, take its place above the salt and not below it? One thinks of such problems unconsciously; a few days, I thought, and I will know; but answer came there none.

The days went by and lengthened into weeks and the only inspiration I had was to think of Carême. Great chefs of the past have always fascinated me, with their control of huge kitchen brigades, using the utmost military discipline, coupled with marvellous inventive genius, which, however, must not get too fanciful or the patrons would be displeased. Alexis Soyer is my favourite, but I admire Carême more than most. He was very much the self-made man and he spent a great deal of his spare time in public libraries trying to better himself and learn more about his *métier*. He took himself most seriously, and a courageous turning point in his life must have been when he actually gave the future king of England notice because the taste of His Royal Highness the Prince Regent, in matters culinary, was not classic enough. 'So I'll take myself to Carême's cook book' I said to myself. 'If there are no cheese recipes, that means that at least cheese as a dish was not much thought of around the time of the Revolution. If there are a good number, then cheese was in vogue'.

He had one recipe, an Omelette au Fromage:

'Grate up a quart of Parmesan cheese and also cut in very small dice a quart of Gruyère which must not be too new. Next break and then beat up a dozen eggs as you would for a *fines herbes* omelette. Add a little salt, grated nutmeg and some butter. Beat it again and add the Parmesan. Melt it all in an oven with 6 oz. of the finest butter. When it begins to cook, throw on the Gruyère; fold over; give the omelette a lovely colour and serve'.

This hardly helped me, for it did not prove anything. Besides, I had been deceiving myself, for I realized that whatever Carême had said or failed to say, certain cheeses were considered gastronomic long before his time, as witness mention of Brie, Roquefort, Maroilles 'and two or three English cheeses not without merit'. Parmesan and Holland cheeses are quoted in the great Parisian work, the *Almanach des Gourmands* of Grimod de la Reynière. Furthermore, one of the 'not without merit' (what chauvinism!) English cheeses would have been Stilton, which as you will see later was never made at Stilton at all – yet which was prized before Carême was born.

This book, therefore, had to be started without one essential piece of information to which research, reflection and luck have perhaps given me the key.

The affluent state! Boredom, striving for something new, combined with the extraordinary if small number of basic foods which exist on this planet.

When there is a struggle for existence you have rye bread, wine from grapes which are surrounded by so many wild yeasts that it soon turns to vinegar, and mousetrap cheese, but when the struggle ends and civilization returns you put caraway seeds on the bread, make Château Margaux and isolate *Penicillium Candidium* to make Camembert.

The point I am trying to make is that cheese has been with us always, but that new varieties have been created when there have been long periods of peace and an upsurge of population, somewhat bored perhaps and wanting something to tickle their palates. It happened as we have seen in Rome with the minor varieties already mentioned. It happened in England in the prosperous days when Stilton came into being; it occurred in Italy with Bel Paese earlier this century, and it is happening in France with new creations being produced yearly.

Cheese, bread and wine have surely one thing in common which is fundamentally different from meat, fish, fruit and vegetables, namely that each comes from a single item – milk, wheat or grapes – and is only made exquisite and fit for Lucullan tables by the ingenuity of man. The other commodities have been there all the time, and the palate of various generations decides whether certain cuts or varieties are staple diets or epicurean. The heron, peacock and porpoise, luxury foods of Plantagenet times, are still with us; and the same applies to chicken. In Victorian times, 'tweenies' would stipulate with great temerity before going into service that they should not have to eat salmon three days a week, while upstairs in the same household whiting *en colère*, that is curled and with its tail tucked into its head, was quite a delicacy. Now the former is well over twenty shillings a pound, while the latter is sold ninety per cent for cats. In the Middle Ages, Winter Purslane was an esteemed vegetable to which we would not give stomach room now. The tomato, first called the love apple and brought over from South America, has been in Britain for three centuries, nearly as long as the potato. Without question, if people had really liked it, more could have and would have been grown.

Cheese and wine, then, will always be changing in texture and flavour to suit various civilizations' palates; some will disappear completely, and no history book will really be able to tell what they tasted like, whereas with meat, fish etc., what our ancestors liked is always there for us to try, though admittedly the sauces they had them with are hard to reconstruct. It is odd to think that perhaps three centuries from now there might be much laughter if someone suggested taking a pet cockerel out of its cage and roasting it!

One cheese which has faded away because others have become much better is – or was – Suffolk. This mousetrap was really unpopular; so much so that servants frequently complained of being served with it too often. Samuel Pepys records how he returned (from wenching and drinking, he secretly recalls) one evening to find that his wife has been very angry 'at her people for grumbling to eat Suffolk cheese'. This was in late seventeenth-century England, when other cheeses were fivepence a pound.

Suffolk was only threepence halfpenny; and it had the nicknames of 'Suffolk Thump' and 'Suffolk Bang'.

Equally unpopular was Essex cheese: both it and the Suffolk were cruelly described in the following jingle:

> They that made me were uncivil
> For they made me harder than the devil.
> Knives won't cut me, fire won't sweat me
> Dogs bark at me but won't eat me.

Going back some four hundred years to the middle of the sixteenth century, we find that there were only four different kinds of cheese. This information comes from a curious book called *A Compēdyous Regyment or a Dyetary of Helth* written by a fun-loving, jovial, much-travelled man, Andrew Boorde – who, incidentally, took himself on the famous pilgrimage to Santiago de Compostela in far north-west Spain and died of drinking bad water on the way back. Writing in A.D. 1542 Boorde tells us that there was green cheese, soft cheese, hard cheese and *spermyse* cheese, which last he says was made of curds and the 'juice of herbs'. These three words give us an extraordinarily interesting insight into cheese making in the Middle Ages, for they lead us to believe that cheese was curdled not only with the rennet coming from the intestines of cows, sheep and other animals but also with certain herbs. One of these, *Gulium verum* ('Lady's Bedstraw'), was also called Cheese Rennet because of its ability to coagulate milk. Another such plant which has a still more interesting history is *Pinguicula vulgaris*, commonly known as butterwort. But it has another country name, 'Earning Grass', and earn is a very old English word (connected with run and rennet) meaning to curdle milk for making cheese.

As for green cheese, this has misled several writers, for it was not one made with herbs like one of my favourites, Sage Derby (which you must eat fresh, as it grows terribly biting) but merely one which was very young.

Between Andrew Boorde and Samuel Pepys came my favourite cheese author of those far-off days. I might not have liked him because, being a self-made man, I do not take kindly to advice from armchair experts; but we do not always run true to style. How Thomas Tusser must have infuriated the small farmer. Up all night with a calving cow, out all day ploughing, cutting firewood by a rushlight at night, he must have had some hard words to say of the author of 'Five Hundred Points of Good Husbandry' who had been a musician, poet, schoolmaster and serving man, and had failed at them all. He had also failed as a farmer, and yet he had had the impudence to tell others how to manage their farms. *And* his book had sold well!

The section on cheese comes into work suggested for April and is in the form of a poem to a dairymaid called Cisley:

> 1. Gehezie his sickness was whitish and drie
>   Such cheeses, good Cisley, ye floted too nigh
> 2. Leave Lot with his piller (good Cisley) alone
>   Much saltness in whitemeat is ill for the stone
> 3. If cheeses in dairie have Argusses lies
>   Tell Cisley the fault in her huswiferie lies
> 4. Tom Piper hath hoven and fluffed up cheekes
>   if cheese be so hoven, make Cisse to seeke cheekes
> 5. Poore Cobbler he luggeth his leatherlie trash
>   if cheese abide tugging, tug Cisley a crush
> 6. If lazer so lothsome in cheese be espied
>   Let baies amend Cisley or shift her aside
> 7. Rough Esau was hairie from top to the fut
>   If chase so appeareth call Cisley a slut
> 8. As Maudlin wept, so would Cisley be drest
>   for Whey in her chases, not lalfe indvgh pest
> 9. If gentils be scruling, call magget the py
>   if chases have gentils, at Cisse by and by
> 10. Blesse Cisley (good mistris) that Bishop doth ban
>   for burning the milk of her cheese to the pan.

A whole host of interest lies in this poem.

1. Until a few generations ago, to 'flot' or 'fleet' was used to describe the action of skimming cream. The utensil used to do it with was called a fleeting dish.
2. Cheese should not be too salt, hence the reference to Lot's wife.
3. Argus was also called Panoptes the All-Seeing and had a hundred eyes. He was placed by Juno to guard Io, and when he died his eyes were transplanted to the tail of the peacock.
4. 'Hoven' is an old word for swollen or puffed up, which cheese should not be. Making Cisley seek cheeks is very far-fetched; it means putting her in a corner, like a dunce.
5. Tough or leathery cheese may arise if it is set too hot, or not worked up, or the curd not broken at the correct time. 'Tug', apart from its meaning of pulling, in those days meant to maul or to pull about amorously.
6. This is interesting: 'lazer' was the old word for leper, but it was also used to

describe cheese made with beastings, the milk of a cow immediately after it had calved.

7. The hairs in the cheese would have come from poor Cisley combing her hair in the dairy.

8. If Cisley had not subjected the cheese to sufficient pressure, it would be too full of whey or too maudlin. Mary Magdalen is often pictured weeping copiously.

9. 'Gentils' are maggots, but the rest of this is a most hideously involved pun. A magpie was commonly called in Provincial England a Magot-pie or maggoty pie from Maggot which stood for Maggie, or Margery or Margaret. That in turn came from the French Margot, an old diminutive of Marguerite. Magot pie meant holy or pious Margery. So the line therefore reads 'If maggots be crawling in the cheese fetch Maggot the py'.

10. This too is involved. It refers to the notorious habit of bishops burning people for heresy.

Shakespeare has a few references to cheese, and in his day those made at Banbury were clearly noted for their skimpiness for, in *The Merry Wives of Windsor* Bardolph says to Slender 'You Banbury cheese!' which tallies with an older quotation 'Like a Banbury cheese, nothing but paring' which comes in *Jacke Drums Entertainment* written in 1600 by John Marston.

Shakespeare makes many a reference to toasted cheese, too, and to the reputation the Welsh had for being so fond of it. 'I would rather trust a Fleming with my butter, Parson Hugh the Welshman with my cheese, an Irishman with my *aquavitae* or a thief to walk my ambling gelding than my wife with herself'.

But the Welsh Rarebit itself was older than Shakespeare for Andrew Boorde has an amusing anecdote on this delicacy:

It has been written in old tales how God made Saint Peter the door keeper of heaven. And furthermore in his infinite goodness God allowed all men into his Kingdom, even those who did not deserve it.

And at this time there was up in Heaven a great company of Welshmen and they babbled and shouted so much that they irritated all those of the other nations so that God said to Peter that he would give almost anything to have got rid of them. To which Peter replied 'Lord, I promise you that this well shortly be accomplished'. And Saint Peter immediately went outside the Gates of Heaven and in a loud voice shouted *'Cause Babe! Cause Babe!'* which is the same as calling out 'Roasted Cheese! Roasted Cheese!'

And when all the Welshmen heard this they all ran out of Heaven. And then Saint Peter went inside and locked the door and kept out all the Welshmen.

If I tell you that Jupiter was supposed to have been in part nourished on goat's milk cheese when Rhea his mother hid him on the isle of Crete; that friezes four thousand years old on a temple at Ur of the Chaldees show a monarch tasting cheese made half of cow's and half of goat's milk; that author John Russell in 1460 in his *Boke of Nurture* states that hard cheeses kept the bowels open; that by 1740 the practice of stamping cheese was common; and that Parson Woodforde records about that time that the latest in cheese was a *ramequin* consisting of 'small slices of bread covered with a farce of pounded cheese and eggs and baked in a dish', then I think I shall have sketched some aspects of its history up to the Victorian era.

One of the times when we shall never know if Queen Victoria was amused or not was in connection with a cheese and for sheer farce there can have been few things before or since to beat it. It shows that the art of public relations is nothing new.

In 1825 a group of farmers gave the then Duke of York a great Cheshire weighing 149 lb. How much His Highness ate of it, history does not relate, but it must have had its share of fame, for when Queen Victoria was married it was decided by the farmers of East and West Pennard in Somerset to put aside for a gargantuan cheese the entire day's milking of 800 cows and to make the largest cheese ever. They succeeded in producing a monster of over a thousand pounds in weight.*

The making was successful and the records are sufficiently accurate for us to know that it was no less than 9 ft 4 in. round and 1 ft 8 in. high. The giant was formally presented to the Queen who graciously accepted it. But the farmers of East and West Pennard couldn't leave well alone, for they next asked Her Majesty if they could borrow the cheese back again as they wanted to put it on show at various travelling exhibitions. The Queen granted the farmers their request. When the cold winds of winter made travelling around with half a ton of solidified milk rather a problem, or when the publicity value had died down, the farmers of East and West Pennard thought that they would extract the final ounce of publicity from the cheese by handing it back again to their sovereign. To their surprise the Queen told them that she was unable to accept the article a second time.

This precipitated a crisis; whether the farmers of the two Pennards had always been at loggerheads but had kept their animosity to themselves in order to show a united front in dealing with royalty we shall never know, but from then on severe quarrels broke out and the cheese became the subject of a Chancery lawsuit.

But, large as this cheese was, America had been thinking along the same lines as far back as 1801, when a huge cheese was made in Cheshire, Massachusetts, and given to their beloved President Jefferson to commemorate his political victory over the Federalists. It created a sufficient stir for the Boston local paper, *The Mercury and New England Palladium*, to publish the following resounding ballad:

*Other accounts give the number of cows as only 750 and the weight 1,232 lb.

THE MAMMOTH CHEESE
An Epico-Lyrico Ballad

From meadows rich with clover red,
A thousand heifers come,
The tinkling bells the tidings spread,
The milkmaid muffles up her head,
And makes the village hum.

In shining pans the snowy flood,
Through whitened canvas pours,
The dyeing pots of otter good,
And rennet tinged with madder blood
Are sought among their stores.

The quivering curd, in panniers stowed,
Is loaded on the jade,
The stumbling beast supports the load,
While trickling whey bedews the road,
Along the dusty glade.

As Cairo's slaves, to bondage bred,
The arid deserts roam;
Through trackless sands undaunted tread,
With skins of water on their head,
To cheer their masters home;

So here full many a sturdy swain
His precious baggage bore;
Old misers e'en forgot their gain,
And bed-rid cripples free from pain,
Now took the road before.

The widow, with her dripping mite,
Upon her saddle horn,
Rode up in haste to see the sight
And aid a charity so right,
A pauper so forlorn.

The circling throng an opening drew
Upon the verdant grass
To let the procession through
To spread their rich repast in view,
And Elder J. L. pass.

Then Elder J. with lifted eyes
In musing posture stood,
Invoked a blessing from the skies
To save from vermin, mites and flies,
And keep the bounty good.

Now mellow strokes the yielding pile
From polished steel receives,
And shining nymphs stand still a while,
Or mix the mass with salt and oil
With sage and savory leaves.

Then sextonlike, the patriot troop,
With naked arms and crown,
Embraced, with hardy hands, the scoop
And filled the vast expanded hoop
While beetles smacked it down.

Next girdling screws, the ponderous beam,
With heft immense drew down;
The gushing whey from every seam,
Flowed through the streets a rapid stream,
And shad comes up to town.

There are records of two other gargantuan cheeses from North America, one at the great Toronto Fair towards the turn of the last century, which weighed 4 tons, and an even bigger one shown at the New York State Fair in 1937.

The Toronto cheese was not only immense but proved exceptionally good to eat; it created an enormous amount of publicity in the whole of the Canadian press, and offers to buy a portion became quite unmanageable.

Undertaker James McIntyre bought a segment after a wait of four hours, but the effort must have been worth it, for James sent in this verse to his local paper:

We have thee, mammoth cheese,
Lying quietly at your ease;
Gently fanned by evening breeze
Thy fair form no flies dare seize.

All gaily dressed soon you'll go
To the greatest provincial show,
To be admired by many a beau
In the city of Toronto.

May you not receive a scar as
We have heard that Mr Harris
Intends to send you off as far as
The great world's show in Paris.

Of the youth beware of these
For some of them rudely squeeze
And bite your cheeks; then song of glees
We could not sing, oh, Queen of Cheese.

I think that early in the nineteenth century ordinary cheeses (that is, non-fancy ones such as Stilton, Brie and perhaps 'Le Chester' as the French called it) were considered rather plebeian and although Lewis Carroll's *The Hunting of the Snark* is pure nonsense we do get a clue in it:

He would answer to 'Hi' or any loud cry
Such as 'Fry me!' or 'Fritter my wig!'
While for those who preferred a more forcible word
He had different names from these.
His intimate friends called him 'Candle-ends'
And his enemies 'Toasted cheese'.

'Toasted cheese'! If we are to believe Mrs Gaskell in *Wives and Daughters* this was one of the most plebeian dishes of all.

'Papa doesn't care what he has, if only it is ready. He would like bread and cheese if cook would only send it in instead of dinner'.
'Bread and cheese? Does Mr Gibson eat cheese?'

'Yes; he is very fond of it' said Molly innocently, 'I've known him eat toasted cheese when he has been too tired to fancy anything else'.

'Oh, but my dear, we must change all that. I shouldn't like to think of your father eating cheese; it's such a strong smelling coarse kind of thing. We must get him a cook who can toss up an omelette or something elegant. Cheese is only fit for the kitchen'.

'Papa is very fond of it' persevered Molly.

'Oh! but we must cure him of all that. I couldn't bear the smell of cheese; and I'm sure he would be sorry to annoy me'.

Mrs Gaskell in another work, *French Life*, written just a hundred years ago, gives us another interesting sidelight on cheese in the provinces of that country:

The *rôti* and the salad follow. The mixing of the salad is too important to be trusted to a servant. Strictly speaking, Madame tells me, the vegetables ought to be gathered when the soup is on the table, washed and cleansed while we are eating the *bouilli* and sliced and dressed with the proper accompaniments while the *rôti* is being brought in.

After this, a chocolate custard or a sweet omelette, a purée of apples perhaps; and then a dressed salad is put on the table – a bit of Gruyère cheese under a glass and the 'Quatre Mendicants', i.e. nuts, almonds, raisins and figs, called after the four begging orders of friars because these foods are so cheap that any beggar can have them.

What is one to make of all this? If the household offered to a foreign visitor a dessert which was so cheap as to be called Four Beggars it would be fair to assume that cheese was in the same category. Yet it was a foreign cheese, and other references lead me to think it was a costly one.

This is borne out by the only reference to cheese in one of the most remarkable gastronomic cook books of all times, Alexandre Dumas' *Le Grand Dictionnaire de Cuisine* which was written around the time of Mrs Gaskell. In its original form it is one of the rarest books in France, but after the death of Dumas, who considered this work to be far greater than any of his novels, an abridged edition giving only the recipes was produced. Called *Le Petit Dictionnaire de Cuisine*, it is still a very long book, and under *Fromages* we read:

There exists a considerable variety of cheeses; the most important are Brie, Holland, Gruyère, Livarot, Maroilles, Camembert, Roquefort and Parmesan.

Not a mention of Stilton, Chester (then highly esteemed), Bleu d'Auvergne or Pont l'Evèque, and yet there is Gruyère linked with Holland. Whatever did they find in the Dutch cheeses in those days?

French literary passages on cheese are frequent but few are memorable; this one is from Emile Zola.

A giant Cantal, seeming to have been chopped open with an axe, stood beside a golden-hued Chester and a Swiss Gruyère resembling the wheel of a Roman chariot. There were Dutch Edams, round and blood-red, and Port Saluts lined up like soldiers on parade. Three Bries, side by side, suggested phases of the moon; two of them, very dry, were amber-coloured and 'full', and the third, in its second quarter, was runny and creamy, with a 'milky way' which no human barrier seemed able to restrain. And all the while majestic Roqueforts looked down with princely contempt upon the others through the glass of their crystal covers.

There is also a very fine poem on cheeses written by Thomas Braun which is so admirably translated into English by Jethro Bithell:

ODE TO CHEESE

God of the country, bless today Thy cheese,
For which we give Thee thanks on bended knees.
Let them be fat or light, with onions blent,
Shallots, brine, pepper, honey; whether scent
Of sheep or fields is in them, in the yard
Let them, good Lord, at dawn be beaten hard.
And let their edges take on silvery shades
Under the moist red hands of dairymaids;
And round and greenish, let them go to town
Weighing the shepherd's folding mantle down;
Whether from Parma or from Jura heights,
Kneaded by august hands of Carmelites,
Stamped with the mitre of a proud abbess,
Flowered with the perfumes of the grass of Bresse,
From hollow Holland, from the Vosges, from Brie,
From Roquefort, Gorgonzola, Italy!
Bless them good Lord! Bless Stilton's royal fare,
Red Cheshire, and the tearful, cream Gruyère.
Bless Kantercaas and Bless the Mayence round
Where aniseed and other grains are found,
Bless Edam, Pottkees and Gouda then
And those that we salute with 'Sir' like men.

The last lines refer to that rich fluffy cheese called Fromage de Monsieur Fromage.
The most famous French saying on cheese is 'A dessert without cheese is like a

pretty woman missing one eye' and was propounded by a man whose book, all these years later, can still be claimed as the only one dealing scientifically and at the same time gastronomically with how the senses of smell and taste work – it is called *Physiologie du Goût* and it appeared in the 1820s. The author was Brillat-Savarin who once was banished to the United States for his views on the death penalty.

Finally in France we come to one of the great gourmands of all time, a man who wrote 'Here we sail from indigestion to indigestion' and records a gastronomic visit to the tables of friends in the provinces with 'Red partridges, quails as fat as chickens, veal for kings, melons for gods, oysters as big as fowls, rabbits fed on sweet-smelling herbs and Roquefort cheese which should be eaten on one's knees'.

The author of these words was Alexander Balthazar Laurent Grimod de la Reynière, born in Paris on 20 October 1758, who lived eating his way through the French Revolution until he died in 1838 in his eighty-first year.

Grimod had hands so badly deformed that he was fitted with two iron contraptions which were then covered with skin. This was done, not so much one gathers to help little Grimod, but because his mother (who thought this was a punishment for marrying below her station) simply could not bear to see the huge bird-like claw which compensated for the fact that the fingers were nothing but stumps. De la Reynière in his youth, thinking that his deformity was all his parents' fault, gave them and his tutors such hell that he was rusticated from Paris and almost literally incarcerated in a monastery, that of Domèore near Nancy. This, it seems, one could legally do with refractory children at that time.

But how well those monks fed him! And it was here that he made the comments on cheese to which I have referred.

Grimod's parents were wealthy, but either they kept their difficult son short of money or they found themselves temporarily short of funds during the Revolution. How lucky for posterity! For de la Reynière turned his hand to editing and writing on the subject of which he was unquestionably the André Simon of his era – wine and food. And with a host of *nouveaux-riches* thrown up by the turmoils of the Revolution, what he produced was bound to succeed. The *Almanach des Gourmands* mentions, under 'Maxims and Reflections', the following:

Cheese we have already said is the biscuit of drunkards; that is, of course, the salted cheeses which, like Gruyère, Roquefort, Sassenage and Gérardmer, provoke thirst and make all pedestrian wine taste good. But between these cheeses and fresh cheeses there is such a difference that one would hardly believe that they were of the same family. The four we have quoted hold a high place among the first group and to these we can add those of Mont d'Or, Franche-Comté, Maroilles, and above all these cheese of Brie, one of the best that is eaten in Paris.

The cheese of Holland and two or three English types are not without merit; Parmesan is hardly used save in *ragoûts*. The fresh cheeses most in demand in Paris are those of Neufchâtel in Normandy and those of Viry. In the housekeeper's room a large amount is made with a base of milk, cream and sugar. But to salted cheeses must be given pride of place; alone they call back the gourmand to the bottle.

The Gérardmer mentioned is now called Géromé, but like the Sassenage (made in the village of that name in the Isère Department) it is now dying out.

Unfortunately the great *Almanach* only came out eight times – the first was in 1803 – since after the death of his parents Grimod became sufficiently well off to devote himself entirely to eating good food and to offering it to his guests. The only disadvantage for the guests was that if, as was usual, they were invited to stay at the old château near Lonjumeau, outside Paris, they found stink bombs going off in their bedrooms, portrait pictures where the subjects either flapped their arms or waggled their tongues, and the likelihood of having to sit next to a dressed-up live pig for dinner – but what a dinner!

To touch briefly on the present century, I feel that *A Little Book of Cheese* by Osbert Burdett is important. Apart from agricultural and technical works this, I think, can claim to be the first discursive book devoted to cheese of the twentieth century and indeed the first of its kind ever in the French and English languages. It is very short, only twenty thousand words, and was beautifully printed by the Curwen Press and published by Gerard Howe Ltd of Soho Square in 1935. One wonders what they thought forty years ago when someone came up with the surely excellent idea of writing a book on cheese. Mr Burdett was an interesting man who had met a number of interesting people – George Moore (I am writing this opposite his house in Ebury Street), John Lane, Robert Ross, C. K. Scott Moncrieff and others – and had recorded his reminiscences of them in two books: *The Art of Living* and *Memory and Imagination together with notes on Suckling Pig, Tavel Rosé and Thoughts on the Corset*. He has dug up a number of snippets on cheese, including this charming one:

> The cheese mites asked how the cheese got there,
> And warmly debated the matter,
> The orthodox said it came from the air,
> And the heretics said from the platter.

Another book deserving of mention is *Cheddar Gorge: A Book of English Cheese* edited by John Squire. My father gave me this fine book for my birthday in 1937, the year it was published, and I confess to treasuring it not only for sentimental reasons but because it is fine, solid and beautifully produced. Sir John Squire took Stilton for himself and then allocated to Horace Annesley Vachell, Vyvyan Holland, Osbert Burdett, Henry Stevens, Ernest Oldmeadow, Ambrose Heath, Moray McLaren, Oliver (*As I was Walking down Sackville Street*) St J. Gogarty and André Simon the following cheeses respectively: Cheddar, Cheshire, Double Gloucester, Leicester, Caerphilly, Wensleydale, Dunlop, Irish and, to the future President of The Wine and Food Society, Blue Vinney. What poor André must have thought of his fellow collaborators, to be given a cheese which was even then so rare as to be well-nigh extinct! But they were wrong; for he has dug up so much cheese lore that his chapter is fascinating. Perhaps an even more difficult assignment was that of the unfortunate Ernest Oldmeadow who was allocated Caerphilly. Like myself he went, on being commissioned, to what he hoped would be the inspiration of his article – the thirty-six-thousand-strong town of Caerphilly in Glamorgan. And like myself he found nothing to help him whatever:

> In that part of Caerphilly town where one waits for the bus, I was heavily depressed. The shops were of the type which by their ugly window-dressing and dogged preference for standardization, do more than anything else to rob industrial towns of such individuality as is within their grasp. The provision stores were displaying 'Canadian Cheddar' but I saw no Caerphilly. Nor did my eye detect anywhere the expected 'Original Shop' which is always to be found in an old place – by the way, Caerphilly is a market town as well as a colliery centre – where some famous dainty has a local habitation and a name. Wherever there is a renowned make of pork pie or sausage, black pudding, cake or toffee, the itinerant epicure counts upon finding in the market place some timber'd and gabled low-ceiling'd establishment called 'Ye Olde Shoppe', where the town speciality is said to be made and sold by the exclusive heirs to the primal recipe. Nor is he surprised or discouraged when, on the opposite side of the market place he comes upon a second 'Olde Shoppe' making the same claim and perhaps urging strangers to be on their guard* against imitators and upstarts. It may be that Caerphilly is likewise furnished. If so I did not chance upon the Shoppe.

Poor Ernest Oldmeadow! He fared no better in Cardiff when, on asking an otherwise intelligent waitress if he could have some Caerphilly, she laughed and 'Evidently she thought it was my little joke; as if I had asked a Piccadilly waiter for Piccadilly cheese or a Lyons waitress for a cheese made of lionesses' milk.'. But he persisted, and the manager was called, who told him that he wouldn't like it, that nobody ever asked for it and that he (the manager) had tried it but that it had gone bad on him.

---

*And it is not only with food that this occurs; when I went to seek the source of the River Loire, I found to my amusement that there were two – or was it three? – farmhouses each claiming that its spring was the one and only true spot.

Much the same was my experience when I paid a special visit to the village of Cheddar some years ago and I found myself describing the place as 'a messy, straggling, dreary little village, one of the worst examples of an unworthy place giving its name to something which is *hors concours* in its class'. The place verily disgusted me: 'At one entrance to the village is a grocer specializing – inevitably – in the product which got its name from the place. The result is deplorable. Single pound and even half-pound 'truckles', those monstrous midgets which all true farmhouse cheese-makers despise, straggle on a slimy marble slab cheek by jowl with processed cheese and (when I was there) a weeping slice of Danish Blue'.

Perhaps the English Cheese Council should make a Model Cheese Town. It might work!

THE MAKING OF CHEESE

There are cheeses, fluffy, feathery and snowy, which are made to last only a few hours, while others like the Saanen in the valley of this name in Switzerland are treated at a very high temperature, have a maturing time of five years and will comfortably last out the century.

How then does one categorize a food of such infinite variety? I would like to divide it into three categories: first, the fresh (i.e. non-fermented) cheeses; second, the fermented, classic ones; third, the packet cheeses.

Let us take Category 1 first. Here the renneting is carried out at a low temperature. Very little rennet is needed, but coagulation takes several days and generally the water is separated out by suspending the cheese-to-be in linen cloths. They always have a slightly acid flavour because the lactic acids have not been fermented out. The French have given designations to these 'fresh' cheeses allowing for the amount of fat in them:

a. Dead white cheeses called 'thin', made with skimmed milk.

b. 'Simple Cream' with 45 per cent of fat, such as Neuchâtel.

c. 'Cream' or 'Heart of Cream' with $55\frac{1}{2}$ per cent of fat.

d. 'Double Cream' with 60 per cent of fat matter such as '*Coulommière Double Crème*'.

e. 'Triple Cream' with 75 per cent fat content such as '*Petit Suisse*'.

To make sure you are getting value for money, look at the label for a sight of the fat content, and pay accordingly.

Category 2, the fermented cheeses, has several varieties:

a. Hard-pressed but not 'cooked' cheeses. (Examples: Cheddar – England; Cantal – France; Tilsit – Germany; Gouda – Holland.)

b. Hard-pressed and 'cooked'. (Examples: Gruyère – Switzerland; Parmesan – Italy.)

c. Soft cheeses which owe their flavour more or less to bacterial growth. Here there are two not very well defined sub-divisions. With Brie and Camembert the curd is not cut, no pressing takes place, maturing occurs over about a month and the flavour comes from the *penicillium* mould. With slightly stronger cheeses like Livarot or Maroilles, the curd is cut, the maturing takes longer and the *penicillium* seems to be washed off to be replaced by another bacterial growth which tends to give off an ammoniac smell.

d. Blue veined cheeses. Here the *penicillium* actually produces a blue mould and is put into the cheese itself during the maturing process in the cellars. For purely commercial reasons, to speed things up, the blue mould is usually grown in the cheese cellars or caves and put into the cheeses by injection (which operation you can often see in Stiltons or Gruyères), but if left to themselves the cheeses will go blue just the same, given time and *if* these bacteria are floating about in the atmosphere.

Category 3, packet cheeses, invite the well-worn cliché that there are packet cheeses and packet cheeses. Some, wrapped in silver foil like America's Philadelphia or a new Continental one which is smooth, creamy and delicately flavoured with Kirsch, deserve to be called great and a variety in their own right. At the bottom end of the scale some of the old-fashioned 'processed' cheeses are an insult to the commodity. When a person feels strongly about something their prose usually gets worse if they write badly and better if they write well. And to my mind one of the finest pieces of splenetic prose has been written by the American gastronome Clifton Fadiman on this very subject:

> We now come to our own land, with which from the cheese point of view we may merge with our good neighbour Canada. A Rembrandtesque picture presents itself, a traumatic picture of light and shade.
>
> The blackest shadow, of course, is cast by processed 'cheese'. The word should always be framed in quotes, for no matter what the law may say I refuse to call this stuff cheese. For me (though it's only fair to say that millions like the stuff) the processed cheeses belong to the same family as ordinary commercial white bread, powdered coffee, cellophaned cake and our more popular carbonated beverages. The most I can say for it is that it is non-poisonous; the worst, that it represents the triumph of technology of science over conscience.
>
> In preparation of this solidified floor wax - often the product of emulsification with sodium citrate, sodium phosphate or rochelle salts; of steaming and blending odd lots of cheese; of paralysing whatever germs might result either in loss of profit or gain of flavour - every problem but one is solved: that of making cheese.

I feel that the phrases 'packaged', 'cellophane wrapped', 'foil wrapped' and especially 'vacuum packed, should be handled with care' are simply ghastly but that the older generation should not become overexcited too readily when they read them.

I used to be violently 'anti' any cigar wrapped in cellophane, even Whiffs, but now, save for a fine Havana (and that is still prejudice), I realize that a wrapped cigar, far from being spoilt, not only retains its flavour but also keeps pleasantly moist.

A Cheshire Cheese is Made – The Modern Way

Modern cheeses made by the English Milk Marketing Board and the other large concerns use oblong stainless steel tanks holding not less than a thousand gallons. These tanks are jacketed, and a turn of the tap brings in steam from pipes from a boiler generally placed in a specially-constructed outhouse adjoining the dairy. The morning's milk is added to the previous evening's milk; rennet is added as a starter whose function is to produce acid in the cheese curd. The curd is cut with an instrument like a huge oblong tennis racket; then it is scalded by turning on the steam. Afterwards the whey is drawn, which is a fancy way of saying that stopcocks are opened to release the whey, which now rushes out along a gulley and eventually goes to feed pigs.

There now remains – in the thousand-gallon tank – a white solid mass which for consistency and looks has a remarkable resemblance to a white rubber sponge. This mass is now cut with a knife into oblong squares the size of a brick. These are wrapped in muslin, stacked and allowed to stand for ten, twenty or thirty minutes according to the acidity content (perhaps the most important point to test in cheese making) of the embryo cheese.

Surprisingly enough, this operation shortly takes place all over again. The muslin bundle containing the large bricks is undone and they are then cut into smaller bricks which are placed on another piece of muslin. A board is placed on this mass, and weights on top of the board.

We can now call the substance cheese, and it is at this juncture that the 'milling' takes place. This consists of dicing it up with an electric grinder with small whirling knives which extract even more whey. At this stage salt is added in the proportion of 2 lb. to every 100 lb. of cheese.

Next the cheese is pressed; not once but three times, and at a higher pressure each time. This takes three days. Then it goes to the maturing room where it is turned, first daily for a week or so, then weekly for a month. At the end of half a year it is ready for eating.

Interior of Cheese Shop: Paxton & Whitfield Ltd, London

Making a Cheshire Cheese – Ninety-Five Years Ago

It was always made in the morning using the last evening's milk. The cream was taken off and half of it was warmed in a shallow pan with a flat bottom until it reached about 100°F. (38°C.), when it was poured into the cheese tub together with the morning's milk and the remaining unheated portion of the evening's milk. The rennet and anatto* were added at this juncture, and of the latter as little as half an ounce (dissolved in warm milk) was sufficient to colour up to seventy-five pounds of cheese. The tube was then closed for an hour to allow coagulation; this started some fifteen minutes after the tube was closed.

The curd was then broken: for cheeses weighing about sixty pounds this would take some twenty minutes. It was then allowed to rest for fifteen minutes to let the whey separate; this was done by gently pressing down a flat bottomed pan on to the curd. The curd was broken up again, and when more whey had been removed a semi-circular perforated board was placed on the curd and a thirty-pound weight put on top which gently squeezed the whey. After this weight was removed, the cheese was cut and pressed, and cut and pressed, and cut and pressed with ever-increasing weights until it was ready for salting, and substantially the same proportion of salt (1 lb. to 45 lb.) was added, as is done today.

The point of giving these two somewhat potted descriptions a century apart is that cheese-making in its essentials is forever unchanging.

A Stilton 'King of Cheese' is Made

In the 1929 Edition of the *Encyclopaedia Britannica* there is a note under the 'Cheese' heading on how to make Stilton cheese. Towards the end, a sentence reads 'The whey drains out and the curd becomes more or less acid and the characteristic blue mould in *due time forms*'.

This is one of those examples when a very careful phrasing has been used to cover up the fact that the author almost certainly did not know all the answers. Of course a blue mould forms, but for the past century at least it has not been formed by accident. It, that is *penicillium glaucum* or *penicillium roqueforti*, has been put there by artificial means.

Stilton is a semi-soft cheese, though up to a point it is made on similar lines to a

---

*Also anatta or annatto; an orange-reddish dye which comes from an Amazon delta plant, the Urulu or anatto. Latin: *Dixa orelana*.

Cheese Warehouse: Paxton & Whitfield Ltd, London

Cheshire or Chester. After warming, renneting, curd cutting and so forth a fair amount of salt (1 oz. to 3 lb. of curd) is added, and the curd goes into round steel hoops 8 in. across and 10 in. high. In the side of these hoops are small holes some quarter of an inch in diameter, for the purpose of draining even more whey. Next the cheeses are turned incessantly and wrapped in linen cloths to rest, always being turned, until the curd is hard enough for the linen to be removed. The Stilton, now white and creamy, goes into the maturing room for the 'blueing' operation to be performed. And operation is an apt word, for each cheese is jabbed or pierced horizontally with a sort of knitting needle attached to a wooden handle. This process is repeated no less than sixty times on three different occasions so that it receives 180 inoculations of the *penicillium*. Actually this operation has now, more often than not, been mechanized in that the cheese is clamped onto a sort of rotating machine and a foot pedal contrivance does the piercing. This inoculation has been done artificially for more than a century, for one can assume that what is described in a book as usual practice and without comment can be assumed to have been practised for at least fifty years.

Here then is how Stiltons (note that they were so creamy that they took at least four times as long to mature as now) got their mould in the last century, from *Farming for Pleasure and Profit* by Arthur Roland (Chapman and Hall, 1879):

Nearly two years is required to bring Stilton cheeses to perfect maturity, which are not generally considered at their best until somewhat decayed. The blue mould may be communicated from an old cheese to a much younger one by removing pieces of the former with a cheese scoop or taster and interchanging them. The operation in fact consists of the transposition of the mould plant from one to the other which grows in most warm cellars, but the cheeses selected for the inoculation should, however, of themselves be dry and the blue mould of the old cheese be quite free from any portion bearing a more decayed aspect.

A Camembert Comes into Being

I quote from a rather enthusiastic handout I picked up in Normandy.

It is very French and the Normans have proof that it was first made in their region even though it is now copied in every part of the world.

And as they have been enabled to reserve exclusive manufacturing rights they have formed themselves into a group called the Union of Normandy Producers with the object of keeping up standards and particularly of seeing that all Camembert offered is a minimum of 45 per cent fat milk.

You will enjoy this table* cheese especially from June to September and of course with bottled cider, but also with innumerable wines such as Clos de Vougeot, Arbois, Jurançon, Riesling and Rhine wines.

I call that one of the most blatant examples of over-egging the cake which I have ever come across. How can any one food go especially well with such widely differing wines as that majestic powerful red Burgundy and those delicate Rieslings?

The brochure tells us that in the making Camembert is neither cooked, nor pressed, nor *malaxée*, which I found means kneading until soft, but as the rest of the description vaguely skirts certain essentials I think my own report may be better, particularly as it was written on the same day as my visit to the heart of the Camembert district and to several factories there.

The thing which is unusual in making this cheese is that hardly any of the whey is drawn off. First the milk (and $3\frac{1}{2}$ pints go into the making of each cheese) is turned into curds and whey which then go straight into the special moulds. These are the most important instruments in the making; in former days they were made of wood, now they are of tin, but plaster is more and more in evidence. They are cylindrical, $4\frac{1}{2}$ in. tall and $4\frac{1}{4}$ in. in diameter, which is only a $\frac{1}{4}$ in. less than the finished product. In the sides of the cylinders are some twenty holes, half the diameter of a very small pea, through which drains the whey. The filled moulds are given around seven to nine hours for the whey to drain away, by which time they are sufficiently firm to allow for the turning. This sounds quite a simple operation but it is in fact a skilled task. At this time a flat piece of metal is dropped on to the mould. It is very light, and not, as I imagined, to press the cheese, but to see that the curd falls evenly.

Twenty-four hours later the salting operation begins. Actually it is quite a simple one to do, for it consists of a woman throwing coarse salt all over the cheese, which she then places on wire slats. These now nearly-completed Camemberts rest here till the early hours (between 4 and 5 a.m., they told me – I was not up in time to see them) of the next day when another worker salts the cheese on the other side. This is done by the men – the women stay in bed.

What is done next is the most curious and unusual operation of all, for now all these small cheeses are sprayed over with a white liquid fungus called *Penicillium Candidum*. This mould may well be grown on the walls of the factory for all I and the producers know, but with such a big industry and with so many cheeses at stake it is necessary to be more sure than this and supplies come from an outside commercial firm. The mould arrives in a metal canister which looks rather like a fire extinguisher. To this a funnel is connected and at the pressing of a button the spraying begins.

*In contradistinction, one supposes, to a cheese you have with 'wallop' and spring onions.

This is not the only method, however, for I visited a factory where they mix the fungus in powder form (it looks very like icing sugar) into the salt. One wonders if a true Camembert expert could detect on his palate the difference between the two ways.

2

A.B.C.
of the World's Cheeses

Aber (Czechoslovakia). A fairly soft ewe's milk cheese made in Bohemia.

Allgäuer Bergkäse (Germany). Also called Allgäuer Rundkäse and Allgäuer Emmentaler. These cheeses, copied from Swiss Emmenthal, are very popular as they come from a fertile district running down into the valley of the Emme in Switzerland.

Allgäuer Emmentaler (Germany). See *Allgäuer Bergkäse*.

Allgäuer Rahmkäse (Germany). Always a splendid cheese. It resembles Limburger but is milder. Sometimes flavoured with caraway.

Allgäuer Rundkäse (Germany). See *Allgäuer Bergkäse*.

Altenburger (Germany). A soft goat's milk cheese made in Thuringia in central Germany.

Anejo (Mexico). The word means 'old'. This cheese, when covered with chili powder, is called Enchilado and is fiercely hot.

Appenzell (Switzerland). Named from the East Canton of Appenzell. Probably produced from the days of Charlemagne (742–814). It is steeped for a few days in a liquor of cider or white wine to which spices are added. The rind and curd are golden, the flavour delicate.

Appenzell Rass (Switzerland). As above, but made with skimmed milk. Steeping in liquor for several weeks results in a pungent cheese.

Asadero (Mexico). The meaning: 'suitable for roasting'. Also called Oaxaca after that state, although usually made today in the state of Jalisco. It is a white, whole-milk cheese melting quickly when heated. The hot curd is kneaded into loaves weighing from 8 oz. to 11 lb.

Asiago (Italy). A semi-cooked Grana-type cheese originating from a commune of that name in the province of Vicenza. The cheese, resembling Pecorino, is flat and round and weighs about 20 lb.

Augelot (France). A Pont l'Evêque cheese made in the Vallée d'Auge.

Aura (Finland). A 'Danish Blue' type cheese.

l'Aunis (France). A triangular, ewe's milk curd cheese seldom made now and eaten only locally around Poitiers.

Backsteiner (Germany). Meaning 'brick'. This cheese is a kind of Limburger-Romadur.

Bagozzo (Italy). One of the numerous varieties of Caciotta; a hard yellow-bodied, sharp-flavoured cheese, the outside of which is often coloured red, made in and near Brescia.

Bandal (India). A cream or soft cheese made on the same principles as Surti, but not smoked. The fat content is high and the flavour mellow, as it is made from cream. It does not keep so long as smoked Dacca cheese. Calcium and phosphate enter the cheese in the original milk, also soluble salts corresponding with the amount of whey not pressed out from the cheese. The amount of milk used in the manufacture of these local cheeses is very small indeed.

Banon (France). These extremely strong goat's milk cheeses are made by peasants in Provence and each pretends to possess a secret recipe. When made, the cheeses, wrapped in herbs, are dipped in *eau-de-vie-de-marc* and then placed in stone jars. They ripen in 2 months.

Barberey (France). A soft cheese resembling Camembert. Commonly known as

Fromage de Troyes, though it derives its name from Barberey near Troyes. Warm milk is coagulated with rennet for 4 hours, then put to drain in a wooden mould with a perforated bottom. After 3 hours the cheese is placed in an earthenware mould and taken out after 24 hours. It is then salted, dried and ripened for about 3 weeks. In summer it is sold without being ripened.

Bath Cheese (England). This cheese is no longer made, but here is the old recipe: Heat fresh milk to 90°F., add rennet to bring it to a curd in 4 hours. When curd no longer sticks to the finger take cheese out of setting vessel and place it in layers in mould on straw mat. Turn mould over on to a board repeatedly until whey has drained and the cheese has become solid. Spread salt over it with a feather. When it is covered with a fine mould it is ready to eat.

Bauden (Czechoslovakia). Also called Koppen. Herdsmen in the Sudeten mountains make a pungent cheese from the sour milk of goats. It is sold in two shapes, one conical, $3\frac{1}{2}$ in. in diameter and weighing about 1 lb., the other cylindrical, 5 in. in diameter and weighing about 2 lb.

Beaufort or Gruyère de Beaufort (France). Made from cow's milk between June and September in the highlands of the Jura and Savoy mountains on the same principles and of same shape as Swiss Gruyère, but it is richer and more buttery. It is like a small millstone and is not supposed to form eyes. Sizes vary from 70–140 lb.

Bellelay (Switzerland). This delicately-flavoured cheese, also called Tête de Moine (Monk's Head) was made in the fifteenth century by the monks of the Abbey of Bellelay near Moutiers in the Bernese Jura, but is now manufactured in dairies of the district. It has a soft buttery consistency and is over 50 per cent fat. Taking more than a year to mature, it will keep for 4 years in a cold cellar.

Bel Paese (Italy). First made in Melzo, Upper Lombardy, but it is a newcomer and was not marketed in Italy much before 1921. Bel Paese (beautiful country) is the trade name for cheeses known locally as Fior d'Alpe (Flower of the Alps), Savoia, Caccio, Reale (Royal) and Vittoria.

It is one of the most popular, uncooked, sweet, mild, fast-ripening, soft cheeses, though it never runs like Brie, Camembert or Pont l'Evêque. It is pearly white and has a rubbery texture which is most agreeable to the palate.

Made from fresh whole cow's milk, preferably pasteurized, it is 'started' with an active lactic 0·25 per cent in strength. At 108°F. rennet is added so that the curd sets in about 20 minutes. This curd is cut, first by hand, then with a rake to prevent matting and to get the whey out quickly, and transferred to moulds, the whole process taking only 30 minutes from the time the lactic acid is added.

When they have been turned for a while the cheeses are given a bath for nearly a day in an 18 per cent brine solution at 55 °F. and are then put in a curing room where the temperature is 40°F. and where they are sprinkled with a little fine salt.

After the curing has begun, a brownish slime appears on the skin. This is desirable and helps give the finished cheese its characteristic flavour. Weight 4½ lb. and 6 in. in diameter. A Bel Paese is ready to eat within 5 weeks of making.

Bierkäse (Germany). Germans sometimes put this small round cheese into a tankard of Munich beer and when it has dissolved they drink it.

Bitto (Italy). First made in Friuli but now also made in the Adda valley and in Lombardy: a firm, semi-cooked cheese similar to Fontina and Montasio, made from cow's milk, ewe's milk or goat's and cow's milk mixed. It is heated to 93–98°F. and enough rennet added to coagulate the milk in 30 minutes. The curd is cut up and heated to 122–133°F., then dipped, pressed and dry-salted for 25 to 40 days. Curing can take as long as 2 years. When not fully cured it is eaten as a table cheese; when fully cured it is grated and used for cooking.

Biza. See *Fajy*.

Bleu d'Auvergne (France). Manufacture began in the middle of the nineteenth century in the Auvergne, south of Clermont-Ferrand. It was intended to copy Roquefort but Bleu d'Auvergne is less piquant and is made from cow's milk only. The best is the blue veined Bleu Fermier. Milk is collected in the summer from many farms in the Auvergne mountains.

From 5 gallons of milk a cheese weighing about 5 lb. is made. It is a rich cheese with 45 per cent fat content, and acquires a sharp, characteristic flavour when mature. As it has no crust, only a filmy skin, each cheese is wrapped in silver paper with a green band. Output 6,000 tons a year, i.e. half Roquefort's.

Bleu de Bresse (France). A small, rich, imitation Gorgonzola made near Lyons.

Bleu des Causses (France). Similar to Bleu d'Auvergne, but made in the Gascony and Guyenne area near Bordeaux. It is matured in caves, as is Roquefort, and the market for it is increasing.

Bleu de Laqueille (France). Made south-west of Puy-de-Dôme in the Bleu d'Auvergne cheese district. It resembles Roquefort but in order to produce a harder crust it is drained and salted at a much higher temperature. Gourmets at Lyons (they think their town is the gastronomic headquarters of France) love it for its curiously scented taste. Faster maturing than Roquefort. Output only 1,500 tons a year.

Bleu de Sassenage (France). Chiefly made in the Isère region, it resembles Gex cheese in texture and flavour. A semi-hard, blue veined, round cheese made from cow's milk and sold in two sizes: one weighing just over 1 lb., the other $4\frac{1}{2}$ lb.

Blue Cheshire (England). The cheese is no longer made with blue veins, though this could probably be done by needling and inoculating a fungus. Some Cheshire cheeses turn blue – if at all – through a lucky fault about a month after manufacture. Manufacturers may deliberately 'blue' the cheese, but as it is well known that blue veins are freaks, they would not advertise the fact.

Blueford (Canada). Blueford and Eremite are trade names for Canadian blue cheeses made from cow's milk.

Blue Vinney (Great Britain). This cheese is sometimes called Dorset Blue and very occasionally Blue Veiny. Vinney is probably not a corruption of 'veins', but is derived from an Old English word meaning 'to become mildewed'. The word is a dialect form of *fenny* or *finny*, which in turn comes from the Old English word *fynig*, meaning 'mouldy'.

During the last 25 years writers on cheese have been fascinated by Blue Vinney. It is the rarest of the genuine district types left in England, and for this reason its flavour is more highly praised than it should be. It can never be a great cheese because it is made from skimmed milk. The cheeses (about the size of a Stilton) can become as hard as granite. It is even said that a train was once run using Blue Vinney instead of metal wheels. When fresh the cheese is rather dry and crumbly.

Bola (Portugal). A semi-hard cow's milk cheese of the Edam type and the most popular in Portugal.

Bondon (France). A small, unripened, whole-milk cheese of the fresh Neufchâtel type. The curd is frequently stirred and when sufficiently drained is pressed in a cloth between weighted boards. Salt is added and the curd placed in moulds $2\frac{3}{4}$ in. deep and $1\frac{3}{4}$ in. in diameter, lined with wax paper.

Bougon (France). A popular goat's milk Poitou cheese very similar to Chabichou.

Bra (Italy). Named after the town in Piedmont where the cheese was originally made by nomads. It is a salty, hard, almost white, compact cheese, sharp and salty in flavour. Partly-skimmed milk is heated to about 90°F., rennet is added to coagulate it in about 35 minutes. The curd is cut into rice-sized grains, the whey drained off, and the curd then placed in moulds for 12 to 24 hours. It is removed several times in the early stages of pressing, broken into coarse pieces and repacked. The cheese is sprinkled with salt and also immersed in brine, after which it is cured. Each cheese weighs about 12 lb.

Brandkäse (Germany). During the ripening process the rind is either moistened with beer or the cheeses put in disused beer kegs, or both. Each cheese weighs only about 6 oz.

Brick (U.S.A.). A genuine American cheese, perhaps so-called because it is made in the shape of a brick or, more likely, because bricks were formerly used in the pressing. It is semi-soft; less sharp and softer than Cheddar and less pungent but harder than Limburger. It has small eyes or holes and has been described as 'The married man's Limburger'.

Bricquebec (France). Bricquebec is a little Normandy town and the priest who shows visitors round the lovely Trappist monastery a mile or so away says there is no such cheese as Bricquebec. A St Paulin (close copy of Port Salut, *q.v.*) is made here and sold under the registered name of Providence.

Brie (France). Has been known for several centuries. Henry IV of France (1553–1610) was given some by Queen Margot. The Great Condé (1621–86) demanded that Brie should accompany a Victory wine. At the Congress of Vienna (1814) Talleyrand sent for a Brie which won a gastronomic competition against sixty cheeses from participating countries. A French historian has even asserted that this victory restored France to the esteem of the other European Powers.

Brie, a soft-paste cheese, is made in the department of Seine-et-Marne and three different varieties are named after Melun, Coulommiers and Meaux. Slightly salted renneted cow's milk is used and the cheese, unskimmed, unheated and unpressed, has no rind, only a reddish-brown mouldy crust marked with white. Its fat content must not be less than 44 per cent and it is always circular in shape.

If Roquefort and Stilton are the kings of cheeses, Brie is the only queen. Like a woman, it is capricious; five times out of six it will be dry and chalky – a sign of unripeness – but the sixth time it will be perfection.

Bruxelles (Belgium). A soft, fermented cheese made from skimmed cow's milk in farms near Louvain.

Bryndza (Czechoslovakia). A ewe's milk cheese called Brinsin in Germany.

Bryndza (Hungary). A typically Hungarian cheese sold in four different sizes, weighing 10, 20, 40 or 60 lb. It is made from renneted ewe's milk and has a fat content of 45 per cent of its total dry matter.

Brynoza or Brynza (U.S.S.R.). A processed cheese made in Russia.

Burgos (Spain). A very popular soft cheese named after the province of Burgos from whence most of it comes.

Buttiri (Italy). A Calabrian variety of a Cacciocavallo. A large knob of butter is put inside the cheese, which is shaped like a huge elongated fir cone, so that each segment contains both butter and cheese.

Cabecou (France). Some three million flat, round, goat's milk cheeses, weighing only a few ounces, are sold yearly.

Cabrales (Spain). Although these goat's milk cheeses are made in the highlands of Asturias and Santander by peasants ignorant of modern cheese-making techniques they succeed in producing 'blue' cheeses similar to Roquefort. Their flavour varies. Some possess a characteristic fragrance which has been described as pestiferous.

Cabrion (France). A goat's milk cheese made in Burgundy at the time of the vintage: it is soaked in *eau-de-vie-de-marc de Bourgogne* and ripened in the fresh husks of pressed grapes.

Cacciocavallo (Italy). Originally made in the province of Sorrento but now comes from the Abruzzi, Molise, Lazio and from many parts of north Italy. It may have acquired its name because the cheeses are dried in pairs, suspended by plaited straw halters, one on each side of a pole, as if astride a horse. It is a hard uncooked cheese made today from whole cow's milk. The curd is drawn, the strands being drawn out in very hot water. Each cheese is shaped by hand into a figure 8, the upper part being from one-tenth to one-twentieth of the size of the lower. The strands terminating at the tip of the upper part are sealed off with boiling water. The cheeses then spend 3 or 4 days in a salt bath and if they are to be eaten they are hung up to mature for from 2 to 4 months, but if to be grated and used in cooking they need from 6 to 12 months. The cheese has a smooth firm texture and keeps and travels well. It is whitish in colour, and in taste a cross between a Gruyère and a Cheddar.

Cachat (France). A cheese that used to come from Provence, where it was made of left-over pieces of cheese put into sandstone pots to ferment with brandy, salt, pepper and mixed herbs.

Caciotta (Italy). Cheeses made on small scale by individual proprietors. They are always put out in flat cylindrical forms and usually weigh from 1–4 lb. Cow's, ewe's or goat's milk is used and the cheese is semi-cooked. There is a wide variety of flavours. The best known are Caciotta Toscana, Caciotta di Urbino, Bagozzo, Cacio Fiore, Chiavari and Fresa.

Caerphilly (Great Britain). The population of this Glamorgan town, seven miles from Cardiff, is 36,900. It is famed for Caerphilly Castle, mighty stronghold of Gilbert de Clun, and is remarkable in that not one shop in the entire place sells Caerphilly cheese. This white, rather crumbly cheese lacks the elasticity of Cheddar, matures in three weeks, and does not keep long. It is probably the most easily digested amongst English cheeses and is popular with Welsh miners in the district, for they can eat great quantities of it and still do a day's work.

The cheeses are made in a flat circular shape, 9 in. in diameter and $2\frac{1}{2}$–$3\frac{1}{2}$ in. thick and weighing about 8 lb. They have recently been copied in other parts of the country, mainly in Leicestershire. In Wales they have been made for longer than can be remembered.

Cambridge (Great Britain). This cheese used to be made in a little village less than twelve miles from the cathedral city of Ely, but is now rare. It was brick-shaped, dented on the top and consisted of alternate layers of firm snowy whiteness and soft, pale buff-coloured cream. Each cheese stood on a small, spotless straw mat.

Camembert (France). You will find how Camembert is made in Chapter I; this is just a background to the cheese.

The place where it all started is in the *commune* of Camembert in the Orme department. If you take the side road from Vimoutiers to Trun you will come, after driving a few miles along beautiful twisty lanes flanked by lush fields, to a crossroads at one corner of which is a square, 8-foot-high tapering stone obelisk, on which an inscription reads: 'EN L'HONNEUR DE MME HAREL NÉE MARIE FONTANE QUI INVENTA LE CAMEMBERT'.

There is no commemorative plaque on the farmhouse where Madame Harel used to live, and no Camembert is made in the commune nowadays. There was once, however, a grand statue of Madame Harel built into the Halle aux Toiles overlooking the enormous square of Vimoutiers. Unfortunately, Madame's imposing image – or at least her head – succumbed along with most of the best parts of the town to the Allies when the town was reduced to rubble a few weeks after D-Day, 1944. This posed an awkward problem for the re-developers later on – what can one do with a headless statue? When I was last there she was being used as a lean-to for a concrete block to cover sewage traps. At that time there was talk of the imminent appearance of a new statue, so perhaps by now she is reinstated.

Camosun (U.S.A.). The method of making this semi-soft, open-textured cheese was developed by Washington State College in order to use up surplus milk on farms. It takes less time than the granular or stirred-curd process. Drained curd is pressed in hoops about 6 in. in diameter and 7 in. deep, salted in brine for 30 hours, then coated with non-odorous paraffin wax and cured for 1 to 3 months in a humid room at 50–60°F.

Cancoillote (France). A curious freak cheese, which is beginning to be made outside its original home in the Jura mountains. Skimmed cow's milk, renneted and cooked in a moderately hot *bain-marie*, is then melted and mixed with white wine, fresh butter and aromatic herbs. The cheese is packed in tin boxes and can be used as a spread.

Canestrato (Argentine). A hard cylindrical yellow cheese made from cow's milk; renneted and moulded in baskets. The rind is uncoloured, the flavour sharp, the smell pleasantly assertive. It takes at least 8 months to mature and weighs from $13-17\frac{1}{2}$ lb.

Canestrato (Italy). See *Incanestrato*.

Cantal or Fourme du Cantal (France). Named after a department roughly at the centre of the Bordeaux-Lyons-Marseilles triangle. In this mountainous region the cheese has been known since Roman times and is France's nearest cheese to Cheddar, being hard and yellow.

Pliny the Elder (A.D. 23–79), Platina and many other men since then have praised these cheeses, of which the best today is Cantal Haute-Montagne. It is made with cow's milk from one herd only, grazed on pastures rich with Alpine flowers.

Cantal is made in cylindrical *fourmes* or forms, 12–20 in. across, average height $15\frac{1}{2}$ in. It ripens in 3 months in the cold caves of the mountainside, should improve with age and weighs from 75–120 lb., but smaller cheeses are made when the best milk is in short supply.

Caprino Romano. See *Pecorino*.

Carentan (France). This is a town of some 5,000 inhabitants half-way between Bayeux and Cherbourg. Carentan and Isigny are the centres of a big Camembert industry, but they do not manufacture types of their own.

Carré de l'Est (France). The square cheese of the east; that is, Alsace-Lorraine's rival to and a good copy of Camembert. Each cheese is about $3\frac{3}{4}$ in. square with rounded corners and weighs from 6–7 oz.

The curd is chopped before draining. The paste is fairly soft, slightly salted, neither pressed nor cooked. Fat content should not be below 40 per cent and it has a mouldy reddish-brown crust. It has the flavour of a mild Maroilles but its 'bouquet' is much more gentle. There are two sorts, Carré de l'Est fleuri and Carré de l'Est lavé.

Casigiolu (Italy). Also called Panedda and Pera di Vacca. It is a plastic-curd cheese made in Sardinia by the same method as Cacciocavallo.

Cassette or Boulette (Belgium). A soft cheese, fermented at a high temperature, seasoned with salt and pepper, hand-pressed and shaped into balls, each wrapped in walnut leaves or pressed into little osier baskets. Made in the Huy, Namur and Dinant districts.

Cebrero (Spain). Cheese named after Piedrafita del Cebrero. It looks like a short-stemmed wide-cap mushroom about 4 in. thick, from 14–16 in. in diameter, varying in weight from 6–10 lb. The rind is pale yellow, the paste free from holes, of fine texture, softish, creamy, slightly sharp, with slight blue veining.

Chabichou (France). A cheese made in Poitou from April to December.

Chabris (France). A goat's milk cheese made in the Indre department by the same method, of the same size and shape as Camembert and packed in similar boxes.

Champoléon (France). A hard cheese similar to Cancoillote made from skimmed milk in the Hautes-Alpes.

Chantelle (U.S.A.). A semi-soft, ripened cheese made in Illinois and cured in the same way as Bel Paese.

Chaourcé (France). Copy of Camembert, but weighs nearly 1 lb. Very small production of only 12 tons a year. Made around the *commune* of Chaourcé in the Champagne district and mostly eaten locally.

Charolles (France). Cheese made wholly or in part from goat's milk, cylindrical in shape and weighing 5–7 oz. (Note: From Charolles farms come the white Charollais cattle famous for beef.)

Chavignol (France). Small goat's milk cheese weighing only 2 oz. They are also called officially Crottin de Chavignol. Crottin means 'dung'. Not a good cheese.

Cheddar (U.S.A.). Every year 900 million pounds of this American Cheddar are made all over the country in many varieties. The technique of producing rindless cheese has increased consumption. Cheeses departing from standard size and weight (i.e. 14 in. in diameter and from 70–75 lb.) are called Daisies, Longhorns, Flats, Twins and Young Americas.

Cheddar (Canada). Cheese production on a commercial basis dates from 1864, when Harvey Farrington built his first factory in Norwich, Ontario. The success was immediate and other factories opened, first in Ontario, then Quebec. In 1868 6 million, in 1885 79 million, in 1900 200 million pounds of Cheddar was exported to England. In 1904 over 1,000 factories, chiefly in Ontario and Quebec, exported 234 million pounds.

The cheese is made from unpasteurized milk (in this differing from American Cheddar) and is sometimes known as Canadian, Store or Bulk Cheese. When mature it equals English Farmhouse Cheddar. Distinctive types are Cherry Hill and Black Diamond, which is a Black Rind.

Cheddar (Great Britain). Some years ago I made a special trip to the village of

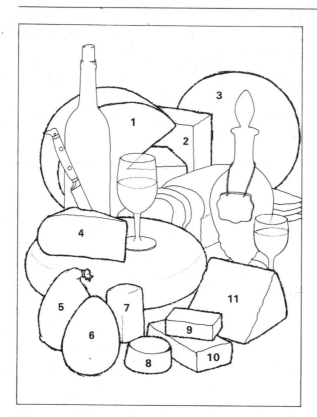

American Cheeses

1. New England Sage
2. Brick
3. Dry Jack
4. Monterey Jack
5. Pineapple
6. Pineapple
7. Schloss
8. Breakfast
9. Pimento Cream
10. Cream
11. New England Sage

Cheddar and the disenchantment was intense. This messy, dreary little village is one of the worst examples of an unworthy place giving its name to something which is *hors concours* in its class; for a firm farmhouse Cheddar, made from the milk of Shorthorn or Ayrshire cows, is superb.

At one entrance to the village is a grocer specializing – inevitably – in the product which got its name from the place. The result is deplorable. Single pound and even half pound 'truckles', those monstrous midgets which all true farmhouse cheese-makers despise.

How the cheese came to be called after the village, not a soul in the place knows or, of course, cares. And furthermore, there seems to be little evidence that fine cheeses have ever been produced in the surrounding countryside.

The true home town of Cheddar is Wells, a beautiful bustling cathedral city with a charm surpassed only by Bath itself. Here trades one of the largest suppliers of cheese-making equipment in the country, also one of the very few private cheese factors left in the industry. A few miles away is Shepton Mallet and if you make

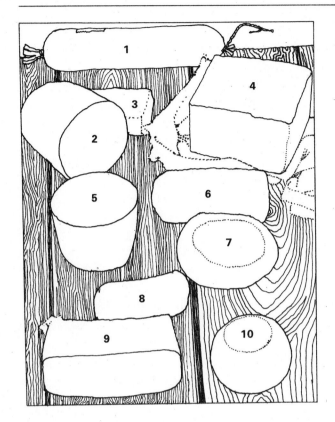

Austrian Cheeses

1. Processed Smoked Cheese
2. Smoked Cheese
3. Kleiner Wachter
4. Edelpilzkäse
5. Smoked with Salami
6. Limburger
7. Handkäse
8. Hartza
9. Trappische
10. Butterkäse

circles on a map around these towns you will find that they take in the best farmhouse Cheddar-making establishments of the district.

The making of the cheese has already been described but another most interesting operation is the testing. When the cheeses are ready for market they will in all probability be purchased by a factor who will store them for a while before passing them on to the wholesaler. The factor's buyer (or now often a Milk Marketing Board inspector) will grade and taste the cheeses, and for this he will use a wooden-handled steel-bladed contraption called a cheese-iron or a cheese-trier. What is less commonly known is that there are different shapes of triers for different cheeses.

The way they work is as follows. Imagine a piece of piping slit lengthwise down the middle, sharpened at one end and attached to a handle at the other, in all it is about eight inches long. This is driven into the cheese with a sharp jab to pierce the linen cloth. When the trier is pulled out it brings with it a circular bore of cheese. The expert looks at this and nicks about a quarter of an inch between his forefinger and thumb and tastes it. He then returns the remainder of the bore to the cheese.

The types of trier are as follows:

For Cheddars and Cheshires there are five designs

    (*a*) blade length 5 in., gauge $\frac{3}{4}$ in., no taper.

    (*b*) blade length 5 in., gauge $\frac{11}{16}$ in., tapering to $\frac{5}{8}$ in.

    (*c*) blade length $4\frac{1}{2}$ in., gauge $\frac{5}{8}$ in., tapering to $\frac{9}{16}$ in.

    (*d*) blade length $4\frac{1}{2}$ in., gauge $\frac{9}{16}$ in., tapering to $\frac{1}{2}$ in.

    (*e*) blade length 6 in., gauge $\frac{3}{4}$ in., tapering to $\frac{1}{2}$ in.

Then there are three designs of soft cheese triers:

For Caerphilly, blade length 5 in., gauge $\frac{1}{2}$ in., tapering to $\frac{3}{8}$ in.

For Stilton (*a*) blade length 6 in., gauge $\frac{5}{8}$ in., tapering to $\frac{1}{2}$ in.

          (*b*) blade length 7 in., gauge $\frac{5}{8}$ in., tapering to $\frac{1}{2}$ in.

There is also a cheese skewer. This is like a 5 in. long, thin paper-knife, with a groove on one side. This is pushed into the side of the cheese and a minute amount adheres to the groove.

Cheshire (Great Britain). Curiously enough, on the Continent, this cheese is usually called Chester from the ancient Roman town of that name. The true cheese-making centre is the town of Whitchurch, 20 miles to the south. This town is quite near the salt-mining town of Northwich and there is little doubt that the saltiness of the surrounding pastures contributes to the special flavour which characterizes Cheshire.

Salt plays an important part in the manufacture of all cheeses. Wensleydale, Cheddar, Lancashire, Stilton and many others of this type all have salt added to the curd at the approximate rate of $2-3\frac{1}{2}$ lb. to 100 lb. of curd. Port Salut, Roquefort, Edam and Bleu d'Auvergne have an equal proportion rubbed into their outer skins.

There is a variation in the amount of salt which is added to Cheshire, depending on the time of year.

a. The Early Ripening. This is a soft Cheshire made in the early spring times of the year, not pressed very hard and sold locally. This has almost 2 lb. of salt to 100 lb. curd.

b. The Medium Ripening. This is made in May, June and September and is ready for eating 6 weeks later. More whey is run off than for the Early Ripener and it is subject to greater pressure. It contains over $2\frac{1}{2}$ lb. of salt to 100 lb. of curd.

c. Long Keeping Cheshire. Made generally in July and August, it is ready for sale 4 months later but will keep for a year. Greater pressure is exerted in squeezing out the whey, and 3 lb. 2 oz. of salt to 100 lb. of curd is used. More crumbly than a Cheddar and less pungent, this cheese has often been rated higher than Stilton for flavour and excellence.

Fortunately, Cheshire has not been copied as much as Cheddar, probably because of the important part played by the soil in the production of its special flavour. At any rate you are safe with Cheshire. If you go into a grocer's shop for a piece of Stilton, Cheddar or Caerphilly, you are likely to find yourself with a piece of white chalk or a substance which takes the skin from your mouth.

Chevreton (France). A goat's milk cheese whose potency varies according to the breed of goat and the time of milking. Feared by many and immensely enjoyed by some, this cheese, placed always on rye straw mats, ripens in 15 days. A hard rind forms, but the inside of the cheese (rectangular and weighing about 12 oz.) is runny, soft and smooth.

Chevrotin (France). Not to be confused with Chevreton. Chevrotin is a fresh goat's milk cheese, sometimes eaten with sugar as if it were a petit Suisse. These cheeses are uncommercial and are ripened in quaint little wooden cages placed on wooden poles some 4 ft above the ground by the peasants. Made all around Lyons.

Cincho (Spain). A hard cheese made from ewe's milk, called Cincho or Campos, is made in the same district that produces Villalon.

Colby (U.S.A.). A cheese similar to Cheddar which can be made from either raw or pasteurized milk, but the curd is not matted and milled. As it has a more open texture and contains more moisture than Cheddar, it does not keep so well.

Comté (France). Owes its name to the Franche-Comté country where from the fourteenth to the nineteenth century it was commonly known as Vacherin, whereas today it is usually called *Gruyère français*. It is made, like its first cousin Gruyère, of cow's milk slowly 'cooked' and its shape is the same. The eyes are few and smaller than those of Emmenthaler and the sides of the 'millstone' are straight instead of curved in. Comté keeps, travels and cooks well.

Coon (U.S.A.). This cheese is a Cheddar cured by a special patented method. Ordinary Cheddars are cured at 40–50°F. and a humidity of 70 per cent. Coon cheese, coloured to a deep chocolate brown, is very crumbly and is cured at 55–70° F. and at a humidity up to 95 per cent. High quality cheese is required for the curing conditions and mould grows on it readily because the temperature and humidity are high. Coon has a strong tang and is a favourite of those who prefer a fully cured, extremely sharp cheese.

Cornhusker (U.S.A.). A cheese similar to Cheddar and Colby, with a softer body, more moisture, and taking less time to make.

Cotherstone (Great Britain). This blue veined cheese is also called Yorkshire Stilton but it is rarely seen. About 1939 a white Cotherstone could be bought which tasted not unlike a cross between a Port Salut and a Bel Paese.

Cottenham, Double (Great Britain). Cottenham is a village about 6 miles from Cambridge and sixty from London. If its inhabitants are asked whether they have ever heard of the cheese, they deny it with astonishment. However, in 1934 or thereabouts, it did exist and Messrs Flack and Judge, Provision Merchants of Cambridge, used to send supplies regularly to London. At that time it was creamier and better than good Stilton. Very few references to it exist.

Creole (U.S.A.). A soft, unripened Cottage-type cheese made in Louisiana for the New Orleans market from equal quantities of Cottage-type curd and rich cream.

Crescenza (Italy). Often called Stracchino Crescenza. Made in Lombardy, Piedmont and Venice, originally from September to April, but refrigeration now makes it possible to produce it all the year round. An uncooked, soft, creamy, mildly sweet, fast-ripening pale yellow cheese made from whole cow's milk. Weight from 1–3 lb.

Crottin de Chavignol. See *Chavignol*.

Cuajada (Venezuela). Cuajada (meaning 'curdled') contains more cream than the similar Queso de Cincho and is generally wrapped in banana or maize leaves. Much eaten by country people.

Dacca (India). Dacca is a small, medium-pressed cheese. Milk is clotted with rennet, the curd broken by hand and put into small wicker baskets and whey pressed out by weighted boards. After 10–14 days the cheeses are sufficiently dry and develop a thin coat of hardened cheese due to evaporation. They are smoked with wood or cow-dung, which has a sterilizing effect, and keep well for a month or two. Some people dislike the tarry flavour due to the smoking.

Damietta. See *Domiati*.

Danblu (Denmark). This cheese was probably sold almost exclusively as a substitute for Gorgonzola. We should be grateful to Denmark for large quantities of it during those lean years. In Denmark it used to be called Danish Roquefort but was made with cow's instead of ewe's milk. French Roquefort is very salty and not often seen in England when most creamy and pungent. Officially a Danblu should have a 50 per cent fat content, when the extreme saltiness of the cheese is offset by its creaminess and the flavour is delicious.

Danbo (Denmark). Used to be called Danish Steppe cheese. Belongs to the Samsoe family and is similar in taste. It weighs only 13 lb. and is about 10 in. square and 3 in. high.

Danish Blue (New Zealand). This country has created no cheese which is exclusively her own. New Zealand Cheddar represents 99 per cent of the cheese made. A copy of Danish Blue has been successfully produced but in very limited quantities.

Danish Brie (Denmark). The Danes have created national names for their copies of foreign cheeses and have produced cheeses very similar to the originals. Danish Brie, however, has no resemblance in shape and little in taste to a French Brie. It is quite excellent, creamy, freely running, intriguing to the palate; but it is *not* a Brie.

Danish Camembert (Denmark). An excellent copy. Usually stays in a runny state longer than a French Camembert and is almost as good.

Danish Edam. See *Molbo*.

Danish Emmenthal (Denmark). A good copy of Swiss Emmenthal.

Danish Gorgonzola. See *Mycella*.

Danish Steppe Cheese. See *Danbo*.

Dauphin, Le (France). So called because Louis XIV, on his way to take possession of the country after the Treaty of Nimeguen, was accompanied by the Dauphin. They were presented with this variety of Maroilles which has retained its name ever since.

This spiced Maroilles, much sought after by lovers of fine old wines, is made by taking a three-day old cheese from the maturing room and mixing in some chopped tarragon, powdered cloves and pepper. Then it is put back to mature. Rarely seen and only made to special order.

Demi-sel (France). A small fresh cream cheese wrapped in paper and made in many parts of France but specially delicious in Normandy. Its salt content is 2 per cent and butter fat content must not be less than 40 per cent of its dry matter.

Derby (Great Britain). The *Grocer's Manual* says 'Like Dunlop'. O. Burdet's *Little Book of Cheese* says 'Resembles Lancaster'. *Complete Book of Cheese* says 'A factory cheese said to be identical with Double Gloucester'. Having quoted these three opinions my own is that it is like a mild, pale, soapy Cheddar. See also *Sage Derby*.

Dil Peyniri (Turkey). Made throughout the country in comparatively small quantities. Turkish cheeses can be bought on the market at Istanbul, Izmir, Mersin, Adana and Ankara. Small quantities are exported to Greece and some of the Greek islands.

Cheese-makers encourage farmers by advancing them cash in the late autumn or early winter (according to the number of their cows, ewes and buffaloes) in return for their undertaking to deliver milk in the coming season.

Domiati (Egypt). This is Egypt's national cheese but is now made in other Arab-speaking countries. An official in the Egyptian Embassy, in a letter explaining how it is made, also calls it Damietta, after the small port on one of the mouths of the Nile.

It is made from whole or partly-skimmed cow's or buffalo's milk and is a soft, white, mild, salty cheese. Salt is added at the beginning of the cheese-making process before renneting: this is unusual. Although mild when young, it can be kept for a year, when it darkens in colour and acquires a marked tang. If the cheese is made in a jacketed vat a constant setting temperature of 95–100°F. is advisable. After a coagulation period of 2–3 hours the curd is poured into metal hoops or wooden forms lined with mosquito netting. Wooden forms may hold 100 lb. of curd or as much as a ton.

If Domiati is to be marketed as fresh cheese it is wrapped in waxed paper; if cured, it is pickled in earthenware containers in salt-whey or salt-brine, and cured for 4–8 months for the local markets. For distant markets it is sealed in tin containers. 100 lb. of cow's whole milk makes about 25 lb. of cheese and 100 lb. of buffalo's whole milk makes 33 lb. to which 7·5 per cent of salt is added.

Double Cottenham. See *Cottenham*.

Dreux (France). This cow's milk cheese, which used to be wrapped in chestnut leaves, is made in the department of Eure-et-Loire.

Dunlop (Great Britain). This, in fact, is Scotland's only national cheese and is made mainly in Ayrshire. It is deep cream and more or less a copy of Cheddar.

Edam (Holland). Was first made around Edam in North Holland and is also called Tête de Maure and Tête de Moine. It is factory made: there is no farmhouse Edam. The fat content is always low and it is copied by every cheese-making country in the world. When these cheeses, shaped like flattened footballs, are exported, they are coloured bright red and then rubbed with wax. The taste is that of pleasant soap. Usual weight: 3–4 lb.

Edam (Australia). Australia produces cheeses copied from types developed in older countries, particularly in Europe, but does not manufacture as much of this copy of Dutch Edam as of Cheddar.

Edelpilzkäse (Austria). A very popular full-cream soft cheese weighing nearly 12 lb. made in the Steiermark. The paste has slight blue veining and may become crumbly if kept. It has a curious mouldy rancid flavour unlike that of any other cheese.

Edirne (Turkey). A soft white cheese made from ewe's milk with a fair proportion of butter fat. The greater the quantity of milk used, the better the cheese. The annual production is about 15,000 tons.

Edirne is named after the *vilayet* or province of that name which borders the Greek-Bulgarian frontier, but the cheese is now also made in the provinces of Trakya, Konya, Afyon, Bursa and Ankara.

Egg Cheese (Finland). Take 6 quarts of milk and 8 raw eggs. Add the eggs to the starter and mix with the milk. Egg cheese is the result. This was probably first done in the province of Nyland.

Elbo (Denmark). One of the Samsoe family, but milder yet full of flavour. Square or oblong in shape. Weighs 12 lb.

Emmenthal (Switzerland). Gets its name from the Emmenthal Valley in the Canton of Berne and has been known as a fine cheese from the sixteenth century.

It is difficult to make; three different types of bacteria are used as starters, *Propionibacterium stermanii* being the one responsible for forming the eyes.

According to regulations, an Emmenthal for export must weigh not less than 145 lb., but these great millstones weigh usually near 160 lb. The minimum fat content must be 45 per cent.

Method of Making. Never less than 2,000 lb. of milk (2,500 lb. makes a cheese of 185–200 lb.) is put into a double-jacketed copper kettle which has a steam chamber at the bottom and is heated to some 86°F. After this, when the curd is firm enough to cut, a remarkable instrument known as a Swiss harp (it is like a very large tennis racket with the strings running only lengthwise) cuts the curd into long rectangular strips of 1 in. thick. Five minutes later the curd is 'harped' again; that is cut and mixed until the particles are some ⅛ in. in diameter. Next the curd is 'foreworked', i.e. stirred, for half an hour. When firm enough it is heated in boiling pans 6 ft across and 3 ft high to a temperature of 125°F. At this moment the Emmenthal-to-be looks like a bubbling mass of boiling breadcrumbs being agitated by a giant electric whisk.

When the moment comes to take the cheese out of the kettle it is scooped up into a coarsely-woven dipping cloth attached to a sort of thick brass rail with a handle. This rail fits snugly round the cauldron, enabling the cheese to be successfully scooped up into the cloth, which hangs for a while above the cauldron so that the remaining whey is strained off.

Then the cheeses are pressed, put into a cold room (temperature 55°F.) and salted in brine. Ten days later they go into another warmer (65–70°F.) room for 6 weeks, when the main maturing takes place, and it is here that the propionic acid starts making the holes. Finally the Emmenthal goes into a colder room for a further 3 or 4 months which can be extended to a year on request.

Emmenthal (Denmark). A good copy of Swiss Emmenthal.

Enchilado. See *Anejo.*

Epoisses (France). Named after a little *commune* south of Dijon in the Côte d'Or, whence the great Burgundies come and where it has been made for many centuries. It is a mould-inoculated small cylindrical cheese 6 in. in diameter and weighing some 12 oz. When it is flavoured with black pepper, cloves or fennel seeds, and soaked in white wine or *eau-de-vie de marc*, it is known as *Epoisses confits au vin blanc* or *au marc de Bourgogne.*

Esrom (Denmark). This used to be called Danish Port Salut and is without doubt one of the finest and approaches most nearly a traditional cheese. No cheese is milder, yet no cheese has a more definite flavour. It is almost white in colour, soft and pliable to the tongue and has small holes in it. It keeps fresh longer than French Port Salut, maybe because of the compact, sensible, brick-like shape. Weight 1–3 lb., 2 in. high, 7 in. long, 4 in. wide. Experts say you should eat the rind.

Faiscre Grotha (Ireland). The name means 'a compression of curds'. A curd cheese eaten when fresh. It is stated that a woman could carry several of these cheeses in a fold of her cloak.

Fajy (Iraq). A rarely marketed cheese made from skimmed milk. Not renneted but heated and flavoured with wild onion, garlic or *caoob*.

Fetta (Greece). A so-called 'pickled' cheese, soft, spicy and usually very salty, made originally of ewe's milk by shepherds in the mountainous region north of Athens, but now produced in many parts of the Balkans. Such soft cheeses should be eaten soon after making because their water content is high and they do not keep.

Fresh milk is poured into large containers, heated to about 90 °F., rennet is added and the curd broken or cut. It is then spread on a coarse cloth for draining. The firm curd is cut into blocks and during the day dry salt is rubbed into both sides. The following day the blocks are cut into 1 in. thick slices, salted and packed in wooden kegs holding from 100–170 lb. or in smaller tin containers. The cheese is ready to eat in about a month.

For small-scale production, the curd is dipped into a cloth bag after the milk coagulates. This is twisted and worked to expel most of the whey and then hung up to drain overnight. The curd is taken out of the bag and cut into slices about 1 in. thick and these are liberally sprinkled with dry salt. About 24 hours later the curd is packed in wooden kegs and the cheese is ready to eat in 4 or 5 days.

Fetta made from pasteurized milk is the best variety for export, as it keeps longer.

Fiore Sardo (Italy). A hard ewe's milk cheese. When immature it is eaten, when fully cured it is used for cooking.

Flavoured Process Cheese (U.S.A.). These cheeses are America's effort to break away, at least partially, from European tradition, although their cheese manufacturers have learned to produce very good copies of traditional European cheeses. I arranged for the Agricultural Department of the U.S. Embassy to fly over a selection and expressed my gastronomic approval to a representative of the Embassy. The young man enthusiastically praised American process cheese and arranged for samples to be sent to me. Six varieties arrived, each in a neat, cellophane packet, one flavoured with pimento, another with pineapple and a third with bacon. I tasted them. They reminded me of soap. I was unable to detect the flavour of any of the added ingredients.

I decided that if all America liked such stuff, it was useless to tilt against it, and I should have left out all mention of process cheese had I not come across the writings of a well-known American cheese-lover, Clifton Fadiman, which I have already quoted on page 31 of my introduction.

Fløteost (Norway). Flote in Norwegian means cream. The cheese is similar, although it contains more cream, to the famous Mysost.

Foggiano (Italy). Made in Apulia from ewe's milk. Resembles Moliterno.

Fontainebleau (France). This is a *triple crème* cheese made in the region of the Île-de-France round Paris. It is a mixture of cream and curd well frothed up. Excellent with strawberries.

Fontina (Italy). One of the fullest of Italian cheeses, made principally in the Val d'Aosta, Piedmont, but also nearby in Switzerland. Yellowish, between semi-soft and hard, made from ewe's milk (milk from separate milkings is never mixed), it is made in the same way as Gruyère and often has a few small eyes. Swiss Fontina is the better as a table cheese and Italian Fontina for cooking. Fontina is the only proper basis for a *fonduta*, a famous Turin dish, because it melts easily. It is perfect, too, on a dish of *polenta*. Summer Fontina, which is the best, has a slightly smoky flavour due to being made in the huts of mountain herdsmen. The individual way in which it is made is responsible for the great variety in size and weight, i.e. from 4–40 lb.

Fordhall Cream Cheese (Great Britain). At first the Hollins family of Fordhall Farm, near Market Drayton, concentrated mainly on soft cheese and yoghourt, then on cottage cheeses, then experiments were made with soft cheese and onion, soft cheese and tomato, soft cheese and parsley. These were successful enough, but still the Hollins were not satisfied; so they tried three really unusual ones, soft cheese with curry and raisins; with horseradish; with nuts and wine. Now they have developed a large number of new varieties, including cream cheeses with watercress; pineapple; cucumber; celery; piccalilli; pickled walnuts; lobster; chives; chutney; and caviar.

All the vegetables used are compost grown.

Fourme d'Ambert (France). A cow's milk cheese, similar to Roquefort in type and shape, made in the Auvergne.

Fourme de Cantal. See *Cantal*.

Fresa (Italy). A Sardinian variety of Caciotta. Fresa di Atunza is the best and is made in autumn for immediate consumption.

Fromage Mou. See *Maquée*.

Frühstückskäse (Germany). A Limburger-type cheese made from cow's milk. It is eaten fully or lightly cured. Yeasts and moulds grow on the cheese surface followed by 'red-cheese' bacteria as in Romadur. These cylindrical cheeses, from 2½–3 in. in diameter, are wrapped in tinfoil or parchment. If wrapped when partly cured the cheese is completed at a temperature of 42–45°F.

Fynbo (Denmark). The cheese is named after a large island situated in the heart of Denmark and used to be called Danish Gouda. Very mild in flavour; one of the Samsoe group. Weight 15 lb. and round in shape.

Gammelost (Norway). Gammel ('old') refers to the old method of making this potent cheese from sour skimmed cow's milk instead of using rennet. The best is produced in the counties of Hardanger and Sogn. The curd is pressed hard in cloth bags, then taken out, broken up and packed into covered forms lined with linen. Boiling in whey for 3½ hours alters the cheese's texture and practically sterilizes it. The next day the cheese is taken out of the forms, dried for a day or two in a warm place and then inoculated. Inoculation with various moulds produces the blue-brown-greenish veining. Heat and humidity are controlled during curing and each cheese is turned daily or every other day and rubbed and cleaned if necessary. The curing period takes about a month or longer.

Gammelost is round and flat, usually about 6 in. in diameter and from 5–6 in. thick, weighing between 5 and 9 lb. Larger cheeses are occasionally produced weighing over 25 lb.

Gautrias (France). A cylindrical cheese resembling Port du Salut produced in the department of Mayenne.

Géromé (France). The town and valley of Gérardmer, some 70 miles south of Strasbourg, give their name to this cheese. It resembles Munster except that its production is dying out. It is one of the most ancient cheeses of France and is mentioned as one of the tithes paid to the old emperors of Germany and the dukes of Lorraine. In size and shape it is similar to Munster, but in order to introduce variety it is often flavoured with aniseed.

Gex (France). Also called Septmoncel or Bleu du Haut Jura. This is a cow's milk, blue veined, Roquefort-type cheese made in dairies, all in altitudes over 2,500 ft in the Jura Mountains and the Pays de Gex. In shape it is like a small millstone and weighs from 13–17 lb. The rind is yellowish or reddish and the paste floury white.

Gien (France). Made in the *communes* of Gien and Châtillon-sur-Loire near Orleans. The cheeses are often made from a mixture of goat's and cow's milk and are quite small, weighing under half a pound. Often they are matured wrapped in leaves.

Gjetost (Norway). *Gjet* means 'goat' and *ost* 'cheese'. Gjetost has been the national cheese of Norway for over 100 years, but now it is usually made with 90 per cent of cow's milk and 10 per cent of goat's milk. I do not know whether goat's milk is added to give a special flavour or whether it is added to justify the cheese's name.

Gjetost does not deserve the cruel epithets which have been hurled at it. Although it has been compared with bad toffee, mouldy hay, sweet manure, patent medicine and tobacco, it is like none of these. It is, however, utterly different from our conception of cheese, and as such it is an acquired taste, and when acquired, delicious.

Whey and cream are boiled in huge stainless steel vats, until reduced to about a quarter of their original volume. Stirring must take place all the time, the better to expel the water. Sugar is added and the result is exactly like a sweet-sour (the sugar taste predominating) fudge. It is marketed in small square blocks and wrapped in thick waxed paper. It keeps indefinitely and has immense nutritive value. I think it delicious with butter and digestive biscuits.

Glarnerkäse. See *Schabzieger*.

Gloucester, Double (Great Britain). Double Gloucester should come from the Vale of Berkeley and the Vale of Gloucester, and can be called one of the most up and coming of England's greater cheeses. In flavour and texture it lies between those other two greats, the Cheshire and the Cheddar, and it is distinctly less crumbly than the former.

Glumse (Germany). A West Prussian cottage cheese.

Gomost (Norway). Curdled milk (French *Caillé*) eaten with salt or sugar in Norway and many other countries.

Gorgonzola (Italy). Gets its name from a village near Milan although, as in the case of Welsh Caerphilly, hardly any is made there now. It is made in Lombardy and cured in the great curing houses of Milan, Novara, Lodi, Cuneo, Pavia and Valsassina. Unique for its creaminess, it is quite unlike the crumbly, salty Roquefort to which some French gastronomes compare it.

Rennet is added to the evening milk at a temperature of 85–95°F. and the curd, obtained in about 15 minutes, is broken up and ladled into a cloth which is hung up in a cool place until morning so that the whey may run off. The morning milk is treated in the same way, but the curd, instead of being left for 10–12 hours, is drained in a bucket after only 10–15 minutes. The cold curd and the morning's warm curd are put in alternate layers and warm curd placed all round. The mould is left in a cool place for 3–4 days. After salting the curd is moved into cool, damp caves where it is left in a strong draught. A red mould sets in and grows over the cheese. From then onwards the cheese must be turned frequently, whilst the mould (*Penicillium Glaucum* – also called *Penicillium Roqueforti*) penetrates and veins the cheese right through. This takes 3 months, but the Gorgonzola should be kept for another 2 or 3 months to be at its best. It is made in round shapes each weighing 14–17 lb.

Gorgonzola (Argentine). A large blue veined cheese weighing nearly 17½ lb.

Gorgonzola. See *Mycella*.

Gouda (Holland). This cheese can be either farmhouse or factory, and was first made around Gouda in South Holland. Cheese-making in the Netherlands is a big industry, but however elaborate the machines or perfect the premises highly-trained men cannot turn out a Gouda to touch a farmhouse cheese in quality.

Gouda, a cow's milk cheese, resembles Edam but contains more fat. It is pressed in cloth-lined moulds, cured in brine and ripened in storage up to 12 months. A farmhouse Gouda when mature becomes an excellent table cheese, straw yellow in colour, strong and attractive in flavour but without bite. It is fairly hard in texture and there should be a few irregular holes evenly distributed. In shape like a wheel, the rind not coloured red. Weight about 12 lb.

Goya (Argentine). Made in the province of Corrientes. A hard Italian-type cheese used for grating.

Grana (Italy). The generic name for a group of hard cheeses which have a granular effect on the palate. They have been made in Italy since the thirteenth century. Among the principal kinds are Parmigiano-Reggiano (see *Parmesan*) and Lodigiano.

Although very occasionally eaten as table cheeses they are most commonly grated and used for cooking such dishes as pasta al forno, pasta asciutta and gratiné.

Grana Padano (Italy). Name officially sanctioned in 1955 and used for all the varieties of Grana cheese made in the valley of the Po, including Grana Lombardo and Lodigiano. The producers have set themselves up in opposition to, and are trying to become quite distinct from, the Parmigiano-Reggiano producers. The output of both groups is about the same.

Green Cheese. See *Schabzieger*.

Gris de Lille. See *Maroilles Gris*.

Gruyère (Switzerland). Has been made in Switzerland for over 200 years and is named after the valley of the Gruyère in the Canton of Fribourg. Today it is also made in the Cantons of Vaud and Neuchâtel and the production is about a third that of Emmenthal, although its manufacture is very similar. Here are the more important differences:

1. A Gruyère weighs on average only 80 lb., whereas an Emmenthaler can weigh 160 lb.
2. The curd is cut into larger pieces and is given a little more heat.
3. The holes are smaller and less frequent.
4. It is more heavily salted.
5. The cheese takes longer to mature.
6. The rind is more greasy than the Emmenthaler and this means that an additional maturing takes place from the outside inwards.
7. The fat content is higher at 48 per cent.
8. The temperature of the curing cellar is distinctly lower and it is this which makes for the smaller eyes.

The texture is firm, almost hard, the taste slightly acidulous. More creamy than Emmenthal.

Gruyère (France). France makes a very good Gruyère in the French Alps.

Gussing (Austria). Like an American Brick cheese.

Hand Cheese (U.S.A.). Made in Pennsylvania (originally shaped by hand) by farming families of German descent and in factories in New York, Wisconsin and

Illinois. A small, sour-milk, surface-ripened pungent cheese, whose curd is finely ground in a curd mill and to which caraway seed is often added.

Harzkäse (Germany). Produced in the Harz mountains. A tiny soft cheese made by hand.

Havarti (Denmark). This cheese used to be called Danish Tilsit, but at an international conference held a few years ago it was agreed to change the name to Havarti in honour of the farm where Mrs Hanne Nielsen, who pioneered the making of this cheese in its present form, lived. This cheese is extremely mild, bland, clean, slightly acid when young, sharpish when older. Flat, round in shape, 8½ lb. in weight.

Herkimer County Cheese (U.S.A.). An excellent, unusual and popular Cheddar. In the 1840s it was made in Herkimer County, N.Y. The cheeses have no added colouring and therefore remain practically white, have a smooth flavour and crumbly texture. They need a whole year in which to mature.

Herrgård (Sweden). This is a close copy of a rather hard Emmenthal but the little gas holes in it are less numerous. It is also called Manor Cheese and is the most popular of typically Swedish cheeses. The best Herrgård, originally made in farms, came from Västergötland, but today it is produced in factories in all parts of the country.

There are two qualities of Herrgård cheese, Herrgård-Elite, which is full-cream, and Herrgård, which is half-cream. Herrgård resembles Gouda in flavour, Elite, Emmenthal. Weight around 26–40 lb.

Herve (Belgium). Probably Belgium's most important native cheese. In type like a soft Limburger, it is sold in blocks 6 in. square and about 3 in. thick. Often the cheeses are peppered with herbs such as tarragon or parsley, or flavoured with olives. They are made in the Herve (with no accent on the final 'e') country just outside Liège.

Holanda (Argentine) or **'Little Dutch'.** These cheeses weigh from 2–4½ lb.

Holsteiner (Germany). Originally made in the turbulent Province of Schleswig-Holstein. It is a skimmed-milk cheese to which fresh buttermilk is added and is subjected to considerable pressure. The cheeses weigh from 9–15 lb.

Ilchester Cheese (Great Britain). The first new English cheese to be developed

Canadian Cheeses

1. Canadian Cheddar
2. Canadian Cheddar
3. Oka
4. Ermite

this century comes, appropriately enough, from the little town of Ilchester in the dairy county of Somerset. But, more surprisingly, Ilchester cheese is the creation of a Yorkshireman, Ken Seaton, who hit upon the recipe almost by accident only six years ago, by devising a blend of cream cheese with chives and other herbs, and Worthington 'E' draught beer. Later a new cheese was added to the Ilchester range. This is the Admiral's cheese, which is prepared from prime English Stilton and Harvey's Hunting Port – its traditional accompaniment. It is made in the same way as Ilchester and is a rich, flavoursome cheese aimed at connoisseurs. Mr Seaton followed these with 'Applewood' which is prime Cheddar smoked, appropriately enough, in applewood and believed to be the only natural smoked cheese produced anywhere in the world.

Ilha, Queijo da (Portugal). (*Queijo* means cheese). A cow's milk cheese made in the Azores, resembling the Cheddar-type known as Derby in its hard texture and cylindrical shape. It is usually smaller, and weighs from 6–8½ lb.

Danish Cheeses

1. Mycella
2. Danish Blue
3. Danbo with Caraway
4. Maribo
5. Danish Blue
6. Samsoe
7. Samsoe
8. Havarti
9. Molbo

Incanestrato (Italy). This is a very popular Italian cheese, similar to or the same as Pecorino, except that it is pressed in wicker moulds, and the imprints of the wicker show on the sides of the cheese. *Incanestrato* means 'basketed'.

Isigny (U.S.A.). Not often seen now. It was intended to be a copy of Camembert but its taste was found to be more like that of a Limburger.

Jack. See *Monterey*.

Kamjak (Yugoslavia). *Kamjak* is a Turkish word meaning 'cream'.

Kareish (Egypt). Similar to Damietta but the curd is salted, not the milk. Skimmed milk is coagulated by souring, the whey drained, and the curd is packed in earthenware vessels in a salt-brine solution.

Kartano (Finland). The Finnish Gouda.

Kaser (Turkey). A medium-hard, ewe's milk, renneted, pressed cheese first made in the mountainous east of Turkey, but now made in the same provinces as Edirne. From $5\frac{1}{2}$–7 lb. of milk are required for a pound of cheese. From 2,500–3,000 tons are produced every year.

Kashkaval (Bulgaria). A cheese made in 3 standard sizes: Balkan – about 4 in. thick; Semi-Balkan – from $2\frac{3}{4}$–3 in. thick; Field-Kashkaval – from 2–$2\frac{1}{4}$ in. thick and about 12 in. in diameter. This cheese made from partly-skimmed milk is also made in other Balkan countries (Kaskaval in Rumania). The ripened curd is worked until it is elastic as in making Provolone. Holes are punched in order to let whey out and to salt the cheese. Curing takes from 2–3 months. Weight $4\frac{1}{2}$–$6\frac{1}{2}$ lb.

Kasseri (Greece). A hard cheese made from ewe's milk.

Katschkawalj (Rumania). In Rumania and in other Balkan countries a Caccio-cavallo type of cheese is made. Ewe's milk is curdled with lab (a rennet-starter preparation). The curd when ripe becomes elastic after heating, is then placed in metal canisters, cooked in water and kneaded like bread dough. Pieces weighing about 6 lb. are worked into spherical shapes, placed in metal or wood forms, cooled, washed with whey, dried, repeatedly rubbed with salt and cured.

Kefalotyri (Greece). About 10 in. across and shaped like a head (Greek *Kefalo*). A very salty, hard cheese with a hard rind; made from either ewe's or goat's milk, used for grating and cooking. Known locally under different names in Thessaly, Epirus, etc.

Kelle Peyniri (Turkey). This cheese is almost extinct. *Peyniri* is the Turkish word for cheese.

King Christian IX (Denmark). This is a mild Samsoe type cheese with caraway seeds in it. When the scented seeds have only partially impregnated the fresh cheese, the flavour is superb. When, however, the cheese is older, the caraway seeds give the cheese too strong a bite. Insist on the fresh cheese.

Kopanisti (Greece). A blue cheese with a sharp, peppery flavour. Curd is produced as for Fetta, then kneaded by hand into round balls. When drying, they soon become covered with mould. The mould and fat are thoroughly mixed in the curd, which is then packed tightly in earthenware containers covered with a dry cloth, changed every day. After ripening for one to two months the cheese is ready to eat.

Koppen (Czechoslovakia). See *Bauden*. This cheese is called Koppen because it is made in cup-shaped moulds. The flavour is pungent and slightly salty.

Laguiole (France). Very like a Cantal, but made in the neighbourhood of Bordeaux. Much used in cooking instead of Gruyère.

La Mothe Saint-Heraye (France). Made in farms between Cognac and Poitiers. Looks like a Camembert but is very different. A semi-soft, goat's milk cheese.

Lancashire (Great Britain). Until the 1914–18 war Lancashire cheese was made in small Lancashire farms as part of the daily routine. This explains the enthusiastic descriptions of its taste and texture. It has the consistency when cooked of a good hot custard, and a wonderful flavour, and it makes the best Welsh Rarebit. More crumbly than Cheshire and Cheddar, it can be spread on butter or toast with a knife. When young it is mild and slightly acid but after maturing for 3 months it becomes mellow and has more flavour than Cheddar or Cheshire.

The method of production is rather unusual. The evening's milk is cooled and placed in a cheese vat where it remains until the following morning. Then the morning's milk is added and the two milkings warmed to renneting temperature. As with nearly all cheeses the curd when formed is cut into tiny cubes. The next stage in the process of making gives Lancashire its special qualities, its unique flavour and crumbliness. The fresh curd is mixed with old curd made the previous day and therefore having a greater acidity. Sometimes the curd of three different days is used.

The shape and size of the cheese vary, from great cartwheels weighing from 40–50 lb. to the now more popular little 12 lb. cheeses, 7 in. in diameter and 10 in. thick.

Lancashire does not come to the south of England nearly enough because although so excellent for cooking it does not travel well and should not be kept long.

In 1913 the first small factory for cheese-making was opened at Chipping. Today there are a good many factories where this cheese is produced of a standard acceptable to Lancastrians. Ten years ago, 17 farms in Lancashire still practised the old craft of making the cheese, but this home skill will probably die out.

Langres (France). This is a soft cheese, rather like a Pont l'Evêque or Livarot, and is named after the old hill-fortress town of the same name north-east of Dijon. Maturing can take 4 months. Weight is about 12 oz. Langres is a very fine creamy cheese but its production is unfortunately dropping rapidly. It is said to have been made since the time of the Merovingian kings.

Larron, Le (France). A poor relation of the genuine Maroilles. It is made from skimmed milk and is ready to eat within 6–7 weeks. Also known as Fromage d'Ors.

Leicester (Great Britain). Until just before the 1939–45 war, when Leicester had a serious set-back, it was the second greatest English cheese. There are signs that it is regaining its popularity. Messrs Tuxford & Tebbut, who also make meat pies, have a great reputation for making farmhouse Leicester cheeses and can sell all they can make. The cheeses resemble a millstone in shape and weigh about 40 lb. The texture is loose and flaky and rather more crumbly than a Cheshire. The lightish red colour is caused by adding anatto dye to the milk.

Levroux (France). An excellent full goat's milk cheese like a Sellessur-Cher made in the districts round Nevers and Bourges. In shape like a truncated pyramid and the rind is slate-grey.

Leyden (Holland). There is Leyden and Old Leyden, named after the university town. Both cheeses contain caraway seeds, but the Old Leyden is well matured and the seeds impart a good 'kick'.

Cow's milk is lightly coloured and, as usual, salted and renneted. The curd is ground and pressed into moulds of a peculiar shape. The cheese crust is hard and branded with the university's coat of arms – two black crossed keys. The paste is light yellow, shot with green, and is firm and without holes. The flat cylindrical cheeses vary in weight from 7–20 lb.

Liederkranz (U.S.A.). This cheese is a trade name for a copy of, and an improvement on, Limburger, those strong smelling cheeses (unpleasantly so in the opinion of many) originally produced in the Province of Liège in Belgium, where they were principally marketed. *Liederkranz* means 'wreath of song', and the art of making it was accidentally stumbled on in the 1890s by a delicatessen shopkeeper, Emile Frey, when trying to produce a copy of the German Schlosskäse (castle cheese) in its turn also a copy of Limburger.

Limburger or Limbourg (Belgium). The Belgian Minister of Agriculture tells me that this cheese was originally produced in the province of Liège. He added that for purposes of propaganda it would be unwise to refer to its noxious smell as 'stink', but better to use the phrase 'something between bouquet and strong-smelling'.

Limburger (Germany). See Belgium (above) for its origins; but this cheese has been made so extensively in Germany – chiefly in the Allgau – that it is considered one of the leading German national cheeses.

Limburger is difficult to make. Sweet milk is set at a temperature of from 91–96°F. with enough rennet to coagulate the milk in 40 minutes. The curd, broken into cubes, is stirred and dipped in rectangular forms that are frequently turned. When firm the cheeses are rubbed with salt until they are slippery, when they are placed in a ripening room at 60°F. The cheese surfaces are frequently rubbed in order to develop the distinctive flavour. The ripe cheese (ripe is the operative word) is wrapped in paper, then in tinfoil and put into boxes, each containing about 50 individual cheeses.

Liptauer (Hungary). This is named after the province of Liptow in the north of Hungary and is normally white. I do not know when it emigrated (especially to Austria) and become the excellent red-coloured mixture we now know.

Ingredients: 4 oz. cream cheese, 4 oz. butter, 1 oz. chopped capers, 5 chopped anchovies, 1 small teaspoonful of French mustard, $1\frac{1}{2}$ teaspoonfuls ground paprika. Mix all together and put into a mould until ready to serve. One can use finely-chopped black olives instead of capers. Another variety has chopped tinned red pimentos.

Livarot (France). The small town of Livarot in the Department of Calvados, one of the least spoilt and most charming in France, lies 30 miles from Caen and 120 miles from Paris and has some 2,500 inhabitants. From this town Livarot cheese gets its name. Two miles away in the hamlet of Sainte-Marguerite-de-Viette is Marcel Desjardins' cheese-making establishment, which is neither a farm nor a factory. Desjardins is not an ordinary producer, as can be seen from the circular, multi-coloured, bright label showing pictures of the medals won at various agricultural shows – Châteauroux a gold one, at Alençon a silver one and at Bordeaux and Rochefort silver again in 1897 and 1898, and finally a Mérite Agricole and Grand Diplôme d'Honneur Hors Concours in Paris, 1899.

M. Desjardins buys his Livarots 'en blanc' and immature from local farmers and ripens them himself. They are salted the first day they arrive with a coarse salt and put in the first ripening room. Then they are turned and salted again and go into another ripening room. Temperature is all-important in cheese-making and M. Desjardins has in his ripening rooms a glass panel protected with a sliding door so that he can look through and see how the cheeses are getting on without having to open the door.

The smell in one of these rooms where lie, on either side, mountains of ripening and browning cheeses is hard to describe. It is certainly overpowering; like the odour of slowly rotting apples, combined with ammonia, a whiff of ripe Camembert and a slight suggestion of seaside ozone, or, if you want to be less kind, of town drains running into the sea.

A good Livarot takes longer to ripen than a Pont l'Evêque, is stronger and perhaps more subtle. The ripening takes place on the surface. There is no spraying or injecting. Before they are sent out, these excellent little cheeses are given a final wash and a touch of reddish-brown colouring and then are wrapped round with a split dried reed to prevent them bursting out. Generally, you will see five of these reed bands round a Livarot and that is why it has been nicknamed 'Le Colonel', for in the French Army, this rank is shown by five bands or stripes on the cuff of the uniform.

Livroux (France). A pyramid-shaped goat's milk cheese made in the northern part of the Indre department; about 3 in. high by $3\frac{1}{2}$ in. square.

Lodigiano (Italy). This is one of the Grana group of cheeses made near Lodi, south of Milan. Used for cooking. The same methods are used for its manufacture as for Parmigiano-Reggiano. The cheese's surface is darkly coloured and oiled and the paste is yellow with a sharp, fragrant, sometimes slightly bitter flavour.

Lour (Iraq). Lour cheese is made from whey for the immediate consumption of those who make it, or given to their livestock. This unpressed, salted soft cheese is eaten as a cheese spread.

Mainauer (Germany). Cheese similar to Radolfzeller cream cheese, and named after an island in Lake Constance.

Mainzerkäse (Germany). A small, round, cured cheese. Curd made from partly-skimmed, naturally-soured milk is kneaded by hand. Small portions are pressed and dried and then cured in a cool cellar from 6–8 weeks.

Majocchino (Italy). Made in the Province of Messina, Sicily. This cheese is similar to Incanestrato but olive oil is added.

Manchego (Spain). An exceptionally nourishing cheese whose fat content is between 57 and 62 per cent of its total dry matter and the total sales are some 32,000,000 lb. It is made from ewe's milk.

The vast bleak central plateau of La Mancha and the highland provinces from Valladolid to Ciudad Real have somehow managed to support large flocks of sheep since the days of Cervantes (1547–1616) and before. The ewes could produce a great deal more milk if the grazing were richer.

Manchego is a renneted, salted and fermented hard cheese, pressed and left to ripen in moulds lined with esparto grass, the clear imprints of which are left on the rind. The quality of the cheeses varies enormously according to the facilities for making it and the ideas and skill of the farmers, the best over such a wide area being in the vicinity of Ciudad Real, where the taste of the citizens is sophisticated. Although all the cheeses are cylindrical in shape and about 50 in. in height, the paste may be dead white or golden yellow, with many small eyes or none.

Manteche (Italy). Manteche is flask-shaped and is a normal Provolone except that, sealed in the centre, is a small quantity of butter. The secret is jealously guarded of how the butter maintains its freshness for long periods and of how it resists melting during the working.

Maquée (Belgium). A soft brick-shaped cow's milk cheese, also known as Fromage Mou. Made in two qualities; one from skimmed milk, renneted, drained in cheese-cloth bags or osier baskets; the other by heating whey.

Maribo (Denmark). A cross between an Emmenthal and a Port Salut in flavour, it is filled with many small irregularly spaced holes. The taste is mild and yet so subtle that in the past it was said that the holes contained the flavour. The cheeses are shaped like cartwheels and weigh 26–30 lb.

Maroilles or Marolles (France). Made in the Nord department and principally round the cantons of Avesnes, Trelon and Candrecies. It gets its name from the famous Abbey of Maroilles, built in the seventh century. In the eleventh century an ordinance obliged the local villagers to convert all their milk into cheese on the eve of St Jean-Baptiste (24 June) and send it to the Abbey.

In shape, texture and taste it is like a Pont l'Evêque, but stronger; it takes four months to ripen and is at its best from May–June and then again from September–October.

Maroilles Gris (France) (also called *Vieux Gris, Gris de Lille, Vieux Lille*). The same as Maroilles, but salted twice and really very strong. Smells slightly of ammonia and takes twice as long to mature.

Mascapone, Mascarpone, Mascherpone (Italy). A very soft, fresh, delicious, cow's milk cream cheese made in Lombardy and Tuscany in winter. Resembles Devonshire clotted cream and is sold in little muslin bags, each cheese weighing

4 oz. It is eaten with fruit, sprinkled with cinnamon, sometimes made with the addition of lemon juice, served as a sweet as in Monte Bianco or beaten up with brandy and sugar. Like Picotta it is occasionally smoked.

Meira (Iraq). Made mostly in the Haj Omran district from milk renneted at milking time and boiled until it coagulates. Drained over night in linen bags with heavy stones on top, then salted, cut into small pieces and stored in sheepskin for 6–12 months. Meira is a better cheese than Roos and keeps longer. It has the largest sale of any cheese in the Baghdad markets.

Mignon (France). Another type of Marolles.

Mihalic (Turkey). A soft cheese whose average annual production is only 500 tons.

Minnesota Blue (U.S.A.). Towards the end of the First World War, when the knowledge of how to identify, isolate and make the blue green mould *penicillium roqueforti* first became known in the States, America began trying to copy Roquefort. Minnesota Blue is agreeable to the palate but perhaps because it is made with cow's – not ewe's – milk and because it is matured in sandstone and not limestone caves, its resemblance to Roquefort is exaggerated.

Mitzithra (Greece). Also called Pot Cheese. Made in primitive conditions near Athens. Whey, a by-product of the famous Fetta cheese, is mixed with fresh ewe's milk in a vat and curdled. After a curdling period of 4–5 days the curd, from which the whey has been removed, is drained and pressed. Shepherds sell the fresh cheese to merchants for sale in Greece and the Greek islands.

Molbo (Denmark). This used to be called Danish Edam and it looks and tastes exactly like a Dutch Edam. It is the most recently manufactured cheese of the Samsoe family and is quite round and weighs 2–6½ lb.

Moliterno (Italy). Also known as Pecorino Moliterno. Similar in general characteristics to Cotronese. Made originally in Calabria and Lucania and now also made in Basilicata.

Monceau (France). Semi-hard cheese of the Maroilles type but smaller. Made in Champagne.

Moncenisio (Italy). A small cylinder-shaped blue-mould cheese.

Mondseer-Schachtelkäse (Austria). Also called Mondseer and Mondseer-schlosskäse. Closely related to Munster and Limburger.

Monsieur Fromage (France). Also called Fromage Monsieur or Fromage de Monsieur Fromage. The paste is fluffy. Fromage Monsieur is made in Normandy and sold in little round wooden chip boxes. When unripe it is never as deadly as Camembert because of its high fat content (60 per cent); but when in first-class condition it is very fine although not quite so fine as a perfect Camembert.

Montasio (Italy). Similar to Asiago and Bitto and made in the Veneto region. When fully matured it is eaten as a table cheese but for use as a cooking cheese it can be cured for as long as 2 years. The rind is sometimes blackened with soot.

Mont d'Or (France). A copy of Munster. A large cheese made to the east of Lyons near Switzerland.

Monterey (U.S.A.). This cheese was first made about 1892 on farms in Monterey County, California. For a time it was called Jack but the original name is now in use, except for the varieties known as High-moisture Jack and Dry-Jack. Factory manufacture began about 1916.

Monterey is a Cheddar made from pasteurized whole, partly skimmed or skimmed milk and no colouring is added.

Monthéry (France). A soft, surface-ripened, cow's milk cheese similar to Brie. Made in Seine-et-Oise in two sizes of $5\frac{1}{2}$ lb. and 3 lb.

Morbier (France). A hard cheese made only in winter in chalets in the French Alps when there is not enough milk to produce giant Emmenthalers or Gruyères. Each cheese weighs approximately 20 lb.

Mothe-St-Héray, La (France). This cheese, which is rarely seen, is made in the Charente from goat's milk cheese during the months from September to March. It weighs about a pound.

Mozzarella (Italy). Originally a Neapolitan cheese made from Buffalo's milk but now made all over Italy from cow's milk. You can eat it fresh like a Scamorza or matured like a Cacciocavallo, both of which it resembles. Weight about 10 oz. It is the basis of Pizza Napoletana and is used for cooking Bolognese Petto di Tacchino alla Cardinale.

Munster (France). This is one of France's greater cheeses and is made in the Vosges Mountains and all over Alsace. It gets its name from the town of Munster (5,000 inhabitants) some 50 miles south of Strasbourg. It is made from whole cow's milk and has a fat content of nearly 45 per cent. The places especially famous for its production are Guebwiller, Kayserburg and Ville, and the valleys of Munster and Lapoutroie.

At present a lot of this powerful semi-hard cheese, not unlike a Pont l'Evêque, is made on little farms up in the mountains. Two slightly different methods are used to make it: in the Munster valley it is made with a mixture of the morning and evening milk and a commercial starter is used, whereas in the Lapoutroie valley the cheese is made twice a day. A popular variety of Munster is produced with cummin seeds. The cheeses are round in shape and 4–8 in. in diameter.

Murol (France). A semi-hard, cylinder-shaped, cow's milk cheese, distinguished by its hollow centre. Made in the Auvergne. 5–6 in. in diameter and weighs about 1 lb.

Mycella (Denmark). Formerly called Danish Gorgonzola. A very good copy of traditional Gorgonzola. The export to Britain is about a fifteenth of that of Danblu. Mycella gets its name from the mould *mycelium* which produces green veins. The paste is yellow and the flavour aromatic. Fat content 50 per cent. The cheeses are approximately 8 in. in height and weigh 11–13 lb.

Mysost (Norway). This is a national cheese of Norway and is eaten all the year round in the Scandinavian countries. It is similar to Gjetost except that it is made from cow's milk whey. The liquid, boiled for 5 hours or more, is stirred the whole time. Albumens solidify and rise to the surface and are skimmed off. As much as 10 per cent brown sugar is then added and some manufacturers flavour with cloves as well.

Nagelkaas (Holland). This cheese is not exported and little finds it way even to The Hague. A Friesian product made with Friesian cow's milk, it is impregnated with cloves. The flavour is delicious, but when the cheeses mature they become extremely strong.

Nantais dit Curé (France). A small square or round creamy and buttery cheese weighing about 6 oz. In 1890 it was first made by a parish priest (*curé*) and comes from the seaport town of Nantes.

Neufchâtel (France). In the department of Seine-Inférieure, in the 'Bray' country, where pasture is exceptionally rich and cattle in consequence very fine, a cylindrical or heart-shaped (*Le Coeur*) cheese is produced. Neufchâtel is a whole-milk cheese, renneted in such a way that the curd takes longer than usual to set: it is then lightly pressed, broken up in a special mill and slightly salted. The cheese, in its moulds, is left in cellars for days, weeks or months. After a few days the cheese becomes covered with a white, velvety down. If eaten then it is soft, creamy and tasteless. If it is left to ferment and ripen the cheese becomes firmer and acquires a fairly pungent flavour.

Neufchâtel is always small, weighing about 4 oz. When cylindrical in shape it is known locally as Bondon, Bondart or Bonde: in other shapes as Le Carré, La Briquette, Le Coeur, Le Gournay and Le Malakoff.

Nieheimer Hopfenkäse (Germany). Named after Nieheim in the Province of Westphalia where it is made. This sour-milk cheese is cured between layers of hops. The milk is heated to a temperature between 100 and 120°F., the whey is drained from the curd over a period of 24 hours. Then the curd is salted and worked until it is mellow. The curd, in the form of cakes, is ripened in a cellar from 5 to 8 days and turned frequently. When sufficiently ripe the cakes are broken up and salt, caraway seed and sometimes beer or milk are added. The mixture is moulded into flat, spherical cheeses weighing about 4 oz. They are then lightly covered with straw and, when dry enough, are packed to ripen in casks with hops.

Niolo (France). A square, round-edged goat's milk cheese tasting strongly of goat and made in Corsica. A very small piece is enough.

Nøkkelost (Norway). An inexpensive cheese frequently obtainable in London; rather like a Dutch Gouda with caraway seeds. This whole or skimmed milk, semi-hard, renneted, salted and spiced cheese used to be branded with St Peter's 'Crossed Keys', the arms of the city of Leyden (*Nøkkel* means 'key'). Cylindrical in shape, it weighs up to 18 lb.

There are four qualities of Nøkkelost ranging from the richest in cream and therefore the most expensive to the poorest and cheapest. By law the four grades are defined as:

1. *Helfet* (whole fat), with not less than 45 per cent fat content.
2. *Halvfet* (half fat), with not less than 30 per cent fat content.
3. *Kvartfet* (quarter fat), with not less than 20 per cent fat content.
4. *Mager* (fatless), with less than 20 per cent fat content.

Nostrale or Nostrano (Italy). Means home made. The local inhabitants apply the name to those cheeses eaten only in the area where they are made. They are usually of the Caciotta or Formaggini varieties. The same names are given to wine and salami not sent outside the area in which they are produced.

Oka (Canada). This cheese is made by Trappist Monks at Oka in Quebec. (See also *Trappist* and *Port Salut*.) In shape it resembles a Brie but is twice as thick and smaller in diameter. Its taste is like that of a Port Salut.

Old Leyden. See *Leyden*.

Olivet (France). This cheese made only in the Orléanais has unfortunately almost disappeared. In order to ripen the cheeses, salt and charcoal (made of burnt vine plants) were rubbed on to their outer surfaces and each cheese then wrapped in walnut leaves.

Olivet is a whole-milk, mould-inoculated, soft, factory-made cheese of the Coulommiers type. There are two sorts of Olivets, the Olivet-Bleu, in season from October to June, and the Olivet-Cendré in season from November to July.

Olivet-Bleu. See *Olivet*.

Olivet-Cendré. See *Olivet*.

Olmützer (Austria). Also called Handkäse, Quargel, Quargeln and Olmützer-Bierkäse. The smell and bite of this pocket-sized cheese is well known. People make vulgar remarks about it. Suffice to say that it is moulded by two hands and not by any other part of the human anatomy. Judging by the ultimate taste that is enough. Ripening time about 9 weeks.

Olmützer-Bergkäse. See *Olmützer*.

Olomouc Hand Cheese (Czechoslovakia). The same as Olmützer.

Pagliarini (Italy). Made only in Piedmont and mostly round Cuneo, Alba and Turin. They are circular, only a few millimetres high and about 4 in. in diameter. Their name comes from the little straw (*paglia*) mats on which they are sold. A cow's milk cheese. uncooked, with an agreeably sharp flavour, it is frequently eaten with the addition of oil and pepper.

Pannarone (Italy). Also called White Gorgonzola and made in much the same way and produced only in Lower Lombardy. Pannarone ferments for 7–8 days at a temperature of 77–82°F. before it is placed in a cold room. It takes from 15–30 days to cure. A flat, oblong cheese, yellow in colour, with a slightly bitter-sweet taste, it is without blue veins but has closely-spaced small eyes. Weight between 17 and 22 lb.

Parmesan (Italy). Italians take as much care in maturing a good Grana as French peasants take to produce a fine wine. Several types of Parmesan are made in Italy but the inhabitants of Parma claim that theirs is the best. In 1954 the name Parmigiano-Reggiano was given to this cheese by a decree of the Government of Italy, which desired to bring peace between rival producers. It was made as long ago as the thirteenth century and is mentioned by Boccaccio (1313–75). It is the only Italian cheese which has no effective rival in any other country.

In making Parmesan the morning milk is always added to the evrning milk which has rested during the night. The two milkings are fermented with whey from the most recently made cheese and then heated to 33°C. After this rennet is added and the coagulated curd is broken into pellets about the size of grains of wheat, then cooked at between 54–58°C., taken out of the cauldrons and put under pressure for 10 hours and finally left to rest for 3 or 4 days. Salting takes 15–20 days in a salt bath. The cheeses are cylindrical, 14–18 in. in diameter, 7½–9½ in. high and weigh about 60 lb., and never less than 48 lb.

The process of maturing takes between 2 and 3 years: the older the cheese the better and the more expensive. Vecchio (old) has been matured for 2 years, Stravecchio (extra old) for 3 years, and Stravecchione (quite old) for 4 years. After 6 months in the first seasoning room, where it is turned, cleaned and oiled, it is given the protective coating which gives it its characteristic appearance. The coating consists of a mixture of lamp-black and burnt umber mixed in wine.

Parmesan is made from the middle of April until the middle of November and is used for grating and cooking. The quality of the cheeses is tested by experts who tap the outside with special little hammers and predict how they will turn out.

Paski Sir (Yugoslavia). This ewe's milk cheese is made in the island of Pag (*Payo* in Italian) and is sold in units of 2–10 lb. It is near to Italian Parmesan in taste and texture.

Pecorino (Italy). The name covers all cheeses made in Italy from ewe's milk and about one sixth of all Italian cheeses consists of some kind of Pecorino. The hard, aromatic Pecorino Romano was the original (it is mentioned in the first century A.D. by Pliny) and is considered the best. When Pecorino Romano is made from cow's milk it is called Vacchino Romano and when from goat's milk Caprino Romano.

For many years the majority of Italian emigrants came from central and southern Italy where the use of Pecorino for both eating and cooking is universal. This explains why such a large proportion of this cheese has been made for export. In 1928 11,334 tons were exported, but by 1953 the export of Pecorino and Parmesan had fallen, due to restrictions on imports and to the fact that the countries to which it had been exported were trying to develop similar types of cheese on their own.

When cured for only 5–8 months Pecorino is eaten as a table cheese, when cured for longer periods it is grated and used for cooking. As well as Pecorino Romano, Pecorino degli Abruzzi, Canestrato, Crotonese, Moliterno and Pecorino Toscano are the best known.

Pelardou (France). One of the best goat's milk cheeses, possessing fragrance and delicacy of flavour. They are made exclusively in the mountains, are usually cylindrical in shape, but as each farmer is an individualist and has his own established routine, they may vary in shape.

Peneteleu (Rumania). Made in the same way as Italian Cacciocavallo and Rumanian Katschkawalj.

Pepato (Italy). This cheese is a spiced Pecorino made in Sicily. The curd is sometimes packed and cured in layers. Pepper is put between the layers or mixed with the curd in the vat.

Pepato (Argentine). This cheese is flavoured with peppercorns mixed with the paste: otherwise it is the same as Moliterno.

Perilla (Spain). Perilla or Teta cheese is pear-shaped and made from cow's milk in parts of the Provinces of Lugo and Coruña.

Petit Suisse (France). This cheese was first made about 1850 in the small hamlet of Auchy-en-Bray, a *commune* of the Oise in the Seine-Inférieure. Madame Herault employed a Swiss cowman on her farm and he suggested that before malaxation of the curd, a little fresh cream should be mixed with it. The idea of the 'little Swiss' was carried out and the cheese created. It is one of the most soft and creamy. Each little cylinder-shaped cheese is wrapped in a thin paper vest and Petits Suisses can be eaten with fine sugar, strawberries and other fruit.

Picodon (France). Shepherds in the Haute Savoie make these goat's milk cheeses and each one varies. They are very soft and take 3 months to ripen in sandstone pots. 'Picodon' comes from the patois 'pico', meaning to prick.

Pineapple (U.S.A.). A rather hard Cheddar, shaped like a pineapple, and first made in Litchfield County, Connecticut, in 1845, although they are now hardly ever seen, even in America, of the size and form they were originally made. From 1845 to the end of the century they were so much in vogue that no American sideboard with its silver bell made to look like a pineapple was complete without one.

The top of the cheese was sliced off as in a real pineapple and the cheese was dug out with a silver cheese scoop. The cheeses used to weigh 6 lb. and not 6 oz. as are the copies of today. The rind was hard, shellacked to a golden brown pineapple colour and when the cheese had been eaten the shell was used to put salads in.

Piora (Switzerland). This cheese is made in three varieties in the canton of Ticino in the Swiss Alps: Tipo Piora and Vero Piora (the latter being the more expensive) are made from cow's milk, whereas Uso Piora is made from a mixture of cow's and goat's milk. The cheeses are flat and round and weigh about 26 lb. Curing takes from 4–6 months, and the cheese is soft to cut like Tilsiter and has small eyes and is of delicate flavour. It is eaten locally but is beginning to find a market in the principal resorts of the Lake of Lucerne.

Pithiviers au Foin (France). A cheese shaped like a small Brie (often called a Coulommiers) and sprinkled with a few strands of hay, but today it is almost extinct.

Poivre d'Ane (France). Made in countryside farms in Upper Provence. It is moulded by hand into small flattened balls and packed with sprigs of rosemary and savory which impart a distinctive and pleasing flavour. Weight varies from 5–7 oz.

Pommel (France). The name given to a commercial brand of *double-crème*, unsalted, paper-wrapped, soft cheese like Gervais and Petit Suisse. It can be bought all the year round.

Pont l'Evêque (France). Map 55 of the Michelin Guide of France gives the small town of Pont l'Evêque a red circle. This means that after the allied landings in Normandy in 1944 the district suffered serious damage. But the attractive Hôtel Lion d'Or, starred by the Michelin Guide, was not hit in the war, and you can enjoy there Bouchée Deauvillaise, Terrine Maison and Poulet à l'Estragon, washed down with the excellent local cider and a glass of Calvados.

You may then wish to buy some of the small 4 in. square Pont l'Evêque cheese

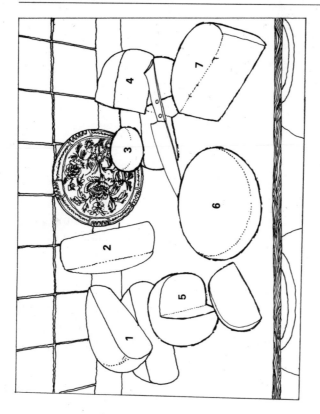

Dutch Cheeses

1. Mature Gouda
2. Leiden
3. Baby Gouda
4. Young Gouda
5. Edam
6. Kernhem
7. Bluefort

sold in wooden chips. The cheese is made of unskimmed cow's milk from only one milking. After renneting for about an hour the curd is placed to drain for a short time on special straw matting, before being shaped in square moulds. A fungoid growth, known as *Monilia candida*, affects the cheese after it has been moved into cellars to be matured. This fungus is not introduced artificially but exists in the walls and on the ceilings of the cellars and is responsible for the distinctive flavour.

The longer a cheese is kept the more pungent it becomes. Pont l'Evêque requires from 15–24 days to reach maturity and in this respect is about half way between the other two great cheeses, Brie and Camembert of the Pays d'Auge. It is made mostly in the Lisieux district and in many farms of the Vallée d'Auge.

Poona (U.S.A.). The origin of the name is unknown. A whole-milk, surface-ripened cheese, round and flat and weighing about a pound. It has the aroma of mild Limburger. During the curing period, which takes 6 weeks, it is rubbed daily to control surface ripening and to produce a fairly firm rind.

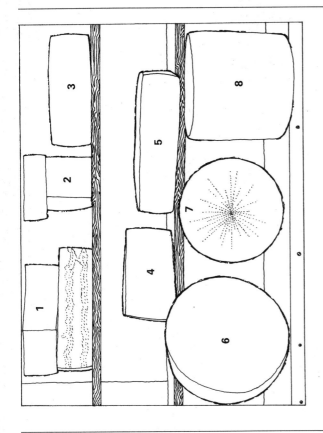

English Cheeses

1. Sage Derby
2. Wensleydale
3. Creamery Double Gloucester
4. Farmhouse Double Gloucester
5. Leicester
6. Cheddar
7. Blue Cheshire
8. Red Cheshire

Port Salut or Port du Salut (France). In 1815 a band of Trappist monks returning from exile were installed in the ancient Port Ringeard priory and the place was henceforth called *l'Abbaye de Notre-Dame de Port du Salut* loosely translated as the Port of Safety. What is not so generally known is that these monks had passed their exile in Switzerland, the home of Gruyère.

At first the monks had 12 cows and the cheeses they made were for their own consumption; perhaps they combined the technique learned in Switzerland with that of making a cheese from lowland milk. At any rate it was good, and one day the Reverend Father gave a present of one to a neighbour. He found it excellent.

In 1873 Port du Salut cheese made its first appearance on Parisian tables and by 1878, the cheese was so well known that the monks decided to register the name at the Tribunal de Commerce in Laval and this was renewed on 15 June 1927.

In taste a rich, ripe Port du Salut is one of the best all-purpose cheeses of France. In flavour, it is a cross between a Bel Paese and a Camembert and in texture it is much nearer the former. By 'all-purpose' we imply that it is sufficiently strong to make it acceptable as a *bonne bouche* at the end of a serious meal and yet sufficiently mild to suit all palates and to go with all wines.

Pot Cheese. See *Mitzithra*.

Pouligny-St-Pierre (France). A small goat's milk cheese, in shape like a pyramid: otherwise the same as Levroux.

Prato (Brazil). A pasteurized milk, semi-cooked, pressed, small-eyed cheese like a Gouda.

Prestost or Prästost (Sweden). (Priest Cheese). A hard cow's milk cheese that has been made in Sweden for 200 years. The milk is set with rennet at a temperature of 90°F. When very firm the curd is coarsely cut and put in a sieve to drain off the whey, then into a cloth and kneaded to expel more whey. Whisky is mixed with the curd and it is then packed in baskets and sprinkled with salt. Three days after maturing in a cool, moist cellar the cheese is washed with whisky. The cheeses are usually cylindrical in shape and weigh from 5–30 lb.

Sweden makes good copies of Stilton, Roquefort, Gorgonzola, Camembert and Port Salut.

Pressato (Italy). A soft cheese, sweetish in taste, not unlike Fontina, and only eaten when fresh. It is of the same type as Asiago.

Provatura (Italy). A soft cheese of the drawn-curd type eaten only when fresh. It was originally made in southern Italy from buffalo's milk, but is now made from cow's milk in much the same way as Cacciocavallo.

Providence (France). A cheese almost the same as Port du Salut made in the department of Seine-et-Oise. Six inches in diameter, $2\frac{1}{2}$ in. thick and weight about $2\frac{1}{2}$ lb.

Provolone (Italy). An uncooked, whole cow's milk, drawn-curd cheese. When it has been cured for about 8 months it is better as a table cheese than Cacciocavallo which it is gradually replacing. There are two main types, Dolce and Piccante, but even the Dolce is strong. The cheeses are sold in a great variety of shapes, including pear- and melon-shaped, and resembling flasks, sausages and truncated cones, etc., but they all have grooves made by the vegetable-fibre cords with which they are hung up. The crust is smooth, thin and shiny, and golden yellow in colour. The paste is creamy-white, solid and without eyes. At Christmas time, particularly in southern Italy and in Rome, groups of Provolone cheeses are to be seen hanging outside grocers' shops. Provolone contains more fat than Cacciocavallo and is smoked before it is salted and dried. These cheeses are made in Aquila, Bari, Calabria, Cosenza, Palermo, Potenza, Rome and Naples.

Provolone (Argentine). There are two qualities of this cheese, one hard and the other semi-hard.

Pultost (Norway). A soft fermented cheese made in all parts of Norway but particularly in the south-east. It is known by many different names, such as Knaost and Ramost, in different localities. Pultost is made from sour skimmed milk which is put in a kettle with 2 per cent of a lactic starter. Sometimes whole milk is added to increase the fat content and sometimes sour buttermilk to increase acidity. The mixture of curd and whey is heated slowly and stirred continually until it reaches 130–140°F. It is kept warm for several hours and stirred frequently to prevent the curd from matting. The whey is then drained and the curd broken up and salted. Sometimes caraway seeds and more rarely thick cream – although this improves Pultost so much – are added to the curd. The curd is put in troughs and stirred occasionally. It can be eaten in a few days as a fresh cheese, but it may also be stored and ripened for later use.

Quargel. See *Olmützer.*

Quart, Le (France). A miniature Maroilles.

Queijo de Minas (Brazil). A chalky cheese made in the State of Minas Gerais.

Queijo de Prato (Brazil). A rather yellow copy of a Dutch Edam made in the River Plate district in the Argentine. Brazilians eat it with a dessert of guava or quince paste. In this way they mask the flavour of the cheese.

Queso de Cabra (Chile). Goat's milk cheese.

Queso de Cincho (Venezuela). A fresh milk cheese eaten young.

Queso Mantecoso 'Chanco' (Chile). A copy of Port Salut. It is made of cream and is the finest Chilean cheese.

Queso de Vaca (Chile). Cow's milk cheese.

Rabaçal (Portugal). Made near the university town of Coimbra. A fairly firm, flat, cylindrical cheese made of ewe's or goat's milk, 5 in. in diameter and about 1 in. thick.

Raclette. See *Valais Raclette.*

Rahmkäse (Austria). These soft farmhouse cream cheeses, usually salt and a little sour, are almost never sold in towns. They have a fat content of from 55–65 per cent of their total dry matter. One variety is known as Imperial-Frischkäse and has a lower butter-fat and salt content.

Rangiport (France). This cheese, made in the department of Seine-et-Oise, is almost the same as Port Salut. Six inches in diameter, $2\frac{1}{2}$ in. thick, weight about $2\frac{1}{2}$ lb.

Reblochon (France). An excellent semi-hard, cow's milk cheese, copied from Port Salut, and made in the Savoie. It was first produced round the popular summer and winter resorts of Thômes and Le Grand St Bernard. This round cheese is about $5\frac{1}{2}$ in. in diameter, nearly $1\frac{1}{2}$ in. in height and weighs about 1 lb. Its fat content must not be less than 45 per cent of its total dry matter and the dry matter not less than 45 per cent of its total weight.

Recollet (France). A type of the square and highly flavoured Carré de l'Est, and it is very popular.

Remodou (Belgium). This cheese has a pungent taste and is very well salted. Similar to, but twice the size of, Herve, it is made in the summer months in the Herve country to be eaten in the winter.

Requeijao (Brazil). This cheese is made in the north of Brazil.

Riceys, Les (France). Also called Le Ricey Cendré, because the cheese is ripened with a coat of charcoal. It was formerly made around the Marne but production has almost ceased.

Ricotta (Italy). Like Scamorza, Mozarella, Broccio, Ziger and similar cheeses,

Ricotta can be eaten fresh, when it resembles a cottage cream cheese, and it can be eaten 'dry' when it is suitable for grating like a Parmesan. Ricotta is sometimes called albumen cheese because of the way it is made. Steam is injected into the whey, albumen then rises to the surface and the curd is put into cheese cloths. When eaten fresh, the cheese is rich, creamy and fragrant. It can be eaten with sugar and is used for stuffing cannelloni, some sorts of ravioli and as the main ingredient in a Roman tart recipe.

Riesengebirge (Czechoslovakia). A soft cheese made from goat's milk in the mountains of northern Bohemia. The milk is coagulated with rennet at about 90°F. The curd is broken up, the whey dipped off, and the curd put into forms and kept in a warm place for 24 hours. The cheeses are then taken out of the forms, salted on the surface, dried for 3 or 4 days and placed to cure in a cool, moist cellar. About 18 lb. of cheese can be made from 100 lb. of milk.

Rigottes (France). Tiny round soft cheeses made from a mixture of cow's and goat's milk in the vicinity of Lyons.

Robbiola (Italy). A type of Stracchino. A soft, rich, quickly-ripening cheese made in the Italian Alps and especially in northern Lombardy. As in the case of Provolone one can buy Robbiola Dolce and Robbiola Piccante; the latter wrapped in foil in quarters of a pound. Robbiola Piccante is an outstanding cheese of its kind.

Robbiolini (Italy). These cow's milk uncooked cheeses, frequently eaten with oil and pepper, come under the general category of Formaggini. They are made in cylinder shape in most parts of northern Italy and weigh from 2–3 oz.

Rocroi (France). Peasants in the Marne in the north-east of France produce only a small quantity of these tiny, soft, white, flat, circular cheeses.

Rollot (France). On May Day in 1678 Louis XIV was given a Rollot for lunch at Orvillers by a Monsieur Debources. He enjoyed it so much that he made the man *maître fromager* on the spot, with a pension of 600 *livres* a year for himself and his descendants. Rollot is a Camembert type of cheese with a reddish crust made in Flanders, but it is now hardly ever seen.

Romadurkäse (Germany). This cheese is similar to Limburger and is made in southern Germany, especially in Bavaria. It is a soft, ripened cheese with a mild aroma produced from whole or partly skimmed cow's milk, to which colour is sometimes added. The curd is put in forms like those used for making Weisslacher, that is they are divided into sections for the individual cheeses. The forms are laid on a screen or mat while the whey drains off and the curd becomes firm. Several times during the 12 hours after the cheeses have been removed from the forms they are rubbed with dry salt. They are cured less intensively and at a lower temperature than Limburger cheeses; sometimes the curing temperature is as low as 42–45 °F. The cheeses are wrapped in parchment and tinfoil and packed in wooden boxes for shipment. Individual cheeses are about 2 in. square, 4½ in. long and weigh about 1 lb., but smaller cheeses are made. 100 lb. of milk makes about 12 lb. of curd cheese.

Roncal (Spain). One of the most popular cheeses in northern Spain. It keeps for a long time and is grated and used for cooking. This hard cheese, one of Spain's few cow's milk cheeses, is quickly renneted, hand-pressed, salted and smoked. Smoking causes the leathery appearance of the rind. The cheeses are cylindrical in shape, about 8 in. in diameter, 3¾ in. high and weigh about 6 lb. The paste is yellow, close grained, hard and with only a few very small eyes. The flavour is sharp. Roncal gets its name from the Roncal Valley in Navarre but is now made in Aragon and the Basque provinces as well.

Roos (Iraq). Is a common type of Iraqi cheese, produced in the Ain Kawa and Haj Omran areas. Made from whole milk, renneted, salted and pressed by hand in the shape of a large orange, it is then stored in goatskins or sheepskins for about 6 months. Its fat content is 22 per cent of the dry matter.

Roquefort (France). How 'King' Roquefort came to be discovered is unknown. Like the tale of the first wine being made when a cave man returned to find his crushed grapes had fermented, the legend as to how Roquefort first appeared, which I explained in Chapter I, may well be true.

Pliny praised this cheese in the first century A.D., and then in the eighth century the monks of St Gall, who were Charlemagne's hosts, found him picking the green bits out and discarding them, and they told him he was wasting the best part. The King tasted the cheese again, realized that the monks spoke the truth, and so ordered a consignment yearly to be sent to Aachen (Aix-la-Chapelle), stipulating that the cheeses should be cut in half so that he could be sure that the blue veins were there.

More officially, perhaps, Roquefort enters into history in A.D. 1060, when the archives of the monastery of Conques record the gift of two cheeses supplied annually by each of the caves in the district.

Casanova has a word, too, about it. In 1757 he writes:

Swiftly as a doe (*leste comme une biche*) she covered a little table, laid two places and set forth all she had: a delicious Roquefort cheese and an excellent glazed ham. Oh, what wonderful food and wine are Roquefort and Chambertin to restore love, and also to bring to maturity a growing love.

In 1407, Charles VI of France, by letters patent, granted to the inhabitants of Roquefort the monopoly of the ripening of Roquefort as it was made 'from time immemorial in the caves of the said village which is so poor that it can grow neither root of vine nor ears of barley'.

From then on and almost regularly twice a century this fabulous ewe's milk cheese became protected and defined.

NOTICE: from the Sovereign Court of Parliament of Toulouse. It is expressly forbidden to travellers, merchants and others of whatever status who have bought cheeses from the neighbouring caves and places in the neighbourhood of Roquefort to sell them either wholesale or retail as genuine Roquefort cheeses, under a penalty of a fine of a £1,000.

This promulgation was issued in 1550 and again on the 31 January 1785.

Gradually the popularity of the cheese caused the area wherein Roquefort could legally be made to be widened and widened until it has now spread to almost the whole of the Causses.

The Causses are a series of arid chalky plateaux south of the Massif Central, and perhaps the most infertile part of France. Here, in these 6,000 square miles, live half a million peasants and it would be a sad day for many of them if Roquefort should lose its popularity. This cheese, made solely of ewe's milk, supports other industries indirectly, such as glove-making and wool. And only sheep could thrive on such barren land. It is true that the making of Roquefort has spread to other parts of France, and to Corsica, but the industry of rearing ewes which give the right sort of milk is a large one and solely confined to the Causses. If anything happened to the makers of Roquefort, 130,000 agricultural workers would suffer.

To make Roquefort, first the ewe's milk is heated and then set. After a coagulation period of 2 hours the curd is cut, the free whey removed and the curd transferred on to a cloth to drain. After this it is put into hoops some $7\frac{1}{2}$ in. in diameter and 6 in. deep with perforated holes at the side. Now comes an important difference from the usual method of making other cheeses. Scooping the curd into these moulds is done in three or four stages and between each scoop a dry blue mould powder is sprinkled which gives the cheese its veins.

The powder, *penicillium roqueforti*, a variety of *penicillium glaucum*, is now commercially made by inoculating bread made of half wheat and half rye flours with the original mould. The loaves become entirely covered with the blue powder if they are left in a damp room for 6 weeks. They are then removed to a hot room to dry and are thoroughly ground, sifted and packed ready to go to the cheese-makers.

The ripening takes place in huge natural caves (though recently others have been dug). They attract tourists to the little village of Roquefort and Michelin's Guide recommends them as worth a visit.

A current of air runs through the caves, where the temperature is low but the humidity high. These conditions permit the cheese to ripen slowly (unwanted micro-organisms do not grow because the cheese is more heavily salted than almost any other) and without the wrong sort of fungi appearing on the surface.

It is claimed that ewe's milk is the richest in fat content, in casein and in minerals. A genuine Roquefort – and at a world conference at Stresa in 1951 the contracting countries agreed that the word Roquefort was a geographical definition exclusively reserved for cheeses of the Causses area – is a very creamy, very pungent and very salty. Personally I find it too strong to consider it as fine as Stilton.

Saanen (Switzerland). Made in the Saanen Valley of the Bernese Oberland. It is sometimes called Hobelkäse because if it becomes very hard a special cheese plane (*hobel*) is used to cut it.

A Saanen takes on an average 5 years to mature. Sometimes a cheese (they are similar to Emmenthal except that the curd is heated at a very high temperature) will be 'laid down' at a child's birth. It is then eaten at all anniversaries and feast days and finished at his burial. A Saanen is known to have kept for 200 years.

Sage or Vermont Cheese (U.S.A.). This American cheese is a type of Cheddar. Originally it was made, in the same way as English Sage in Derby, by crushing fresh sage to get the colouring and the flavour, and by adding chopped sage to appeal to the eye. Later, for factory production, a sage extract was added and instead of the attractive speckles of chopped sage the effect was obtained by chopping up succulent green corn and putting this in the cheese. First of all the green juice was pressed out and added to the curd at the beginning of the making. Today some makers are again using real sage: they find it cheaper than the extract.

Sage Derby (Great Britain). Chopped sage is spread between layers of curd, making the cheese look extraordinarily appetizing.

Saint-Benoit (France). See also *Olivet*. A soft cheese only differing from Olivet in its outside colour: charcoal is added to the salt which is rubbed on the surface of the cheese.

Saint-Claude (France). A goat's milk cheese (4–8 oz. in weight) made in the Department of Jura. The milk is curdled with rennet, and the curd placed in moulds for 6–8 hours. The cheeses are salted on the surface and can be eaten fresh or ripened in a cool, moist cellar.

Saint-Florentin (France). Made for local consumption since the year 1100 in the Auxerre. A creamy mild cheese like Brie, made only recently in sufficient quantity for export. Round or half-moon shaped, it is wrapped in foil and sold under the name of Saint-Flo.

Saint-Marcellin (France). Famous soft cheeses made in the Savoie district. Drained milk is salted: no heating, no kneading, no pressing. Six small cheeses weigh about a pound.

Saint-Maure (France). This cheese is made in Touraine and in the Cantons of Saint-Maure and Loches in the Department of Indre-et-Loire. It is a goat's milk cheese shaped like an elongated cylinder and made somewhat in the same way as a Camembert. It is particularly to be enjoyed with the wines of Vouvray.

Saint-Nectaire (France). This delicious cheese is made only in local farms near the old town of Clermont-Ferrand in the Auvergne district from the milk of Salers cows. It is matured on rye mats and in the most picturesque cool, damp caves which used to be used for wine. Only 1,500 tons are made each year and Parisian gourmets go to enormous trouble to procure one of these cheeses. Each one weighs about 20 oz.

Saint Paulin (France). St Paulin and Port Salut are almost one and the same, for they are both cheeses of the monasteries in the north-west of France.

For example, take the Abbaye de Melleraye, just south of Laval. The monks here are nearly self-sufficient. They have their own herd of cows, with a modern electrical milking installation; it looks somewhat bizarre to see a monk in his long flowing black and white robes (the brothers in black and brown are of a less high order and do far fewer hours of prayer) milking the cows whose names are all neatly stencilled above their stalls – Grenue; Gageure; Banquise; Diabète.

From these beasts comes the milk and the butter used to sustain the monks. No meat is eaten save when one of them is ill and only the minimum milk is allocated for personal consumption, leaving the rest to be made into St Paulin which is sold, the proceeds going towards the upkeep of the monastery.

The place where the St Paulin is made might be thought primitive, but it is scrupulously clean. In one corner there is an ordinary copper boiler where $\frac{2}{3}$ milk and $\frac{1}{3}$ skimmed milk are heated to $32\,°$C. Next comes the pressing. This is done on a very old-fashioned wooden press and by means of a weight suspended from an iron bar above the press. On this bar are 6 notches and as the pressure is increased so the weight is moved notch by notch outwards along the iron bar.

The taste of these little cheeses is almost exactly the same as that of Port Salut.

Saloio (Portugal). Made near Lisbon from skimmed cow's milk by peasants. These tiny, strong-smelling, hard, moulded cheeses have a definitely home-made appearance.

Samsoe (Denmark). Named after the island of Samsoe in the Kattegat, this is Denmark's Cheddar, the national standby, and more is produced than of any other cheese. Samsoe is not a copy and used to be called Danish Swiss in order to identify it. Although not unlike Cheddar in flavour it has a slightly sweet taste of nut kernels. It weighs about 30 lb., is 17 in. in diameter and 4 in. high. It is at its best when about 6 months old.

Samsoe (Australia). Australia has not produced a cheese of a truly Australian character, but makes cheeses of types developed in older countries, particularly those of European origin.

Ninety per cent of her cheese is Cheddar with blue vein, Samsoe, Edam and Fetta coming a long way behind.

San Simon (Spain). Named after San Simon de la Cuesta in the province of Lugo where it is generally made. Shaped like a conical shell, the rind is very thin, shiny and dark yellow. Sizes vary from 2–10 lb. In flavour and consistency San Simon resembles Teta cheese.

Sapsago. See *Schabzieger.*

Sardo (Italy). Pecorino Romano made on the island of Sardinia is called Sardo. Formerly it was made from ewe's milk, but now from cow's milk mixed with ewe's milk.

Sassenage (France). A blue veined cheese like Gex made in the department of the Isère. It is made in two shapes and weighs either 1 lb. or 4½ lb.

Sbrinz (Switzerland). Gets its name from the town of Brienz in the Bernese Oberland. It is one of the oldest hard cheeses of Europe; the *caseus helveticus* mentioned by Columella was probably a Sbrinz. The production is less than a fifth that of Gruyère which it resembles, but –

1. It takes 3 years to cure and in consequence is very hard and therefore grated and used in cooking.
2. The fat content is higher than that of Gruyère, nearly 50 per cent.
3. Holes are either absent or only the size of a pin's head.
4. The dealer stores the cheese vertically not horizontally, and after a year the rind is rubbed with linseed oil to prevent further evaporation and loss of weight.

Sbrinz (Argentine). A hard cheese made from cow's milk; renneted and cylindrical in shape. The paste is smooth, firm and straw-coloured and the taste rather sharp. The minimum ripening period is 8 months.

Scamorza (Italy). This cheese has become so popular that it is now produced all over Italy, but it was first made in the Abruzzi from buffalo's milk. It is made with cow's and goat's milk today. In shape it is like a large turkey's egg.

Scanno (Italy). One of the better known of the Pecorino degli Abruzzi or Pecorino cheeses.

Schabzieger (Switzerland). Also called Green cheese, Glarnerkäse and, in America, Sapsago. The word Schabzieger comes from the German word *schaben* to grate, and Zieger, a kind of cheese. The American Sapsago is also derived from *schaben*.

This cheese is made from slightly sour skimmed milk heated to boiling temperature. Then cold butter-milk is added. In order to precipitate the casein (the albuminous matter which is the chief constituent of all cheese) sour whey is stirred in. This is an important moment in the manufacture of Schabzieger, for if too much whey goes in, the curd will be too soft; if too little it will be too hard.

Dried powdered leaves of blue melilot (*mililotus coerulea*), a sweet smelling kind of clover called honey lotus by the Greeks, is then mixed into the cheese. This gives it an aromatically pungent flavour and makes it an excellent ingredient to grate on to well buttered bread for sandwiches. Schabziegers are shaped like flat-topped cones.

Selles-sur-Cher (France). A goat's milk cheese made in the Sologne countryside, south of Orleans. It is shaped like a flattened cone and the rind is slate-grey. This cheese is considered one of the best goat's milk cheeses in France because of its delicate nutty flavour. Average weight 7 oz.

Serra (Portugal). The generic name for a typical and popular Portuguese cheese made in all the mountainous regions of Portugal. It is usually made from ewe's milk, but sometimes from ewe's milk and goat's milk mixed or from goat's milk only. The texture is compact and sometimes there are minute almond-shaped eyes. The consistency varies from harder to softer according to whether it is summer or winter.

Serra de Estrella (Portugal). Called after a mountain range of the same name and the best cheeses of this type are produced in the region. It is usually made from ewe's milk or occasionally from a mixture of ewe's and goat's milk. Flavour sharp and rather acid.

Silivri (Turkey). Is the name of the better of the two grades of Yoghourt and it is rich in cream.

Sir Imjesani (Yugoslavia). '*Sir*' means cheese and '*Imjesani*' mixed which refers to the spices in the cheese.

Sir Masni (Yugoslavia). A heavy cream cheese. '*Masni*' means fat.

Sir Posni (Yugoslavia). A pleasant cheese but not for the gastronome. '*Posni*' means meagre or low in fat content.

Slipcote or Slipcoat (Great Britain). Slipcote is an old English word (probably from the Norwegian *slipa* – slime) meaning (*a*) a soft semi-liquid mass, (*b*) curdled milk. Cote is an old word for a shed where things were made or stored. Salte-cote was the place where salt was made on the sea-shore. It is therefore unlikely that slipcote means a cheese that has slipped or fallen out of its coat.

Stilton cheeses sometimes burst and spill down in a soft mass. When this occurs they are eaten without waiting for them to ripen and are called Slipcotes or Slip-coats. More commonly the word was given to a very old cream cheese made in Rutland and Yorkshire, rarely seen in London, and, when ripe, not unlike a Camembert.

Smoked Caraway Cream Cheese (Denmark). This cheese can be bought only in Denmark. Its smell is most appetizing; the taste disappointing.

Snow Brand (Japan). When I asked the Japanese Embassy whether they had any national cheeses I was sent by air mail samples of Japanese copies of traditional European cheeses. They were excellent copies, superbly packed and were all called 'Snow Brand'.

Japan began research in 1915 and in 1925 embarked on making cheese 'for sale in markets'. I do not know in what markets the cheese was sold, but in 1955 Japan produced 2,698,621 lb. of cheese.

Sorbais (France). One of the types of Maroilles. A cheese about 5 in. sqaure and $1\frac{3}{4}$ in. thick.

Soumaintrain (France). Only 18 tons produced yearly. Made in Champagne in the Communes of Beugnon, Neuvy, Santour, and Soumaintrain in the Department of the Aube. Soumaintrain is a semi-hard cheese like a Munster.

Spalen (Switzerland). These cheeses get their name from the wooden containers (*spalen*), first made in the canton of Unterwalden, in which they are shipped abroad. They are in every way similar to Sbrinz, except that the Spalen are a younger, less mature variety and may not by law be sold as Sbrinz.

Steppe. See *Danbo*.

Stilton (Great Britain). Stilton cheese was never actually made at Stilton but it was probably at The Bell at Stilton that many travellers on the coach from London to the north had their first experience of what Daniel Defoe, in his *Tour through England and Wales*, calls 'this magnificent cheese'.

The cheese which was offered to the tired and hungry passengers as they tumbled out of the coach at The Bell was in fact made by a Mrs Paulet, daughter of Elizabeth Scarbow, who was married to a farmer who lived at Woldenham. Mrs Paulet's sister was married to the landlord of The Bell at Stilton, Mr Cooper Thornhill, and one Christmas in the late eighteenth century, about 1790, they received a gift of some splendid cheese from the farm. Mr Thornhill, perhaps realizing that he had the chance of acquiring for The Bell a reputation for offering their visitors a really splendid cheese, promised his sister-in-law that The Bell would be able to use all the 'Stilton' she could supply them with.

In fact the name of Stilton was already fairly well known, at any rate in London, as much as 50 years before Mrs Paulet introduced it to The Bell. In Alexander Pope's *Imitation of Horace* the following lines appear:

'Cheese such as men in Suffolk make
But wished it Stilton for his sake'.

So, in spite of the fact that there was a strong move to erect a statue to Mrs Paulet at one time, along the lines of the one in honour of Madame Harel, the inventor of Camembert, she cannot be heralded as the inventor of Stilton, but undoubtedly she and Mr Thornhill did a great deal to popularize it.

There are further references to Stilton in English literature.

In the course of one of those interminable Jane Austen strolls we find Mr Elton giving some young lady 'an account of yesterday's party at Cole's, and that she was to come in herself for the Stilton cheese and the North Wiltshire, the butter, the celery, the beetroot and all the dessert'.

Charles Lamb writing to his friend, Thomas Allsop, in 1823 is also very complimentary, 'Your cheese is the best I have ever tasted. Mary has sense enough to value the present; for she is very fond of Stilton. Yours is the delicatest, rainbow-hued, melting piece I have ever tasted'.

Enough about the history of Stilton; now let me tell you a little about eating it.

Cutting, Serving and Storing

Up until now you may have thought that the proper way of serving a Stilton, socially and gastronomically, was to cut it in half and wrap half round with a fine lawn napkin and then to dig into the centre with an ivory handled silver cheese scoop. Along with this treatment goes the tradition of pouring a generous noggin of port into the centre of the cheese. These practices have sometimes been questioned by serious gastronomes over the years but by and large have always been held to be sound. Now the Stilton Manufacturers Association has produced a pamphlet which states:

'It is widely assumed that the correct method of serving Stilton is with a spoon from half a cheese and that port wine poured into it improves the flavour. Both these assumptions are false. The use of the spoon causes a large amount of waste and as for the port, if the cheese is good it requires no port, whilst if it is not good, no amount of port will improve it, though of course Stilton cheese and port wine go well together'.

The Americans have also discovered that Stilton and port are united just as Leicester cheese and watercress are, and on the other side of the Atlantic a mixture of port wine and Stilton is marketed in a tube with a screw cap. 'A gentle squeeze and with all the smooth controlled facility of toothpaste consigning itself to the brush, a distillation of the pastures of the Leicestershire vale of Belvoir and an essence of the sunny alien vineyards of Spain (sic) is delivered in a gastronomic alliance'.

If the Stilton Manufacturers Association is not comprehensive enough on the subject of the addition of port to Stilton, an acknowledged expert of the district, T. G. W. Wiles, is. 'A fair drenching of port will mask the faults of an imperfect grade, but there is not a vintage in the world that will improve a good one'.

As far as cutting a Stilton is concerned, it all really depends on how quickly you are going to eat it. If it is going to be consumed fairly rapidly, by a house-party over Christmas for example, then you can afford the aesthetic extravagance of a silver scoop without risking the cheese becoming too dry. If, however, the cheese is to be preserved in perfect condition for as long as possible then the method of cutting recommended by the Association is that it should be cut in half and then that slices should be made across the face. Not only is this method far less wasteful, it has the advantage that none of the cheese is exposed to the air for too long before it is cut.

The Stilton cheese-makers have very good advice regarding the storage of cheese and I could not do better than quote them verbatim.

'Keep the cheese at room temperature covered with a cloth. Cheese which has been allowed to go dry should be covered with a cloth which has been damped with brine (a handful of common salt in a basin of water). The recovery of texture and flavour will be assisted by a little warmth. A fluctuating temperature will ruin a good cheese. The optimum temperature is approximately 58°F.'.

Stracchino (Italy). Stracchino can designate a very rich, uncooked, soft, creamy, white cheese, practically without crust, rather like a Bel Paese. As a generic term Stracchino is applied to cheeses made since 1100 from the milk of cows passing through the Lombardy plains on their way south at the onset of winter, and whose milk was affected by their fatigue; *stracca* being a dialect word for *stanca* 'tired'. Dolce and Piccante Stracchino is made; of the latter Gorgonzola is the best known. The main difference between the Dolce and the Piccante forms is that the former is made from the milk of a single milking only, while in the Piccante forms (including Gorgonzola) the morning milk is added to the previous evening's milk.

Sueciaost or Sveciaost (Sweden). Both words simply mean Swedish cheese. It is a moderate copy of a Gouda, but there are many varieties throughout the country. Nearly always Sueciaost is of open texture. 'Open' is the best translation of the Swedish word *grynpipig*, an adjective describing small mechanically made holes and not 'gas holes'. Sweden eats about twice as much of this cheese as she does of all her other varieties put together. A spiced Suecia is made with caraway seeds and cloves.

Surati (India). A soft cheese named after Surat in Bombay State. Whole milk

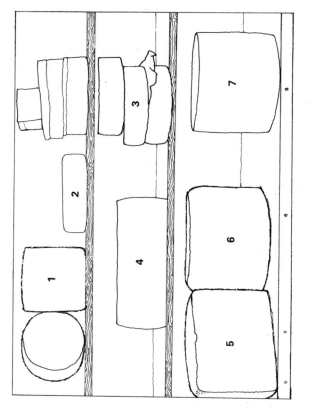

English Cheeses

1. Stilton
2. Derby
3. Caerphilly
4. Dunlop
5. Blue Cheshire
6. Blue Cheshire
7. White Cheshire

is clotted with rennet and the unbroken clot placed in wicker baskets to drain. The curd is turned to aid drainage. The cheeses are immersed in acid whey containing salt, after which they are drained dry. Surati, which is like a cottage cheese, should be eaten before it is 10-14 days old.

Swaledale (Great Britain). A soft white cheese made in Yorkshire. Swale comes from an old Norse word meaning a low-lying place, somewhere cool.

Taffel. See *Tybo*.

Taleggio (Italy). Named after the Taleggio Valley in Lombardy. It was not created until after the 1914-18 war. Taleggio is a quite soft variety of Stracchino made with whole milk. Square in shape; weight 3-4 lb.

Tanag (Ireland). A hard-pressed, skimmed milk cheese.

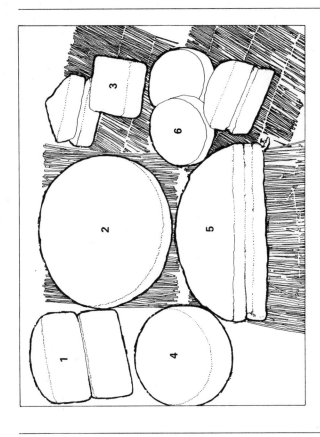

French Cheeses

1. Roquefort
2. Brie
3. Maroilles
4. Roquefort
5. Brie
6. Coulommiers

Teleme (Greece). A very quickly ripening cheese made all over Greece, Turkey and Bulgaria. Teleme is a Fetta cheese made in squares, weighing about 2 lb. each. These cheeses are sold in tins containing 30 squares packed in layers, with plenty of salt between each layer. 100 lb. of goat's milk makes about 20 lb. of cheese and the same quantity of ewe's milk makes about 30 lb. of cheese.

Thenay (France). Thenay, a soft, whole-milk cheese, resembles Camembert. It is made, and the larger part eaten, in the region of Thenay in the department of Loir-et-Cher. Rennet is added to a mixture of evening and morning milk at a temperature of about 85°F. During the 20 days when the cheeses stand in a well-ventilated room, they become covered with mould. This is cleaned off and the cheeses removed to a cool, moist cellar to cure for another 15 days.

Tignard (France). A hard, blue veined cheese, which resembles Gex and Sassenage, made from ewe's or goat's milk in the Tigne Valley in Savoy.

Tilsiter (Germany). It is rather like a Port Salut even to the small holes, but stronger. An excellent, full-bodied cheese, pleasant to the taste and Germanic in its respectability.

Toggenburger (Switzerland). Also called Bloder cheese. It is Switzerland's only sour-milk cheese and is made in the Alps of St Gall, in Toggenburg, and in the Werdenberg district, but it is also made in the Principality of Liechtenstein. Toggenburger is made of skimmed milk and takes from 6–9 months to cure. It does not form a rind but what is called a *Speckschicht* or a layer of fat. This cheese hardly ever leaves the district where it is made, being consumed by the farmers whose income derives from the butter they make.

Tome au Marc de Raisins (France). Also called Tome au Marc and Tome de Raisins. This excellent cheese fascinates many people. It is white, rather waxy, extremely solid, and is made in the shape of a flat cylinder or tiny millstone, each cheese weighing about 3½ lb. What gives the cheese its distinction is that the rind is made of dried pressed grape skins and grape kernels. It is made in the Savoie.

Tome de Savoie (France). Same as Tome de Raisins.

Trappist (Yugoslavia). This is one of those cheeses which is now made and sold far beyond its original boundaries, but was first made in 1885 in a monastery near Banjalaka in Bosnia. It resembles Port Salut and the great Canadian Oka. Although semi-soft, it is cured like a hard cheese and ripens all through and not only on the surface. Cheeses are made weighing 3 lb., 5 lb., and others over 10 lb.

Travnik (Yugoslavia). Also called Arnautski Sir. A soft whole milk cheese with a little goat's milk added.

Tybo (Denmark). This cheese used to be called Taffel. It is of the Samsoe family, brick shaped and rather nondescript in flavour. Weight 4½–6½ lb.

Ulloa (Spain). Ulloa cheese comes from Galicia. Its paste is soft and reminds one of that of a ripe Camembert.

Vacherin (Switzerland). Made in the autumn only – at least in Switzerland – in a dozen or so mountain dairies in the Joux Valley of the Vaud Canton. It is a curious very soft, creamy, white cheese, with a wonderful taste when ripe, almost like a runny Brie, but with a very hard rind. Often it is eaten with a spoon. The cheeses take 2 or 3 months to mature, are from 6–11 lb. in weight, 8–12 in. in diameter and 2–3 in. in height. The marketing period ends with the warm weather, therefore the summer tourist seldom sees this fine cheese, but it makes a great treat for the winter skier.

Vacherin des Beauges (France). This is probably the rarest great cheese still made in France. Judging from descriptions of cheeses which are no longer produced, better cheeses may have existed, and many of the great cheeses (Brie, Camembert, Roquefort, etc.) made in large quantities are as good, but Vacherin des Beauges occupies a place between the extinct cheeses and these great ones.

It is made with full cow's milk and only from October–December. This is because during the rest of the year the beasts graze on *alpage* (high-up mountain grass) and from their milk a modest cheese is made. But in October they feed on *regrain*, which is second crop hay; their milk yield decreases, but up goes the fat content.

These Vacherins are shaped like tiny millstones and weigh about $2\frac{1}{2}$ lb. They take 3 months to ripen. The rind is firm, but the inside is like the most runny Camembert ever seen. You eat this enjoyable cheese with a spoon.

Vachino Romano. See *Pecorino*.

Valais Raclette or Raclette du Valais (Switzerland). Is made only in the Canton of Valais and is used mainly for a special dish of melted cheese called Raclette and in Valais fondue. The fat content in all cases is in excess of 50 per cent. The temperature in the curing cellars does not exceed 12–15 °C., and the curing takes 3 months.

Valençay (France). Indentical with a Levroux only larger. It is made in pyramid shape from goat's milk in the Indre Department.

Västerbottensost (Sweden). Västerbotten cheese is now made all over Sweden. A slow maturing hard cheese, it weighs from 35–40 lb. and ripens in 8–12 months. It is highly flavoured, somewhat pungent, and can be a little bitter when stored for a long time.

Västgötaost (Sweden). Made in Västergötland. A semi-hard, pressed cheese, like a Svecia or Emmenthal, but more aromatic in flavour and the paste is less compact. It becomes deliciously piquant if kept for a fairly long time. The ripening period is from 4–6 months and the cheeses vary in weight from 20–30 lb.

Vendôme (France). A soft cheese made by a very small number of producers in the Valley of the Loire near Vendôme. It is ripened in charcoal and can occasionally be bought in Paris and Blois.

Veneto (Italy). Better known as Vezzena. One of the Parmesan type cheeses. Made in the same way as – but considered superior to – Asiago, it usually has a sharp flavour and is sometimes bitter. Eaten fresh when fully matured and used for cooking when old and dry. The paste is granular and usually greenish-yellow, although when made in the spring it may be straw-coloured and when made in the winter almost white.

Vermont Sage. See *Sage*.

Vezzena. See *Veneto*.

Vieux Gris. See *Maroilles Gris*.

Vieux Lille. See *Maroilles Gris*.

Villalon (Spain). Like Manchego, this is made of ewe's milk in many parts of central Spain but especially in the province of Valladolid. Milk is renneted in 2 or 3 hours and the curd drained in little bags called *fardeles*, then pressed in wooden moulds and, after salting and washing, the cheese is ready to be eaten. It is sold in the shape of small, long cylinders.

Villebarou (France). Made in the *communes* of Marolles and Saint-Denis-sur-Loire at Villebarou. Each cheese weighs about 1 lb. and is about 8 in. in diameter and a good inch high. One gallon of milk makes three such cheeses. They are soft, mildly salted, a cross between a Camembert and a Port Salut. Formerly they were wrapped in the leaves of plane trees. Most of them are now sold on Saturdays in the market square of Blois.

Vosges, Crème des (France). These small fresh cream cheeses can be bought in Alsace, but only during the summer months.

Wensleydale (Great Britain). Wensleydale, the valley of the Ure in Yorkshire, is the home of what some call the rival of – and others say is better than – Stilton. Most Wensleydale cheese is made today in local creameries; the bulk of the production is of the white variety. Wensleydale is also made in the neighbouring dales.

Wensleydale is of the same shape as Stilton, only often a little smaller and the rind, instead of having a mottled crinkly appearance, looks corrugated: this is because of the way the cloth is bound round the young cheese. Some say that blue veined Wensleydale (the white cheese is also excellent and popular) is a little more tangy than Stilton, others that it is more creamy. The two cheeses are certainly very similar.

Westphalia Sauermilch (Germany). This is a wonderful cheese. When it is well made, kneaded by hand, the right amount of butter, egg yolk, pepper and caraway seeds added, and when it has ripened – dare one say putrefied? – just the correct amount, it makes a superlative spread.

White Gorgonzola. See *Pannarone*.

Wiltshire (Great Britain). There are two kinds of Wiltshire: the first is made in almost the same way as Gloucester, but the curd is heated twice, as in making Cheddar. Fermentation is thereby increased, causing the texture and flavour to differ from Gloucester. The second is the 'Wiltshire Loaf', a cylindrical cheese of about 9 in. in diameter, prepared without a second heating of the curd.

York Cream (Great Britain). Another name for Cambridge.

Yorkshire Stilton. See *Cotherstone*.

French Cheeses by Provinces

Alsace
Carré de l'Est
Munster
Petit Munster

Anjou
Beauvoir
Saint-Maure
Toucy

Artois
Boulettes d'Avesnes
Maroilles

Béarn
Croute Rouge
Laruns

Berry
Crottin de Chavignol

Selles-sur-Cher
Valençay Levroux

Bourgogne
Epoisses
Saint-Florentin
Soumaintrain

Bresse
Bleu de Bresse

Bresse (continued)
Rigottes
Saingorlon

Bretagne
Nantais dit Curé
Saint Paulin

Causses
Rocamadour
Roquefort

Champagne
Chaource
Croute Rouge
Langres
Petit Camembert
Triple Crème

Corse
Asco
Niolo

Dauphiné
Saint-Marcellin

Flandres
Gris de Lille
Mimolette
Paunt Macère
Saint Paulin

Franche-Comté
Comté
Maconnais

Guyenne Auvergne
Bleu d'Auvergne
Cantal
Croute Rouge
Fourme d'Ambert
Saint-Nectaire

Ile-de-France
Brie
Coulommiers
Pointe de Brie

Normandie
Bondon Neufchatel
Camembert
Demi-Camembert

Livarot
Pont l'Evêque
Triple Crème
Triple Crème Aromatisé

Picardie
Croute Rouge
Galantine
Rollot

Poitou
Chabichou
Pyramide (croute blanche)

Provence
Banon
Pelardon
Poivre d'Ane

Savoie
Bondes aux Raisins
Emmenthal
Fondue au Raisin
Petit Reblochon
Reblochon

3

Wine with Cheese

Wine's affinity to cheese is remarkable. There is a wine to go with every cheese. But let us not exaggerate: every wine does not go with every cheese by a long chalk. Indeed there are a growing number of people who experience a marked dislike of their red wine after they have had a mouthful of a certain cheese. I put this down to too much propaganda on the part of cheese publicists, who have realized what a wonderful opportunity the growth in popularity of wine and cheese parties has been to their cause and have thus oversimplified too much.

But first let us note how many genuinely different basic wines there are to marry with cheese. Such a list must, of course, be fairly arbitrary; one could suggest any number from twelve to a thousand. We must therefore confine ourselves to those principal varieties which are likely in practice to be met by the readers of this book.

The following list of wines, to be married at a later stage in this chapter to various cheeses, has been compiled with the reader – a knowledgeable person who does not care for fantasy – constantly looking over my shoulder. The wines of 'different flavours' with which I deal here amount to thirty-seven.

Red Table Wines

1. **Claret** Bordeaux *ordinaire* quality, through Côtes de Blaye, Medoc, Medoc Supérieur and up to St Julien, including plain Margaux, St Emilion and Pomerol.
2. **Claret** Crus Bourgeois of notable years; Fourth and Fifth Classified Growths of fair to good years, and the First to Third Growths of very light, fast-maturing vintages.
3. **Claret** The Fourth and Fifth Classified Growths of great years.

Note : These three will have been made with grapes containing a fair amount of tannin, thus giving the wine a harsher or firmer flavour than Burgundies.

4. **Burgundy** Minor Commune names of the Côte de Beaune, such as Côtes de Beaune Villages, Beaune, Santenay, Pommard and Volnay.

5. **Burgundy** The really good Côte de Nuits wines, perhaps bottled in France and of good years, such as Clos Vougeot, Chambertin, Vosne-Romanée, Flagey-Echezeaux, etc.

6. **Burgundy** (Southern) Mâcon, Juliénas, Beaujolais, Moulin-à-Vent.

7. **Rhône** (Deep Southern). Hermitage, Châteauneuf-du-Pape, Côte Rôtie.

Note : The Côte de Beaune and Côte de Nuits wines are made with the Pinot Noir grape which is gaining more ground in Europe and, indeed, throughout the world, than any other. The southern Burgundies are made with the Gamay grape, not such a fine wine-making variety as the Pinot Noir, but one which does make a good red wine in the Mâcon and Beaujolais areas. The Rhône wines are made from several varieties of grape combined.

8. **Italian Reds** Chianti, Barolo, Barbera, Nebbiolo.

Note : I do not mean to infer that all these Italian wines are the same – indeed, they have definite individual flavours – but they are distinctly sweeter than the French wines which I have mentioned.

9. **All Other Reds** Australian, Spanish (Rioja), Portuguese, French Midi, South African, Californian, Algerian, Tunisian, Moroccan.

White Table Wines

10. **Rhine** Minor whites such as Oppenheim, and Nierstein.

11. **Rhine** Good medium-sweet wines, and all the branded Liebfraumilchs on the market.

12. **Rhine** The great names: Rüdesheim, Johannisberg, Marcobrunn, Hallgarten, Vollrads, Hochheim, Hattenheim, Winkel, Geisenheim, Erbach, Eltville, Kiedrich, etc.

13. **Palatinate** The great sweet Palatinate wines such as Wachenheim, Forst, Deidesheim, Ruppertsberg, etc.

14. **Moselles** The wines of the Lower Moselle (from Coblenz to Alf) and the Upper (Trittenheim through Trier to the Luxembourg frontier), and also the less great names of the Middle Moselle such as Zeltingen, Enkirch, Erden, etc.

15. **Moselles** The great Middle Moselles with vineyard names attached. Wehlen (Sonnenuhr, Feinter Münzlay), Brauneberg (Juffer, Lay, Kammer, Falkenburg), Bernkastel (Doktor, Rosenberg), etc.

16. **Franconia** The wines made around Würzburg.
17. **White Bordeaux** The low-priced, old-fashioned flavours of Graves, Graves Supérieur, Entre-deux-Mers, etc.
18. **White Bordeaux** The newer, drier white Bordeaux, sometimes made with grape varieties from other parts of Europe to give them an up-to-date scented, yet dry, flavour.
19. **White Bordeaux** The great ones – Barsac and Sauternes in the classified growths class.
20. **Alsatian Wines** Sylvaners and Rieslings.
21. **Alsatian Wines** Traminers and Gewürztraminers.
22. **White Burgundy** Minor wines such as Bourgogne Aligoté, Pouilly-Fuissé, Mâcon Blanc, etc.
23. **White Burgundy** The greats: Chablis, Montrachet, Corton Charlemagne.
24. **Loire** Dry wines such as Muscadet, Pouilly Fumé, Sancerre, Quincy.
25. **Loire** Sweet wines such as Vouvray, Quart de Chaume.
26. **Sparkling Wines** For the purposes of tasting cheese, I include Champagne with all the others.
27. **Yugoslav Wines** All.

Rosé Wines

28. **The dry, full-bodied Rosés** Rosés from Spain, Portugal, Tavel and Bordeaux.
29. **Medium Sweet Rosés** Anjou Rosé.

Sherries

30. **Dry** Finos, Manzanillas, Montillas.
31. **Medium Sweet and Sweet** Amontillados, Olorosos, Old Brown.

Ports

32. **Tawny**
33. **Ruby**
34. **Vintage**

Madeiras

35. **Sercials**
36. **Sweet** Bual, Verdelho, Malmsey.

So, with nearly forty wine flavours to choose from, let us see what different sorts of cheese and wine parties we can give. As I see it, there are three. The first kind, which I shall call 'very light eating and social', is an informal one when you are all going on somewhere else later to have dinner, and it does not much matter how many or how few cheeses there are, so long as everybody enjoys himself Next there are the more serious 'tasting' parties, when you and your guests are keen to learn more about the cheeses or the wines, but at which you are not serving a big meal; and, finally, there are the parties at which you intend to serve a substantial meal which may either be a social occasion or a more informative one.

Before giving suggestions for these parties it does behove me to say more about this question of certain cheeses giving certain red wines (and, indeed, certain white wines) a most unpleasant flavour. I do not claim to have the world's best palate, but boiled fish (fried is usually all right) does make claret taste horrible and I cannot abide French mustard with bacon or roast beef. But neither of these palate clashes is as bad as a very strong Camembert or Pont l'Evêque with a light claret or a delicate white wine. The only way to avoid this at a party when, for business reasons, you have to show all or a great number of wines and cheeses, is either to leave out all cheeses of this type or to have only very cheap or very expensive and potent table wines.

Light Eating and Social

A party to hold early on a summer evening when you will be having dinner later:

Cheeses
Bel Paese; Tome au Marc de Raisin; Caerphilly; Pommel; Fontainebleau; Double Gloucester.

Suggested wines
A Moselle such as a Zeltingen Riesling; an Alsatian Sylvaner; a Fino for those who want something stronger.

Extras
Bath Oliver biscuits; cream crackers: Vita-Wheat; Hovis; black olives; radishes; watercress; cucumber and cream salad with capers; Danish or Dutch butter; Cheese Dip made from cream cheese with finely-chopped pimentos, green olives and chopped chives.

Ice the wines and chill the sherry.

Another summer party, but this time a late evening one:

Cheeses
Bel Paese; Brie; Danish Blue; Cheshire; Gruyère.

Suggested wines
A Franconian wine such as a Randersacker Teufelskeller; as it is late, something to hit the palate like a Gewürztraminer Reserve Exceptionelle; Tavel Rosé; Oloroso Sherry – this is for those who want the Brie but don't want it with a table wine.

Extras
Cream crackers; crusty French bread; toasted Hovis; tangy salty biscuits; apple and celery salad; olives; lettuce; watercress; Danish or Dutch butter; endive and chopped egg mayonnaise.

Light Eating, Informative about Cheese

We might suppose here that your grocer has told you about some whole Brie cheeses which are coming over and will be in sensational condition in a few day's time. You suddenly feel you must share with friends the gastronomic experience of tasting one of these cheeses at its peak creamy condition (without exaggeration I don't believe that the period is more than some 6–12 hours). When they have started to run all through right up to the rind, and before that acrid flavour has taken over, they can marry exceptionally well with a magnificent red wine.

Cheese
Brie only.

Suggested wines
Only one wine, as it is the cheese you want to concentrate on. I would suggest a not-too-old Hermitage or a Nuits St Georges or a Gevrey Chambertin of a recent year; if you want a white wine then choose a Corton Charlemagne or another really fine white Burgundy.

Extras
Bath Olivers; best Normandy butter; thick white toasted bread with the crusts cut off.

Another interesting, informative party is a comparison between the classic French soft cheeses and their Danish and German copies. On this occasion I imagine that your guests will be going on somewhere afterwards and, though most of those whom you invite will be interested in the cheeses, some may not, so you need not be too earnest in your choice.

Cheeses
Brie; Camembert; Pont l'Evêque; Munster; Fromage de Monsieur Fromage; Maroilles; Port Salut; Reblochon; Tome au Raisin.

Suggested wines for summer
Dry sherry; Pouilly Fuissé; Oppenheimer; Côte de Beaune Villages; St Emilion; Schloss Johannisberg; or, if only a few people are coming, a Lafite or a Latour.

Suggested wines for winter
For a large number: a Cru Bourgeois or Châteauneuf-du-Pape or a Yugoslav Riesling or a Fino sherry. For a small number: Chablis or a Richebourg or a sweet Palatinate wine such as Durkheimer Annaberg or a very fine Moselle such as a Bernkastel Doktor or even a Wehlener Sonnenuhr, though these two will have to be younger vintages and the cheeses not too ripe or they will be swamped.

Extras
Bath Oliver biscuits; cream crackers; curly fried bread; water biscuits; watercress; Danish or Normandy butter.

A blue cheese party: for this party, when you want to try out all the blue veined or mould-inoculated cheeses, I am going to assume that it is either midday or early evening and in the winter. The cheeses to be tasted are Danish Blue, Roquefort, Blue de Bresse, Stilton, Bleu d'Auvergne, Pipo Crème; some of these cheeses are very 'bitey', others are milder than they appear and I would suggest that you marry a certain wine to a certain cheese and have a table set aside for each. The order of the tables presents a problem. It would be a pity to go from the mildest to the most pungent, which would mean that of the blue cheeses perhaps the best of all would have to come first. This would not be fair, as it deserves a fine wine to go with it, but this wine would overshadow the sound but less great wines. You might like to explain this to your guests and tell them that they can wander from one table to another in any order they choose.

Cheeses
Danish Blue; Roquefort; Bleu de Bresse; a mild, slightly unripe Stilton; a pungent and fully ripe Stilton.

Suggested wines
An Algerian red wine; Tawny port; medium sweet sherry; Moulin-à-Vent or another red Burgundy; an old Tawny port.

Cheese
Blue Cheshire.

Suggested wine
Claret, perhaps Château Lynch-Bages of a good year.

Cheese
Bleu d'Auvergne.

Suggested wine
Sercial Madeira.

Cheese
Pipo Crème, rather creamy and not pungent.

Suggested wines
This could taste better with either a Yugoslav white or, if well iced, a good Barsac of a recent year.

Extras
A nice change with these cheeses is fatted bread, i.e. dried slowly in the oven, and a very slightly sweet wholemeal biscuit. New Zealand butter is recommended.

Light Eating and Informative about Wine

This group may not rightly belong in this book, so I will be brief. I feel that I should perhaps make the point that this chapter is devoted to parties and not to straight tastings because I am not a great believer in having much cheese at tastings, and when one does it should only be when switching to a completely different wine. Let us imagine that you are invited to a wine merchant to taste some young clarets still in cask and just about to be bottled; some very fine old Burgundies of which a couple may be getting a little tired; a collection of branded lines of Liebfraumilch to see which is the best value; and, finally, some Rosé wines from the Loire Valley. Now the interesting thing about this tasting is first that there is no cut and dried order in which to take the four categories. If you put the old Burgundies last your palate may well be tired before you get to them. If you put the hocks first (and usually whites come before reds in a tasting) the sweetness may kill your taste buds for the other, drier wines. The second thing to note is that, though there is a vast difference *between* each category, *within* each category the wines will be very similar. What I would do under the circumstances – and I have attended tastings all my life – would be to have a good mouthful of some mild cheese on bread or biscuits while running through the wines in each group. Having a nibble between two or more *similar* wines is a great mistake and not enough people ever realize this.

But this is an aside; we are concerned here with parties which can be instructive without being too severe. You could give an interesting wine party around most of the thirty-seven categories I have listed, though some might be rather cloying or restricted. I have chosen twelve tastings for you, sometimes running two categories into the one *dégustation*.

How many wines should you give at such a party? Not less than six, I feel, and never more than ten. Between these numbers I feel you must be guided by availability and your pocket, for it is unfortunately true that the more different wines you have, the more you consume.

First tasting – Burgundy

A comparison between Domaine bottled and English bottled.

Cheeses
Port Salut; Cheshire; Cheddar.

Wines
Two bottles each: Nuits St Georges; Chambolle Musigny; Clos Vougeot.

Second tasting – Claret

Cheeses
Cheshire; mild Stilton; Munster, not too ripe.

Wines
Red Bordeaux; St Julien; St Emilion; Cru Bourgeois Médoc, approximately three years old; Cru Bourgeois St Emilion, approximately three years old; a Fifth Growth, approximately four years old; a Fourth Growth, approximately four years old.

Third tasting – Claret

Cheeses
Blue Cheshire; mild Camembert; Saint Paulin.

Wines

Eight wines, all of the Third and Second Growth of the Médoc, all of the same year (say, five years old).

Fourth tasting – Claret

Cheeses

Caerphilly or White Wensleydale.

Wines

The four First Growths of the Médoc and Château Mouton-Rothschild, all of the same year (say, around eight years old).

I know I suggested six wines as a minimum, but there is an exception to every rule, and the single cheese is *not* a mistake. With wines like these, the cheese should take a very minor place.

Fifth tasting – Red wines

Cheeses

Gorgonzola; Gruyère; Brie; Liptauer.

Wines

Barolo; Nebbiolo; Barbera; Chianti; Provence; Cahors; Algerian Red; Tunisian Red; Spanish Rioja; Portuguese Red; California Red; Bulls' Blood (Hungarian).

These red wines appear to the palate to be somewhat sweet and, to me, Gorgonzola tastes so bland as almost to impart a sweetish taste itself. I feel that marrying Italian wines with this cheese is a suitable touch.

Sixth tasting – Ten different brands of Liebfraumilch

Cheeses

Port Salut; Bel Paese; Lancashire.

Wines

The reason I suggest such a high number of wines here is that most Liebfraumilch is pleasantly round and soft and does not demand a tremendous amount of concentration.

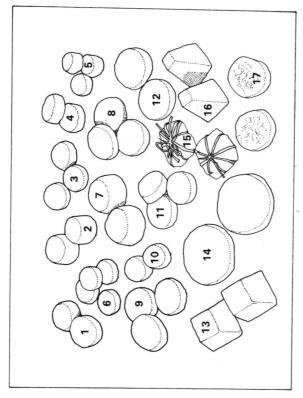

French Cheeses

1. Crottin de Chavignol
2. Chabi
3. Saint-Marcellin
4. L'Ardechois
5. Rigotte de Condrieu
6. Monchoy
7. Pouly
8. Selles-sur-Cher
9. Saint-Heray
10. Cabécou
11. Romans
12. Bougon
13. Valençay
14. Chévre à la Feuille
15. Banon
16. Pouligny-Saint-Pierre
17. Poivre d'Ane

Seventh tasting – Rhinegau wines

Cheese
Caerphilly.

Wines
Eltviller Sandgrube; Johannisberger Erntebringer; Winkeler Hasensprung; Hall-gartener Würzgarten; Rüdesheimer Bischofsberg or any other similar five.

Eighth tasting – Franconian wines

Wines from this district are being exported more and more as their popularity increases. Being harder and more earthy than Rhines or Moselles, they can stand up to a stronger selection of cheeses.

Cheeses
Mild Danish Blue; Cheddar; Brie; Boursin à l'ail.

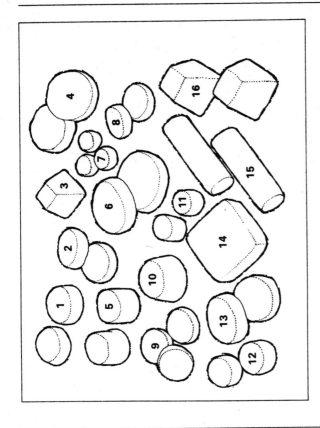

French Cheeses

1. Rougeret
2. Thoissey
3. Saint-Loup
4. Chevroton
5. Bonde du Vercors
6. Vézelay
7. Bouton de Culotte
8. Picodon
9. Pélardon
10. Chevrotin
11. Jumeaux
12. Chabichou
13. Tome de Raisins
14. Niolo
15. Sainte-Maure
16. Levroux

Wines
Würzburger Leisten; Horsteiner Abtsberg; Escherndorfer Lump; Randersacker Teufelskeller; Iphofener Kalb; Sommeracher Katzenkopf.

Ninth tasting – White Bordeaux and Alsatian wines

As value for money, the lower priced white wines of Bordeaux are the best buy in France; but they do lack that tangy, titillating acidity on the palate which typifies Anjous, Alsatians and white Burgundies. For this reason, Bordeaux growers are experimenting with making wine from the Riesling grape. To compare these at a wine and cheese party might be amusingly instructive. I suggest the following:

Cheeses
Tome au Marc de Raisin; Blue Cheshire; Munster; Gjetost (for fun).

Wines
2 'new' white wines from Bordeaux (e.g. Riesling); 1 Sylvaner; 1 Riesling (non-

vintage); 1 Riesling (of a good year); 1 Traminer; 1 Gewürztraminer. All except the first wines listed are Alsatian.

Tenth tasting – Loire wines

With this tasting, starting with dry white wines and working through to Rosés and reds, I suggest a selection of cheeses from the north of France.

Cheeses
Camembert; Port Salut; Maroilles; Pont l'Evêque; Livarot.

Wines
Gros Plant (dry); Muscadet (dry); Pouilly Fumé (dry); Sancerre (dry); Quincy (dry); Vouvray (medium sweet); Quart de Chaume (sweet); Anjou Rosé (sweet); Chinon (red).

Eleventh tasting – Sherries

Cheeses
Brie, almost over-ripe; Camembert, almost over-ripe; Tilsiter; Blue Wensleydale; Bleu d'Auvergne; ripe Stilton.

Wines
Montilla; Manzanilla; Fino; Amontillado Fino; Oloroso.

Twelfth tasting – Vintage ports

Cheese
Ripe Stilton.

Wines
Five vintage ports from five different shippers, all of the same year.

Substantial Cheese and Wine Party

Here I am going to assume that you want to make an evening of it with your friends, that you want them to leave feeling replete and that cheese is the peg on which you wish to hang your party. Personally, I feel that to drink very fine wine on such occasions is unwise, but some readers may want to cater for their guests a little more expensively than others and so I have given two suggestions for the summer months and a further two for winter.

Summer, inexpensive

Cheeses
Caerphilly; Danish Blue; Edam; Cheddar; Lancashire.

Wines
A dry Loire wine such as Muscadet; medium dry South African sherry; Anjou Rosé.

Extras
Wholemeal bread; cream crackers; French bread; butter; watercress (plain); lettuce (plain); Russian salad; potato mayonnaise; cold tongue; cold ham; chutney; plenty of both English and French mustard; a salad of broad beans, French beans and carrots, with tomatoes cut in quarters and an oil, vinegar and garlic dressing. If you live in the country add nasturtium seeds – which are very good to eat. Follow this choice with:

Cold open spinach flan; a flan of hard boiled eggs and anchovy fillets; cold open cheese tart and bacon: fresh fruit salad and cream; any fruits you can get hold of.

Summer, more expensive

Cheeses
Cheshire; Brie; Port Salut; Bel Paese; Stilton; Pommel; Tilsiter; Walnut Cream Cheese.

Wines
Liebfraumilch – medium dry; Manzanilla sherry; Tavel Rosé; Sparkling Vouvray.

Extras
Bath Oliver biscuits; French bread; cream crackers; Ryvita and Vita-Wheat; English farmhouse butter; Normandy butter; cheese and anchovy flan; salade Niçoise; fennel salad; radishes (plain); watercress (plain); lettuce (plain); egg mayonnaise; potato mayonnaise; Avocado pears; cheese straws; asparagus flan; chicory and egg mayonnaise; cold tongue; cold beef; smoked salmon; cold chicken breasts; cold smoked trout; cold smoked eel fillets and scrambled eggs.

Winter, inexpensive

Cheeses
Danish Blue; Cheddar; Liptauer; Gjetost (The cost of this cheese per pound is high, but it goes a long way, has no rind and keeps forever.)

Wines
Rioja Spanish Red; Marsala; Yugoslav Riesling.

Cold extras
Brown wholemeal bread; cream crackers; butter; Russian salad; potato salad; potato, onion and cheese pie.

Hot extras
Cheese, potato and bacon flan; garden pea and bacon soup with fried bread snippets; chipolata sausages.

Winter, more expensive

Cheeses
Stilton; Blue Cheshire; Gjetost; ripe Camembert; Port Salut; Munster.

Wines
Manzanilla sherry; Meursault; Châteauneuf-du-Pape; Old Tawny port; dry Sercial Madeira; Tavel Rosé.

Cold extras
Bath Oliver biscuits; Hovis; Vita-Wheat and Ryvita; Normandy and English butter; cheese straws; salade Niçoise.

Hot extras
Hungarian goulash with fresh peppers; stuffed aubergines; fondue; fresh hard-boiled eggs with salsify ('poor man's oyster') on top; asparagus flan.

Substantial and Informative

Personally I would approach a party of this sort in a different way from the others and divide the evening into two sections, beginning with the tasting and serving a more substantial meal later. Such a party could, I feel, only be given in wintertime.

Cheeses
Brie; Camembert; Pont l'Evêque.

Wine
Very old in the wood Tawny port.

Extras
Watercress; French bread; Normandy butter.

Later I would serve creamed chicken in a white sauce, creamed potatoes and cauliflower polonaise with Champagne and finish the rest of the cheese with a vintage port.

Another menu might be:

Cheeses
Blue Cheshire; Stilton; Bleu d'Auvergne; Roquefort; Mountain Gorgonzola.

Wine
A young, robust vintage port.

Extras
Bath Olivers; English farmhouse butter.

For the main meal I should serve steak, kidney and oyster pie with sauté potatoes and red cabbage. The wine is not an easy choice after the port and blue cheeses but, improbable though it may sound, I suggest Sparkling Burgundy.

Variations on the Theme

Tasting Sheets and Competitions

I have often added an element of competition to my own wine and cheese parties and I feel that, if skilfully done, this can make the evening pass even more enjoyably. I must point out, however, that there are those who disagree with me as they think it shows up people's lack of knowledge. This is only the case if you start your competition in such a way that a guest can make a fool of himself. With a little thought, all should go smoothly. Here are some suggestions: remember that the best sort of competition is based on opinion rather than fact; or, if the competition has to be based on fact, then arrange it so that if a person is wrong there is no reflection on his gastronomic taste.

An interesting competition is to take the rind and wrapping from two German, two Swiss and two French cheeses and let people guess what they are. There is a definite correct or incorrect answer here, but it would not be very serious if most people got them hopelessly wrong. A more imaginative type of tasting competition would be to take five or six different sorts of cheese with the same number of wines and have your guests marry them up. As this is entirely a matter of opinion you would have to provide an expert's adjudication and the winner's paper would be the one most nearly approximating to it.

Never make the prizes (if you decide to give them) too good. The reason for this is that as most competitions will be questions of judgment or opinion, a lot of guests will feel that they should have won which will not matter if the whole thing is treated in a light-hearted manner and there are plenty of prizes.

With wine the possibilities and variations multiply a hundredfold, because there are so many different varieties and vintages. Wine is also much more easily masked than cheese and you can most easily do this by putting a piece of paper with a number round the label and making a key for yourself.

Always end any competition, whether of cheese or wine, long before the party itself ends. The reason is that you are bound to have a number of guests who will want to savour again whatever was the object of the test in the light of what the expert considered to be correct. If very fine wines are involved I would give the answers within an hour of the party starting, because it is very annoying for a guest to discover at the very end of the evening that he has missed tasting a Lafite or Steinberger of a year he has always been particularly interested in.

For sheer simplicity you may like to have just a single cheese or wine, with the prize going to the first person who hands in the correct name.

Finally, it is quite a good idea to hand out tasting sheets with the cheeses listed down the left-hand side of the paper and a space for comments. If you offer prizes for the best written comments and then gather them in you will find something which will amuse your guests far more than any paid entertainer. Among your serious guests you will find some extraordinarily interesting descriptions but, in addition to this, at such parties there is bound to be a handful of facetious people who cannot resist having a tilt at what you are doing, and some of the entries, especially if you read aloud the unkind ones before the serious ones, can be very funny indeed.

Equipment

I am assuming that all parties will be of the buffet type, but one must nevertheless allow for at least three-quarters of the guests to be able to sit on a chair, stool or the edge of a sofa, because having to manage a glass in one hand and a plate and a fork in the other is so tricky that it spoils all enjoyment in eating.

I know that cheeses are very salty, but one in ten of your guests will, like myself, combine an addiction to vast quantities of salt with a passion for radishes or water-cress. One should therefore have plenty of salt cellars about – a point that is usually forgotten.

Glasses for table wines should be large and generous enough to allow you to give the wine a good rotation and so to enjoy the bouquet. For table wines I recommend glasses of a 5 oz. capacity (i.e. if only two-thirds filled one obtains almost eight glasses to the bottle) and for sherries, ports and Madeiras glasses of $3\frac{1}{2}$ oz. capacity.

If you expect from ten to twelve at the party and only four or five very fine wines are to be served you must be prepared to hire some five dozen glasses, otherwise you should have a good supply of rinsing bowls filled with luke-warm water and an equally good supply of drying cloths.

The larger the number of wines to be tasted, the more important is the provision of a number of empty bottles with funnels in the neck. In Wine Trade tastings spittoons are always provided and the best improvized ones are empty wooden champagne cases filled with sawdust and, ideally, raised some three feet from the ground.

If you are supplying Gjetost, then one of those flat stainless steel cheese planes with a cutting slit in the middle (and which you pull towards you) is essential, for the cheese shows at its best when wafer-thin.

Last of all, butter knives. Assuming – it looks so much more appetizing – that you will let people help themselves to butter from bowls, do see that your knives have blunt, rounded ends; the butter is hard to get out of the dish otherwise.

4
The Classic Chefs and their Cheese Recipes

How finely ground was flour when Escoffier was writing his great recipe book?

What was the butterfat content of a Camembert when Francatelli was at work on his tome?

Then, take Parmesan; it may have been considerably sweeter – or more, or less, pungent – when Alexis Soyer was in the throes of composing his work, than it is now. As for eggs, we do know that they were smaller than they are now, but how much smaller they were in Carême's time is still not known.

It is because we are so very much in the dark on this question of flavours of foods and taste of dishes of the past, and because I am certain that many of us have a strong desire to try out historic dishes, that I had the notion to comment on some of the recipes, having taken on each occasion the most expert advice of professional chefs and Cordons Bleus. Sometimes my comments will include an additional or alternative spice which will give the recipe added piquancy or, indeed, prevent it from being too pungent, the general idea being to bring the 'Old Masters' up to date. After all, the skilful and sympathetic cleaning of great paintings is no bad thing.

Master William Verral (died 1761)

One hardly thinks of Thomas Gray as a gastronome, but a unique book in the British Museum Library is his copiously-annotated copy of *The Cook's Paradise, Being a Complete System of Cookery* by William Verral, Master of the White Hart Inn, Lewes, Sussex, which was published as early as 1759.

Verral was in his day somewhat worried that he might have overreached himself in writing a cookery book, for he says in his uproarious preface that 'To pretend to wish for fame would illy become a person in my sphere of life (who am no more than what is vulgarly called a poor publican').

He was obviously enthusiastic about French cooking and was most impressed by his 'friend and patron', one Clouet, who appears to have taught him all he knew. Clouet was to Verral what Carême was to Francatelli, the Great Instructor.

When they reached the top of their profession these eighteenth- and nineteenth-century chefs were in reality itinerant culinary advisers. In modern times the nearest and closest equivalent position is that of the Army or Air Force Catering Officer created at the beginning of the last war.

Verral set great store in having the correct culinary equipment – 'kitchen furniture' as he calls it – so much so that on one famous occasion he sent off for his own, saying that 'A surgeon may as well attempt to make an incision with a pair of shears or open a vein with an oyster knife as for me to pretend to get this dinner without proper tools to do it'.

One article of furniture which seems to have been far more important then than now was the sieve and, on this same occasion, he is disgusted with what he is offered by Nanny, the cook:

> But at length wanting a sieve I begg'd of Nanny to give me one, and so she did in a moment; but such a one! – I put my fingers to it and found it gravelly. Nanny, says I, this won't do, it is sandy; she look'd at it, and angry enough she was: rot our Sue, says she, she's always taking my sieve to sand her nasty dirty stairs. But, however, to be a little cleanly Nanny gave it a good thump upon the table, much about the part of it where the meat is generally laid, and whips it into the boiler where I suppose the pork and cabbage was boiling for the family, gives it a sort of rinse, and gave it to me again, with as much of the pork fat about it as would poison the whole dinner; so I said no more, but could not use it, and made use of a napkin that I slyly made friends with her fellow servant for; at which she leer'd round and set off; but I heard her say as she flirted her tail into the scullery, hang these men cooks, they are so confounded nice. I'll be whipt, says she, if there was more sand in the sieve than would lay upon a sixpence. However, she came again presently, and I soon coaxed her into good humour again.

On these occasions, when Verral or any other chef in a similar position had been instructed by the Master to 'dress a dinner' for some dozen guests, although the chef would have full authority, the greatest tact was necessary when dealing with the permanent resident cook. I consider his account of how he soothed down 'Nanny' the cook to be as funny a thing as I have ever read.

After he had been commissioned to prepare a good meal Verral used to work out the bill (menu) which 'was vastly approved of'. He had previously been shown the larder which had a 'vast plenty' of good provisions so that he had nothing further to do in the way of shopping, but only to get on good terms with the cook.

> My next step was to go and offer a great many compliments to Mrs Cook about getting the dinner; and as it was her master's order I should assist her, I hoped we should agree; and the girl ,I'll say that for her, returned the compliment very prettily, by saying, Sir, whatever my master or you shall order me to do, shall be done as far and as well as I am able. But Nanny (for that I found to be her name) soon got into such an air as often happens upon such occasions. Pray, Nanny, says I, where do you place your stewpans, and the other things you make use of in the cooking? La, Sir, says she, that is all we have (pointing to one poor solitary stewpan, as one might call it) but no more fit for the use than a wooden hand-dish. Ump, says I to myself, how's this to be? Here's neither stew-pan, soup-pot, or any one thing else that is useful; there's what they call a frying pan, but black as my hat, and a handle long enough to obstruct half the passage of the kitchen. However, upon a little pause I sent away post haste for my own kitchen furniture. In the meantime Nanny and I kept on in preparing what we could that no time might be lost.

The gentleman was clearly so pleased with the meal that he went out and bought a basting ladle, iron skewers, a drudging box and a brazier, invited more friends and asked Will Verral to cook another meal the next week 'for a clerk, a tailor, and a journeyman perriwig-maker who are much about as great epicures' as the host. They may have thought they were gastronomes, but the author of *The Cook's Paradise* has a low opinion of them.

> There was no ceremony for clean plates; but at it they went, just as they do at one of our country club-feasts; the turkey was strip in a minute, and the poor hare tore all to pieces (for there was not a carver amongst them) and a most profound silence there was for a long time, except only a very pretty concert of growling, smacking their chaps, and cracking of crusts.

After this came a pudding with a curious reference to cheese:

> Now the two puddings (improperly called so) were made as follows: I took a few potatoes boiled, and thump'd them to pieces, with an egg or two, and a little sugar, for one; the other was a few old mackeroons I had in my house perhaps twenty years: I soak'd 'em well, and put them into a little milk and flour, instead of cream and eggs, seasoned it high with plenty of onions, etc., to which I added a large clove of garlick, which is enough for the dishes of a fifty-cover table served twice over, and covered it over with some good old Cheshire cheese instead of Parmesan; so that the colours were alike, and sent up, as said before.

One extraordinary thing about Verral's recipes is the amount of oranges he uses. I am not referring to the sweets, of which there are very few, but to the savoury dishes

(Partridge pie with endives, chicken in the Dutch way, Goose pie and bacon, Turkey in a braize with chestnuts, etc.), and then in twenty-five recipes in succession a squeeze of orange (or lemon) is recommended. Were oranges less sweet than now-adays?

Des Macarons au Parmesan (Macaroons with Parmesan cheese)

For this too you must boil them in water first, with a little salt, pour to them a ladle of cullis, a morsel of green onion and parsley minced fine, pepper, salt and nut-meg; stew all a few minutes, and pour into a dish with a rim as before, squeeze a lemon or orange, and cover it over pretty thick with Parmesan cheese grated very fine, bake it of a fine colour about as long a time as the last, and serve it up hot.

The French serve to their tables a great many dishes with this sort of cheese, and in the same manner, only sometimes with a savoury white sauce, such as scallops, oysters, and many of the things you have among these *entremets*.

This is not what we call macaroons of the sweet biscuit sort, but a foreign paste, the same as vermicelli, but made very large in comparison to that.

Comment. A delightful recipe. It makes a good luncheon or supper dish. Almost any pasta is suitable – try 'Conquilla', a medium-sized shell-shaped pasta, say about 12 oz. for 4 servings.

Cook in fast boiling water (well salted, and with a fresh bay leaf) until slightly soft (8–12 minutes) then drain very carefully. Melt 4 oz. unsalted butter in a heavy pan, throw in the drained pasta, and ½ cupful very rich well-flavoured stock, (try adding a few coriander or caraway seeds at this stage) and simmer for a few minutes.

Add 2 tablespoonfuls chopped chives and one of coarsely-chopped parsley, salt, milled pepper and a grating of nutmeg, and a few mushrooms sliced and lightly sautéed in butter. Toss well, then add the juice or a lemon or orange and toss again. The orange must be very sharp and well flavoured – a mixture of orange and lemon juice is often better in England.

Combine some grated cheese with the mixture during the second tossing – top thickly with Parmesan or Mozarella and brown lightly in a hot oven or under a very hot grill. Do not overcook or the chives and parsley will lose their savour.

By the way, cullis is a very thick rich broth, almost a gravy.

Des escallopes en coquilles, aux onions (sic) (Scallops in shells, with onions)

Take your scallops from their shells, blanch them well, and take off the beards, provide some small old onions, peel off the two outermost skins and fry them of a nice colour, and tender, cut the scallops in thin pieces, put them into a stewpan, with the onions well drained, a little cullis, and pepper, salt, parsley and nutmeg; stew all together a few minutes, squeeze the juice of orange or lemon, and put into the shells, sift over a little fine grated bread, but not to hide what it is, colour with a salamander, or in an oven, and serve 'em to table.

This is a genteel good *entremets*, with sauce *à la Benjamele*, with a little Parmesan cheese nicely coloured.

Comment. The flavour of onions would perhaps overpower the delicacy of the scallops: try leeks for this recipe.

Chop the white part of two large leeks finely and cook very gently in butter until soft and slightly golden, then add the sliced scallops – eight for four people.

The cullis should of course be a really good *court bouillon* and very little is required. Add a pinch of powdered mace and a few drops of Tabasco sauce, as well as the parsley, salt and pepper then the orange or lemon juice.

Top scallops with cheese, but preferably a more mildly flavoured one than Parmesan – sometimes Fetta, sometimes Mozarella.

Scallops are so delicious that they are the ideal thing if one wants to whip up a first course in about five minutes. Simply clean and de-beard scallops, add salt, milled pepper, Tabasco and lemon juice; wrap in very thin streaky bacon; cook under a hot grill for about two minutes – turn the wrapped scallops over, top thickly with cheese and cook until lightly brown. Garnish with parsley and lemon wedges and serve at once with thin brown toast.

Des anchois au Parmesan (Anchovies, with Parmesan cheese)

Fry some bits of bread about the length of an anchovy in good oil or butter, lay the half of an anchovy, with the bone upon each bit, and strew over them some Parmesan cheese grated fine, and colour them nicely in an oven, or with a salamander, squeeze the juice of an orange or lemon, and pile them up in your dish and send them to the table.

This seems to be a trifling thing, but I never saw it come whole from the table.

Comment. Use large anchovies for this dish – most good delicatessens sell the large salted ones loose. Wash very well under a running tap until the salt completely dissolves. Drain well, then soak in vinegar (with a blade of mace, a few allspice and a fresh bay leaf) for an hour or two.

Dry the anchovies very well, split and cover with a good olive oil before placing on the fried bread. Use brown bread and unsalted butter.

Add a generous squeeze of lemon juice, then cover with Parmesan or Mozarella before finishing under a very hot grill. Garnish the dish with lemon wedges and parsley).

Antonin Carême (1784–1833)

Born in Paris in June 1784, Carême in later years, and in his cookery books, always called himself Antonin, though his real Christian names were Marie-Antoine.

His father was nothing more than a poor workman who (and one likes the touch of one biographer) was 'overwhelmed by progeniture', so much so, that even Carême himself records that he was one of twenty-five.

In any event, father Carême was so poor that finding food for his family soon became impossible and, indeed, almost to save Antonin from starvation the two had a final farewell meal at a local bistro when the son was told to fend for himself.

'Go, my son, and God be with you. There are many prosperous trades to take up in the world, leave us to languish and die while you flourish. This is an affluent period'.

Stirring words from a father who had so signally failed to make the grade himself but that is just what young Carême did – he prospered exceedingly.

M. Bailly; Talleyrand; the Congress of Vienna; in England with the Prince Regent at Brighton; in Russia with the Emperor Alexander; back in England with Lord Stewart, and finally with M. de Rothschild, who was then reputed to have the finest table in Europe. These were just a few of the people and places that Carême visited in his youth and early middle age.

If Soyer and Escoffier were demons for work, what adjectives are left to describe Carême? He was prodigious. To understand his greatness we must understand that what was important about luxury cooking at that time was, apart from the preparation of the dishes, the conception of huge *Pièces Montées* (perhaps best translated as mounted sculpted show pieces) made of fruit, flour pastry or sugar, which were placed on the tables at great banquets. They were popular before Carême's time, but he carried them to fantastic lengths, to such an extent that he became virtually an architect in sugar. This is not my exaggeration; much of Carême's time was in fact spent studying classical architecture in public libraries, and at one time he put a grandiose scheme to Emperor Alexander for the embellishment of the Palace at St Petersburg. For his pains the Emperor gave him a ring studded with diamonds.

Carême died quite poor in Paris in July 1833, working to the last on his cookery books.

Eggs au Gratin Camerarni

Place in a frying pan 2 oz. of excellent butter, 2 large tablespoonfuls of *sauce Allemande**, a quart of grated Parmesan and a little chicken stock with a pinch of

---

*According to Escoffier this is not what he calls one of the leading sauces but is a thickened Velouté – a sauce of flour and veal stock – with a vast number of egg yolks, lemon and mushroom stock.

mignonette and one of grated nutmeg. Melt all the above until they have blended into a whole and then throw in a dozen hard boiled eggs which have been cut into rounds. Roll them in the sauce and then dress them in a fine silver casserole dish.

In this dish make a bed of your eggs and around each one put a dessertspoonful (*cuillerée à bouche*) of Gruyère cut into small dice and a dessertspoonful of purée of tomatoes and continue doing this until all your eggs have been used up. Cover the whole with chicken stock which has been considerably thickened by simmering and into which has been blended some grated Parmesan cheese. Place under the grill and serve.

Comment. This is quite a straightforward dish which would serve as a main course for a luncheon or as a hot hors d'oeuvre for a more formal dinner at night. The chicken stock could easily be replaced by a *bouillon* cube without spoiling the recipe, especially as the cheese would give it a fairly potent flavour.

The nutmeg could be left out or replaced by ground mace or allspice. Fresh tomatoes peeled and skinned would not change Carême's original conception if this were easier.

Alexandre Dumas (1802–70)

In 1870 the author of *The Three Musketeers* and *The Count of Monte Cristo* produced a book which he himself thought would be his greatest work. Entitled *Le Grand Dictionnaire de Cuisine*, it was a work of immense length and written in remarkable circumstances. Dumas had had written into his contract with the publishers of his novels a clause that expressly allowed him to write a cookbook and place it wherever he pleased. After fifteen years of writing novels at a feverish pace, in order to pay off a gigantic debt (he states in a long preface to the cookbook that he averaged during the time 'three volumes a month'), Dumas felt the need to 'seek temporary periods of rest and sea air to provide me with the strength I need'. What a way to set about rehabilitating yourself – to write the longest gastronomical treatise in the French language! Unfortunately the work was only partly set in type when the disastrous Franco-Prussian war broke out, the year also that Dumas himself died. When the war was over the book was seen through the press in its unabridged form and became extremely rare. Later the recipes were extracted from this jungle of gastronomic knowledge and were published as *Le Petit Dictionnaire de Cuisine*.

Fresh Cod Italian Style

Stuff the cod with chopped, pounded whiting and anchovies. Put into a shallow dish with butter and parsley. Add a bottle of white wine. Sprinkle with breadcrumbs mixed with grated Parmesan cheese. Pour melted butter over. Bake. If necessary, brown under the grill to a golden colour.

Eggs Parmesan

Beat your eggs with grated Parmesan cheese, salt, pepper. Make five little omelettes. Sprinkle them with Parmesan, roll, and arrange on a platter. Sprinkle again with Parmesan, wipe off the clear part of the platter, and put in the oven to glaze the cheese. This should not take more than 15 minutes. It is important that this dish be served very hot.

Eggs à la Philippsburg

Make a forcemeat with finely chopped and mashed cooked fish or meat, and line the bottom of the platter you will use for serving. Break your eggs over this as for mirrored eggs. No salt is necessary. Sprinkle with grated Parmesan. Cook on the stove. Pass under the grill at the last moment to glaze the Parmesan, but not long enough to harden the egg yolks.

Oysters Parmesan

Drain your oysters and put them on a buttered platter. Sprinkle with coarse pepper and chopped parsley. Pour over them ½ glass of Champagne, cover with grated Parmesan cheese, and bake. When they are a good golden colour, and the cheese glazed, remove, pour off any excess butter, clean the edge of the platter, and serve.

Comment. This oyster dish served at a dinner party is a great success. Keep back some of the parsley to decorate at the end, for the parsley sprinkled over the oysters will probably discolour somewhat during cooking.

Charles Elme Francatelli (1805–76)

We learn a little about Francatelli from the 1846 edition of this book *The Modern Cook*:

> The Author hopes he shall be excused for alluding to himself and his pretentions for writing a book of this kind. Although bearing a foreign name, he is happy in being an Englishman.
>
> He received his professional education in Paris and acquired a knowledge of his art in some of the most celebrated cuisines of that capital, and was so fortunate as to become the pupil of the renowned Carême.

and, later,

French Cheeses

1. Bleu du Haut Jura (also called Gex)
2. Tome de Savoie
3. Tome de Savoie
4. Bresse Bleu
5. Livarot

And he shall ever consider it the greatest honour to which he could aspire to have served as chef cook and Maître d'Hôtel to Her Most Gracious Majesty the Queen.

In this Preface, Francatelli 'ventures to offer a few suggestions for the consideration of Epicures'.

One of these is a strong hint that gourmands in England were well behind their French friends in the number of courses they demanded and that fish, hors d'oeuvres, patties and croquettes should form part of the fish course and not a distinct course, as they are considered 'east of Temple Bar', a dig at the gluttony at City Banquets. He also felt that turtle and venison should be served less indiscriminately in London. 'They are both so excellent that instead of having them as side dishes, they should, when they form part of a *recherché* dinner, be served with very light entrées and on such occasions indeed it would be preferable to arrange the dinner in the Russian fashion, placing the dessert on the table first while the whole dinner is served from side tables'. This meant, he continued, that the extravagant number of first course dishes served could be cut down and the dinner 'has a better chance of being hot'.

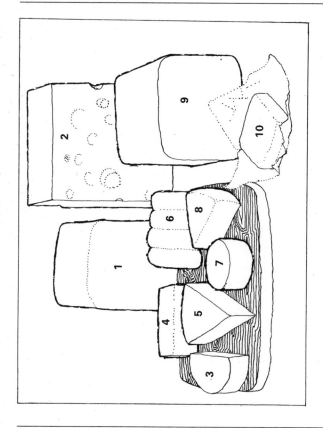

German Cheeses

1. Tilsiter
2. Allgäuer Emmenthaler
3. Camembert
4. Romadur
5. Brie
6. Harzer-Mainzer
7. Weinkäse
8. Butterkäse
9. Edamer
10. Frischkäse

He is exceptionally sound on wine, begging his English readers to desist from serving sweet Champagne with the first course for 'this wine from its sweetness naturally counteracts the flavour of savoury dishes'.

With such sound advice as this on wine, I feel he is equally to be trusted on cheese.

The first six recipes are from the 1846 edition; the last six from the 1911 edition.

Braised Fillet of Beef, à la Milanaise

Braise a larded fillet of beef in an oval braising pan garnished with the usual quantity of vegetables, etc.; moisten with a bottle of sherry or Malaga; when the beef is done, glaze and dish it up, and garnish it round with macaroni prepared as follows:- Boil ¾ lb. of macaroni, cut it into 2 in. lengths, and put it into a stewpan containing some scollops of mushrooms, truffles, tongue, and the fillets of one fowl: to these add a ragout spoonful of Béchamel sauce, 4 oz. of grated Parmesan cheese and a pat of butter; season with a little grated nutmeg and mignonette pepper, toss the whole well together over the fire until well mixed, and use it as directed. Surround the fillet with the essence (clarified in the usual manner), and send the remainder to table in a sauceboat, to be handed round with the fillet of beef.

Polpettes of Rabbits, à l'Italienne

Roast two rabbits, and when they are cold, cut off all the meat and chop it up fine; put this into a stewpan with a tablespoonful of chopped mushrooms, an equal proportion of parsley and 2 shallots, also chopped, 4 oz. of grated Parmesan cheese, a little grated nutmeg, and 2 gravy spoonfuls of reduced Velouté sauce; stir these together over the fire until well mixed, then add the yolks of 4 eggs, and spread the preparation out in a square, about $\frac{1}{2}$ in. thick, upon an earthenware dish; when this has become cold, stamp the Polpettes out with a circular tin mould about $1\frac{1}{2}$ in. in diameter; breadcrumb them twice in the usual manner, place them in a sauté pan with some clarified butter, and fry them to a light colour over a brisk fire; when done, drain them upon a napkin, dish them up in double circular rows, pour some brown Italian sauce under them, and serve.

Potatoes, à la Crème, au Gratin

Cut some boiled potatoes in slices, about 1 in. in diameter. Prepare an *au gratin* mixture as follows:- Put a large *ragoût* spoonful of Béchamel or Velouté sauce into a stewpan, with 4 oz. of grated Parmesan cheese, 2 oz. ($\frac{1}{4}$ cup) of fresh butter, the yolks of 4 eggs, a small piece of glaze, some lemon juice, nutmeg, pepper and salt; stir this preparation over a gentle fire, until it be well mixed, without boiling. Place some neatly-cut pointed *croûtons* of fried bread round the bottom of the dish, in the form of a coronet; place a close circular row of the slices of potatoes within this border of *croûtons*; spread a layer of the mixture over them: then repeat the row of potatoes and the mixture until the dish is complete. Smooth the top over with some of the sauce, shake some fried breadcrumbs and grated Parmesan cheese over the surface, so as entirely to cover it: put the potatoes in the oven for about 20 minutes, to be warmed through, and serve.

Cauliflowers, with Parmesan Cheese

Prepare cauliflowers. Put a large *ragoût* spoonful of Béchamel or Velouté sauce into a stewpan with 4 oz. of grated Parmesan cheese, 2 oz. ($\frac{1}{4}$ cup) of fresh butter, the yolks of 4 eggs, a small piece of glaze, some lemon juice, nutmeg, pepper and salt; stir this preparation over a stove-fire, until it be well mixed, without boiling then pour it on to the cauliflowers, so as to mask them entirely with it. Smooth the dome over with the blade of a knife, and cover the top with a coating of grated Parmesan cheese; place them in the oven to cook for about a quarter of an hour; when they have acquired a bright yellow colour, put a border of *croûtons* of fried bread round the base, and serve.

The *croûtons* may be set round the bottom of the dish in the form of a coronet, previous to serving the cauliflowers, so as to prevent them from spreading.

Eggs, au Gratin

Boil the eggs hard, and when done, take off the shells, cut them in slices and set them aside on a plate. Next, put a large *ragoût* spoonful of white sauce into a stewpan to boil over the stove-fire, and when it is sufficiently reduced, add 2 oz. of grated Parmesan cheese, a small pat of butter, a little nutmeg, mignonette pepper, the yolks of 4 eggs, and the juice of half a lemon; stir this quickly over the stove until it begins to thicken, and then withdraw it from the fire. Place the eggs in close circular rows in the dish, spread some of the preparation in between each layer, observing that the whole must be served up in the form of a dome; smooth the surface over with the remainder of the sauce, strew some fried breadcrumbs mixed with grated Parmesan cheese over the top, put some fried *croûtons* of bread or *fleurons* round the base, and set them in the oven to bake, for about 10 minutes, then send to table.

Comment. This makes an excellent first course for lunch or dinner and has the merit of being easily and quickly prepared.

Allow 6 eggs for 4 persons and about ¾ pint (2 cups) white (Béchamel) sauce. The Béchamel sauce is greatly improved by adding ½ teaspoonful dry mustard (first mixed to a thin paste with cold milk) and a few drops of Tabasco sauce. My preference is for a pinch of powdered mace in place of the nutmeg. The oven should be hot for the 'gratination' and 5 minutes is quite long enough.

Omelette, with Parmesan Cheese

Break 6 eggs into a basin, then add a gill of cream, 4 oz. of grated Parmesan cheese, some mignonette pepper and a little salt; beat the whole well together; then put 4 oz. of fresh butter in an omelette pan on the stove-fire; as soon as the butter begins to sizzle, pour the eggs into the pan, and stir the omelette, as the eggs begin to set and become firm; when the whole has become partially set, roll the omelette into the form of an oval cushion, allow it to acquire a golden colour on one side, and then turn it out on its dish.

Comment. The eggs should not be over-beaten, but rather lightly whisked (use a fork so that air is not beaten into the eggs). Add the seasoning, then lightly fold in the cheese before pouring the mixture into the pan. Use a spatula to lift the mixture as it sets, and then allow more to run underneath. This avoids over-cooking, which can produce a leathery omelette.

Perhaps one should use rather less butter than the proportions given – 3 oz. ($\frac{1}{3}$ cup) for 6 eggs would be ample.

Finish for a few seconds under a very hot grill rather than over the heat.

Garnish the omelette with a little more grated Parmesan and fresh green parsley.

Cheese Fondue

Ingredients: 2 oz. fresh Parmesan cheese grated, 1 oz. flour, 3 yolks and 4 whites of eggs, 1 oz. butter, 1 gill ($\frac{1}{2}$ cup) milk, a pinch of mignonette pepper, and a very little salt.

Mix the flour, butter, pepper, and salt well together with the milk, and then stir this over the fire until it boils; work the batter quickly with the spoon until perfectly smooth, then add the grated cheese and yolks of eggs; whip the whites quite firmly, and fold them in very lightly. Fill the soufflé dish with the *fondue*, bake for about 30 minutes, and send to table as soon as it is ready.

Note—half the quantity of Gruyère with the other half of Parmesan cheese is sometimes used. It is also customary to season *fondues* with mustard, lemon juice, cayenne pepper, and essence of anchovies for those who prefer high seasoning to the more delicate flavour of the Parmesan cheese.

Cheese Aigrettes

Melt 1 oz. of butter in a saucepan, add $1\frac{1}{2}$ oz. flour, stir over the fire, and add 1 gill ($\frac{1}{2}$ cup) of milk, 2 tablespoonfuls of water. Stir till it boils, and work to a smooth paste adding 3 yolks of eggs. Fold in when cooled the whisked white of 1 egg, season to taste, and add 2 oz. grated Gruyère cheese. Drop the mixture from a dessertspoon into hot fat or clarified butter, and fry to a light brown colour. Drain, dish up, and serve at once.

Cheese Darioles

Whip up $\frac{1}{2}$ pint ($1\frac{1}{4}$ cups) of cream and mix it with $\frac{1}{4}$ pint ($\frac{1}{3}$ pint) of semi-liquid aspic, and 4 oz. grated Gruyère cheese. Season with cayenne or paprika and a little made mustard. When well mixed, fill the required number of small paper or china dariole or soufflé cases; place these on the ice to set. Before serving, sprinkle over each a little grated cheese.

Baked Cheese Ramequin

Stir 2 yolks of eggs into 1 gill ($\frac{1}{2}$ cup) of cream, and mix with 4 oz. grated Gruyère cheese, and season with salt and pepper. Whisk the whites of 2 eggs, and mix with the above. Fry about 6 slices of bread in hot butter, and put them into several buttered fireproof china pans or dishes. Pour over the prepared mixture and bake in a hot oven to a golden brown.

Golden Buck

Grate or chop $\frac{1}{2}$ lb. of Cheddar cheese. Put in a saucepan $\frac{1}{2}$ gill of water or ale, or – if you prefer – cider; add the cheese, $\frac{1}{2}$ teaspoonful of salt, a dash of cayenne, a teaspoonful of onion juice, and stir with a wooden spoon over the fire until it becomes smooth and creamy; then stir in 1 yolk of egg. Pour hot on pieces of buttered toast placed on a hot dish, and serve.

Cheese Talmouses

Half a pint ($1\frac{1}{4}$ cups) of milk, $2\frac{1}{2}$ oz. scraped Brie, 2 oz. butter, 4 oz. cream-curd, 2 or 3 eggs, a very little salt, 6 oz. puff pastry, 2 oz. flour.

Put the milk, butter and salt into a stewpan on the fire, and as soon as these begin to simmer, gradually add the flour and stir the whole with a wooden spoon for 2 or 3 minutes; then add the curd (from which all superfluous moisture has been extracted), and work in the eggs one after the other, remembering that this paste must be kept to about the same consistency as for *petits-choux*.

Make 6 oz. of puff pastry and give it seven turns, roll out to $\frac{1}{4}$ in. thickness, stamp out about a dozen circular pieces with a cutter 2 in. in diameter, and put these on a baking sheet an inch apart from each other; put a good teaspoonful of the Brie in the centre of each, wet round the edges, and then turn up the sides so as to form each of them in the shape of a three-cornered hat; egg over with a paste-brush, bake a light-brown colour, and when withdrawn from the oven, dredge over some fine grated Parmesan. These cakes should be served hot.

Comment. The flour must be stirred well when added to prevent lumping, and the eggs added slowly in case they are not all required to achieve the desired consistency. Take care to put the Brie into the centre of the pastry only, to allow for the mixture spreading during cooking. If there is too much mixture in the pastry it will ooze out when cooked.

Alexis Soyer (1809–58)

Alexis Soyer wrote a book which sold over a quarter of a million copies, and invented a stove which saved thousands of lives and was the standard equipment of a great army for over a century. He was more frequently caricatured in *Punch* than any Cabinet minister, catered and cooked equally well for kings and beggars, invented sauces, naval kitchens, pantomime illusions, teapots, kettles, and a gadget for keeping golden sovereigns in the heels of dress boots. He would send to Paris one week for ortolans for a dish costing a hundred pounds and the next would supervise soup kitchens for starving Irish peasants. He was vain, yet popular; married to a woman who became a very fine artist, he sang superbly, wrote a ballet and then dashed off to ruin his health helping Florence Nightingale in the Crimea. When a man has done all this – dying, incidentally, at only forty-nine – he can say that he has lived. Such a man was Alexis Soyer.

Appropriately enough, this truly great chef and lovable personality was born at Meaux-en-Brie, a small village twenty-five miles north-east of Paris, where that queen of cheeses is made. The date was 14 October 1809, and he was the third son of a small shopkeeper. His mother was anxious that he should become a priest but the vocation was so distasteful to him that one night, at midnight, he rang the great church bell which, in those days, was the alarm for a fire, was expelled from school and almost by accident became a chef in Paris.

By the time he was twenty-one he had reached London, which was to be his home for the rest of his life. Here he went from success to success until the great moment when he was invited not only to become the chef of the new Reform Club, but also to advise on designing the kitchens which were to become world-famous. One biographer of Soyer has even suggested that he contributed to the revival of the Whig party.

Once established, Soyer wore himself out with activities of every kind – and not, be it noted, only those which were financially profitable to himself. By far his greatest invention was his Soyer stove, which had a fantastic reception when it arrived in the Crimea. The first day they tried it out the Coldstream Guards used only 47 lb. of wood instead of 1,700 lb. and found that two cooks were sufficient to prepare their lunch where previously they had needed seventeen. Soyer refused to patent his stove lest it should be thought that his offer to improve the soldiers' lot had been made only for his own profit, but he could not resist insisting that his name should appear on each and every one.

When he died, Florence Nightingale wrote: 'His death is a great disaster. Others have studied cooking for the purpose of gourmandising, some for show, but none but he for the purpose of cooking large quantities of food in a nutritious manner for great numbers of men. He has no successor'.

But though I have stressed his humanitarian side, he was first and foremost a great creative chef, as his many recipe books show.

Turbot à la Crème (gratiné)

Put ¼ lb. (1 cup) of flour in a stewpan, mix it gently with a quart (5 cups) of milk, be careful that it is not lumpy, then add 2 shallots, a bunch of parsley, 1 bay leaf, and a sprig of thyme tied together. If cut in loose these would spoil the colour of your sauce (which should be quite white). Then add a little grated nutmeg, a teaspoonful of salt and a quarter teaspoonful of pepper. Place it over a sharp fire and stir it the whole time, boil it till it forms rather a thickish paste, then take it off the fire and add ½ lb. (1 cup) of fresh butter and the yolks of 2 eggs, mix them well into the sauce and pass it through a sieve. Having the remains of a turbot left from a previous dinner, you lay some of the sauce on the bottom of a dish, then a layer of the turbot (without any bone), season it lightly with pepper and salt, then put another layer of sauce, then fish and sauce again until it is all used, finishing with sauce; sprinkle the top lightly with breadcrumbs and grated Parmesan cheese; put it in a moderate oven half an hour, give it a light brown colour with the grill and serve it in the dish it is baked on.

Fillet of Beef à la Milanaise

Prepare and lard the fillet, then make a stiffish paste of flour and water, roll it about ½ in. in thickness and fold the fillet in it, fold it again in three sheets of paper, tie it up at both ends, run a small spit through it, and, just as you are going to put it down to roast, open the paste, pour in three glasses of Madeira wine, close the paste well, tie it up securely, roast it 2 hours, take it up and remove from the paste, glaze it, brown lightly with the grill, dish it plain, and have ready the following sauce: cut ¼ lb. of blanched macaroni into pieces an inch long, likewise 2 oz. of very red cooked tongue, 6 large blanched mushrooms, and 4 middling-sized French truffles, put 20 spoonfuls of white sauce* in a stewpan, stir it over the first 5 minutes, season with half a teaspoonful of salt, a small quantity of cayenne, and a little sugar, add all the other ingredients, with ½ lb. grated Parmesan, stir the whole over the fire to get hot, but do not break the pieces; moisten with a little cream, pour the sauce in the dish, lay the fillet upon it, glaze and serve.

*White sauce. Cut 12 lb. of knuckles of veal into large dice, with 2 lb. of lean ham; butter well the bottom of a large stewpan, into which put the meat, (some of the bones of the knuckles may be included in the weight of the meat, but not much), with 3 large onions, 1 carrot, a blade of mace, 4 cloves, and a bunch of parsley, 2 sprigs of thyme, and 2 bay leaves; pour in ½ pint (1¼ cups) of water, and place the stewpan over a sharp fire, stirring it occasionally, until the bottom is covered with a clear white glaze, then fill it up with 10 quarts (25 pints) of stock, or 9 (22½ pints) of water; add 3 oz. of salt, and when upon the point of boiling, place it on the corner of the fire; let it simmer 2½ hours, keeping it skimmed and adding cold water occasionally, to keep the quantity, then pass it through a fine cloth into a basin; then in another stewpan have 1 lb. of fresh butter, melt it over a slow fire and stir in 1½ lb. (3 cups) of flour, stir it over the fire 10 minutes, but do not let it change colour; then take it from the fire, stirring it until half cold, then pour in the stock, stirring it quickly all the time; place it over a sharp fire, keep stirring, and boil it for ½ hour; add 2 tablespoonfuls of chopped mushrooms, and a quart (2½ pints) of boiling milk; boil it 10 minutes longer, then pass it through a sieve into a basin; stir it occasionally until cold, and use it where required.

This sauce is easily made, full of flavour, and has a very good appearance.

Cotelettes de Porc à la Bolognaise

Prepare 12 pork chops, mixing some grated Parmesan cheese with the breadcrumbs and frying them in oil; then cut 80 pieces of blanched macaroni, about $\frac{3}{4}$ in. long, with 20 pieces of cooked ham or tongue, and 20 mushrooms the same size as the macaroni; put them into a stewpan, with two spoonfuls of tomato sauce and a piece of glaze the size of a walnut; place over the fire and when quite hot add 2 oz. each of grated Parmesan and grated Gruyère cheese, mix well together by shaking the stewpan round, season with a little salt, pepper, and cayenne to taste.

Croustade de Fondue au Parmesan et Gruyère

Put $\frac{1}{2}$ lb. (8 oz.) of butter and $\frac{3}{4}$ lb. (3 cups) flour in a stewpan, mix them well together (without melting the butter) with a wooden spoon, then add rather more than a quart (5 cups) of boiling milk, stir over the fire, boil 20 minutes, then add the yolks of 10 eggs (stir in well), 1 lb. grated Parmesan, and $\frac{1}{2}$ lb. grated Gruyère; season with half a teaspoonful of salt, a quarter teaspoonful of pepper, and half a saltspoonful of cayenne; if too thick add 2 or 3 whole eggs to give it the consistency of a soufflé, whip the 10 whites of egg firm, stir them gently into the mixture, have ready a *croustade**, pour in the above mixture, and bake it in a moderate oven; it will require half an hour longer than the soufflé, i.e. $1\frac{1}{2}$ hours.

Petites Fondues (en caisse) au Stilton

Put 6 oz. ($\frac{3}{4}$ cup) of butter and $\frac{1}{2}$ lb. (2 cups) of flour in a stewpan, blend well together with a wooden spoon, add a quart (5 cups) of warm milk and stir over the fire for a quarter of an hour. Next add the yolks of 8 eggs, $\frac{3}{4}$ lb. grated Parmesan, and $\frac{1}{2}$ lb. Stilton cheese in small dice, season rather highly with pepper, salt and cayenne, add the whites of the eggs whipped very stiff, and stir them lightly in. Have ready a dozen and a half small paper cases, fill each one three parts full, place them in a moderate oven and bake for about 20 minutes. When done, dress them on a napkin on the dish and serve very hot.

---

*Croustade. Put 3 lb. (6 cups) of best flour upon your pastry slab, make a hole in the centre, in which put 1 oz. salt, 2 lb. (4 cups) of fresh butter, 6 eggs, and sufficient water to form it into a rather stiffish paste (it will require about $\frac{1}{2}$ pint ($1\frac{1}{4}$ cups)), mix well together, drawing in the flour by degrees. When well mixed, roll out four times as for puff paste, leave for $\frac{1}{2}$ hour and it is ready for use.

Line a raised piedish with the above, filling with breadcrumbs, and finishing the edges as for a raised pie; bake it (to a very light brown colour) about an hour in a moderate oven. When done, empty out all the breadcrumbs without taking it out of the mould, then tie a band of buttered paper (4 in. wide) round the top, and put it by until wanted.

Georges Auguste Escoffier (1846–1935)

Temperamental chefs? Not always. In fact, quite a number who have climbed to the top of the culinary tree have been calm men who led simple, well-ordered lives. Such a one was Escoffier, of whom Lord Northcliffe, his great friend, said, 'I love Escoffier, a fine chap and such a restful man', and who, in Sarah Bernhardt's view, made the best scrambled eggs in the world, though he never disclosed his secret.

Georges Auguste was born in 1846 in the village of Villeneuve Loubet, not far from Nice. His father was the local blacksmith, who made far more money by growing tobacco plants and selling them to the wholesale cigarette manufacturers. His years of apprenticeship as a chef were divided mainly between Paris, the suddenly popular Monte Carlo, and the German spas, until these were put out of business by the German government's edict prohibiting gaming, a pastime which had become alarmingly popular.

The turning point in Escoffier's career came when he first met the dynamic César Ritz, who gave his name to Ritz hotels and all that was the latest in luxurious refinement and cooking in Paris, London, New York, Montreal, Pittsburg, Philadelphia and Madrid. The two men had met in France some years previously, but in 1888, when D'Oyly Carte, after a considerable struggle, managed to secure the services of Ritz to open his new Savoy Hotel, Ritz in turn secured Escoffier, who by then was beginning to command substantial sums for his services.

In the world of professional chefs Escoffier is worshipped and revered as the man who, if one may coin a phrase, brought lightness and took away gaudy brightness from menus. He was to the kitchen what Lister was to medicine or W. O. Bentley to motor-cars – a man in advance of his times. He cut down the number of dishes he served his clients (for such they were – each individual dinner being personally planned by Escoffier) and banished from the *plats* the indigestible and garishly-coloured trimmings which were hardly ever eaten. To get some idea of what Escoffier did, we must go back to the idea of a good menu at the time of that other great chef, Carême. What a grand dinner in an English country house can have been like before him is unimaginable for he, in turn, had brought in a number of refinements and did away with 'certain culinary vulgarities and their preposterous names'.

In Carême's day the all-important thing was the art of dressing the table; everything was piled on to it, together with a massive display of heavy silver gadgets and 'weird complicated architectural virtuosities'. Guests (far too many) were seated round immense tables nearly three yards in diameter and found themselves

contemplating a hundred different dishes from which they could not even choose. Their chance placing at table alone decided whether they should try Capon in Aspic or

Rouen Duck, Quenelles d'Ortolan or Doudin de Lievre. As for the young partridges served on a bed of truffles or the Venison Cutlets à la Gelée d'Oranges, one could only regret that they were out of reach. One could of course console oneself with the dishes placed by chance at close quarters – Jambon de Sanglier Trempé au Vin de Madère or Petits Patés aux Hachis de Cailles. What torments the unfortunate gourmet must have endured in finding himself barred by fate or protocol from his favourite dishes!

The whole conception of the table at these gargantuan feasts was in reality what we nowadays think of as a cold buffet, and although weird and wonderful and incredibly heavy heaters were placed under the dishes so that they could be served hot, very few *plats* and still fewer sauces were ever served at their right temperature. That was why – to bring all the food hot to the table – the kitchens themselves towards the end of the eighteenth century were such infernos that they made the stokehold of a coal-fired liner seem like an Arabian pleasure garden by comparison. Here is Carême on the subject:

> It is rush hour in the kitchen. Imagine a large room and in it twenty or so workers all busily at work, hastily coming and going in this gulf of heat. One range a yard square is reserved for the cooking of entrées and another for soups, sauces, stews and fried dishes. Over a smaller range turn four spits . . . In this furnace everyone works at high pitch and not a whisper is heard. Lastly to heighten our suffering all doors and windows are closed for about half an hour before serving to prevent the food from getting cold. This is the way we spend the best years of our lives. Our greatest enemy is coal.

Toward the end of his working life (he died in Monte Carlo, aged 89) Escoffier, a lively little man, became quite a figurehead in London when he was christened 'The King of Chefs and the Chef to Kings'. In spite of his advancing years, fascinating new delicious culinary inventions continued to come from his brain – he created, say the chefs of the world, more dishes than any other chef before or since. He it was who created Pêche Melba for Nellie Melba after seeing her in the role of Elsa in *Lohengrin*, and it was he who . . .

Now I must be careful for there seem to be conflicting facts. When I was studying mid-nineteenth-century characters I noted that neither Francatelli nor Soyer had a cheese soufflé but that a re-issue of Francatelli's cookbook published in 1911, some seventy years after the first edition, did have one. I mentioned this to chef Rusconi when I was lunching at the Mayfair and he said that it was Escoffier who popularized the dish in England.

Poached Eggs Mornay

Coat the eggs with Mornay sauce, and sprinkle with grated Gruyère and Parmesan cheese, mixed with cheese slivers. Then, by means of a slice, carefully transfer the eggs to pieces of toast fried in oil. Arrange them in a circle on a dish, sprinkle each egg with a few drops of melted butter, and set to glaze quickly in a fierce oven.

Eggs en Cocotte à la Lorraine

Put a teaspoonful of breast of pork, cut into dice and fried, into each cocotte, also 3 thin slices of Gruyère cheese and 1 tablespoonful of boiling cream. Break the eggs, season, and poach in the usual way.

Neapolitan Moulded Eggs

Make a preparation consisting of scrambled eggs and Parmesan cheese, keeping it very soft; add to it, for every 5 scrambled eggs, 2 raw eggs. Fill some little, well-buttered brioche-moulds with this preparation, and poach in the *bainmarie*. As soon as the contents are properly set, turn out the moulds on to a buttered gratin dish, sprinkle with grated Parmesan cheese, and coat the eggs with reduced and buttered half-glaze, well flavoured with tomato essence.

Scrambled Eggs with Cheese

Break the eggs, beat them, season, and add to them, for every 2 eggs, $\frac{1}{2}$ oz. fresh grated Gruyère, and as much grated Parmesan. Cook the eggs in the usual way on a very moderate fire, in order to keep them creamy.

Scrambled Eggs à la Piédmontaise

Add grated Parmesan cheese to scrambled eggs, in the proportion of $\frac{1}{2}$ oz. to 2 eggs, with a coffeespoonful of raw, grated Piedmont truffles. Serve in a timbale, and garnish with a fine crown of sliced truffles of the same kind.

Tournedos Valentino

Prepare for each *tournedos* a piece of turnip of the same diameter, but $1\frac{1}{2}$ in. thick. Cut it neatly, stamp it with an even, circular cutter and parboil it until almost completely cooked. Hollow it out, by means of a spoon, inside the mark left by the cutter, and stuff with a preparation of semolina and Parmesan. Put these stuffed pieces of turnip in a sauté pan; add a little water, butter, and sugar, and glaze them while finishing their cooking. Fry the *tournedos* in butter, and serve them in a circle, each on a section of stuffed turnip.

Pommes de Terre Duchesse au Chester

Prepare the necessary quantity of 'Croquette' pastry* and combine it with 2 oz.

Potato Croquettes. Cook quickly in salted water 2 lb. of peeled and quartered potatoes. As soon as they seem soft of grated Cheshire per pound. Mould it to the shape of very small *galettes*; set these portions on a buttered tray; gild them with beaten eggs; cover each with a thin slice of Cheshire, and set them in the oven for 7 or 8 minutes before serving.

Comment. These are a real winner with children of all ages. They provide an easily prepared-in-advance potato to accompany any meat dish, and are excellent with any veal or ham dish. Served with mushrooms and bacon rolls, they form a meal in themselves.

Tomates Farcies à la Provençale

Prepare the tomatoes as follows: Cut them in two; remove their seeds; season them, and place them, cut side undermost, in an omelette pan containing very hot oil. Turn them over when they are half-cooked; cook them for a little while longer; lay them on a gratin-dish, and stuff them with the following preparation: For 6 tomatoes, fry 2 tablespoonfuls of chopped onion in oil; add 4 peeled, pressed and crushed tomatoes, a pinch of chopped parsley, and a crushed clove of garlic, and cook under cover for 12 minutes. Complete with 4 tablespoonfuls of breadcrumbs, soaked in consommé and rubbed through a sieve; two anchovies also rubbed through a sieve, and finish with some somewhat fat, braised-beef gravy. When the tomatoes are stuffed, sprinkle them with breadcrumbs combined with grated cheese; sprinkle with oil, and set the gratin to form. These tomatoes may be served either hot or cold.

Soufflé de Tomates à la Napolitaine

Prepare ½ pint (1¼ cups) of very reduced tomato purée, and combine therewith 2 oz. grated Parmesan, 2 tablespoonfuls of very stiff Béchamel sauce, and the yolks of 3 eggs. Add the 3 whites, beaten to a stiff froth, and spread the preparation in layers in a buttered soufflé timbale, setting upon each layer a bed of freshly-cooked macaroni, covered with butter and grated Parmesan. Cook like an ordinary soufflé.

Macaroni à la Napolitaine

Prepare a beef *estouffade* with red wine and tomatoes; cook it from 10–12 hours, that it may be reduced to a purée. Rub this *estouffade* through a sieve and put it aside.

---

to finger, drain them, place them in the front of the oven for a few minutes in order to dry them, and then tilt them into a sieve lying on a cloth, and press them through the former without rubbing.

Place the purée in a sauté pan; season with salt, pepper, and nutmeg; add 1 oz. of butter, and dry; i.e., stir over a brisk fire until the purée becomes a consistent paste.

Take off the fire, complete with the yolks of 3 eggs, well mixed with the rest, and turn the paste out on to a buttered dish, taking care to spread it in a rather thin layer, so as to precipitate its cooling. Butter the surface to prevent the preparation's drying.

Parboil some thick macaroni, keeping it somewhat firm; drain it; cut it into short lengths, and stir butter into it.

Sprinkle the bottom of a timbale with grated cheese; cover with a layer of *estouffade* purée; spread a layer of macaroni upon the latter, and proceed in the same order until the timbale is full. Serve the preparation as it stands.

Soufflé Piédmontais

Boil 1 pint (1¼ pints) of milk with ⅓ oz. salt; sprinkle on it 2 oz. maize flour; mix well; cover, and cook in a mild oven for 25 minutes.

Then transfer the paste to another saucepan; work it with 1½ oz. butter and as much grated Parmesan; mix therewith 1 egg, 2 egg yolks, and the whites of 3 eggs beaten to a stiff froth.

Place in a buttered timbale; sprinkle with grated cheese, and cook like an ordinary soufflé.

Soufflé au Parmesan

Mix 1 lb. (4 cups) of flour and 2½ pints (6¼ cups) of milk in a saucepan. Add a little salt, pepper and nutmeg, and set the preparation to heat, stirring it constantly the while.

As soon as it comes to the boil, take the saucepan off the fire, and add 1 lb. of grated Parmesan, 3 oz. butter, and 10 egg yolks. Rub the whole through a sieve and then combine with it the whites of 10 eggs whisked to a stiff froth.

Mould in a silver timbale, lined with a band of buttered paper, and bake in the oven for 20–25 minutes.

Beurrecks à la Turque

Reduce the required amount of Béchamel sauce to a thick consistency; mix with it an equal quantity of grated Gruyère; season with cayenne, and spread the preparation on a dish to cool.

Then divide it up into portions the size of fine walnuts; shape these like cigars, wrap each portion in a very thin layer of noodle paste; treat them *à l'anglaise**, and fry them at the last moment in very hot fat.

Choux au Fromage

By means of a piping-bag, form some *choux*, a little larger than the St Honoré ones, from ordinary *choux* paste. Gild them with beaten eggs; bake them in

Anglaise: i.e. dip them in a mixture of well-whisked eggs, with salt and pepper. Add 1 dessertspoonful of oil per 2 eggs.

a moderate oven, and keep them dry. When cold, cut them at the top; garnish them with *Fondue au fromage* seasoned with cayenne, and complete with some Chantilly cream, combined with grated Parmesan; this should be laid on by means of a piping-bag, as in the case of *choux à la crème*.

Camembert Frit

Free the cheese from its crust, and cut it into elongated lozenges. Sprinkle the latter with cayenne, treat them twice *à l'anglaise* (see footnote to *Beurrecks à la Turque*) and fry them at the last moment in hot fat.

Ramequins and Gougère Paste

Quantities: 1 pint (1¼ pints) of milk; 8 oz. (1 cup) butter; ⅓ oz. salt; 1 lb. (4 cups) sifted flour; 16 fair-sized eggs.

Procedure: Put the milk, butter and salt in a saucepan and heat. When the liquid boils and rises, take the saucepan off the fire; add the flour, and mix. Return the saucepan to a moderate fire, and stir the paste until it ceases to stick to the spoon, and the butter begins to ooze slightly.

Take the saucepan off the fire; add the eggs, 2 at a time, taking care to mix each couple thoroughly with the paste before inserting the succeeding couple. When all eggs are added, cut into dice 8 oz. fresh Gruyère, and add to the paste.

Comment. Many people think choux paste difficult to make, but in fact that is not the case, although a common fault is to have the paste too moist. The bigger quantity one is making, the fewer eggs one needs to use, for example in the above recipe when using 1 lb. (4 cups) flour you will probably not need the full amount of eggs. Probably the quantities in the above recipe are due to the different texture of flour now, and when this recipe was written. The secret of choux paste is good beating as the eggs are added.

Crème Frite au Fromage

Mix together 4 oz. (1 cup) flour, 2½ oz. ground rice, 3 eggs and 2 egg yolks. Dilute with 1 pint (1¼ pints) of milk; season with salt, cayenne, and nutmeg; boil, and cook for 5 minutes over an open fire, stirring incessantly the while.

Add 4 oz. of grated Gruyère; spread this preparation on a buttered tray; leave it to cool; and then cut it into elongated lozenges. Roll the latter in beaten egg and breadcrumbs mixed with grated cheese, and fry them at the last moment. Serve them on a napkin.

Comment. The *crème-de-riz* (which can be found in most good grocers) adds texture and lightens the mixture. Take care not to over-season with nutmeg – some prefer powdered mace. A pinch of dried celery leaves pounded finely is a pleasant addition.

The *crème* mixture is often improved by somewhat longer and slower cooking. Use a double saucepan so that there is no possibility of the mixture burning slightly and ruining the delicate flavour. Allow it to cool slightly before adding the cheese.

Serve this on thin fingers of toast rather than in a napkin.

Croquettes de Camembert

Dilute 2 oz. ($\frac{1}{2}$ cup) of flour and 2 oz. ground rice with $\frac{1}{3}$ pint ($\frac{3}{4}$ cup) of milk.

Add 1 lb. cleaned Camembert, cut into disc, 5 oz. (about $\frac{2}{3}$ cup) of butter, salt, cayenne, and nutmeg.

Cook the preparation, stirring it the while; cool it; spread it on a tray; mould it to the shape of small quoits; treat these twice *à l'anglaise*, and fry them.

Comment. This is a delicious, rather expensive dish. Only a touch of cayenne and nutmeg should be used, otherwise the delicate flavour of the Camembert is lost. You can also add a very few caraway seeds and milled black pepper.

Use a double saucepan and do not allow the mixture to boil while it cooks.

Three boxes of Camembert are sufficient to produce 1 lb. cleaned Camembert, and the cheese should not be over-ripe.

The croquettes are very good if rolled in matzos crumbs (finely crushed) before frying. Serve on very thin fingers of toast and garnish well.

Paillettes au Parmesan

Prepare some puff pastry with 10 oz. ($1\frac{1}{4}$ cups) of butter; roll it out ten times, dusting it and the table well the while with grated Parmesan and a little cayenne, that the pastry may absorb as much as possible of these. Then roll it into square layers 4 in. by $\frac{1}{8}$ in. thick; cut these up into ribbons $\frac{1}{8}$ in. wide; set them on buttered trays; bake them in a very hot oven, and serve them on a napkin.

Comment. Puff pastry must be well rolled to achieve the desired effect. Roll with quick sharp movements, always away from you, and always 'fold' the pastry as neatly as possible. Cut the pastry quickly with a sharp knife dipped in flour to prevent sticking.

Pudding de Fromage au Pain

Set some thin slices of stale, buttered and cheese-sprinkled bread in a piedish. Having three-parts filled the dish, cover the slices with a preparation consisting of the yolks of 4 eggs mixed with $\frac{1}{4}$ pint broth – which quantities are suited to a pint dish.

Sprinkle well with grated cheese; bake in the oven, glazing at the last moment.

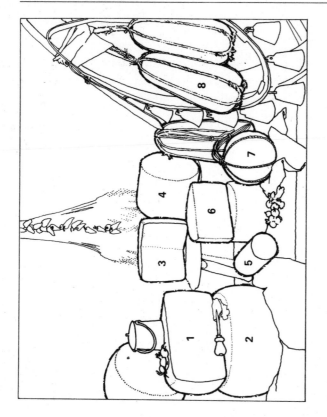

Italian Cheeses

1. Parmesan
2. Parmesan
3. Pecorino
4. Pecorino
5. Provolone
6. Gorgonzola
7. Provolone
8. Provolone

Comment. This is another excellent recipe, and a slight variation on it is to add a small quantity of fine breadcrumbs to the mixture of egg yolks and broth (stock). This will produce a slightly more solid pudding.

Swiss Cheeses

1. Sbrinz
2. Emmenthal
3. Appenzell
4. Schabzieger
5. Gruyère
6. Tilsiter
7. Processed Gruyère
8. Brie
9. Vacherin du Mont d'Or

5
Twentieth-century Chefs and their Cheese Recipes

For many years I often wondered why it was that I always went back to restaurants which I liked. It seemed to me that I should try out other restaurants which my friends told me were excellent. The answer came some years later, when André Simon was asked which he considered to be the best restaurants in London (or elsewhere) and he answered that they were the ones you always returned to. Since then I have never felt guilty when I find myself going back again and again to restaurants I particularly like.

The cheese recipes on the next few pages are my particular favourites from my favourite London restaurants. I hope the reader will enjoy them as much as I have.

Apéritif Grill, Jermyn Street, London

It was all a glorious mistake. A press invitation arrived for me for the opening of a night club just behind St James's Square. I duly presented myself, and after waiting for some 20 minutes while a young lady took my overcoat, I eventually found myself in almost pitch darkness in a basement where the only drink was whisky, something which I have never yet drunk in my life. It was impossible to get out and so I sat there for nearly an hour, stone cold sober. When I did emerge into the spring air, it was a question of where to go for dinner. Although I had consumed no alcohol, I had been stuffing myself with excellent canapés, but this was hardly enough.

I took myself to the Apéritif Grill, where I had been so many times in my youth, and rather grumpily ordered the omelette of the house and half a bottle of claret. It was so marvellous that I was back the next day to see if it had been as good as all that. It was; so I went downstairs to see the chef.

OMELETTE MAISON

6 oz. haddock	Cook the haddock. Beat up 2 eggs, salt and pepper and
2 eggs	add the flaked haddock. Butter the omelette pan (a
salt	large one as the omelette is open). Put in the egg
pepper	mixture (this is the knack and one must be courageous),
butter	turn the whole omelette over on to a plate so that the
Béchamel sauce	brown side is uppermost. Now pour on a little Béchamel
Hollandaise sauce	sauce, and also some Hollandaise sauce. On this
	sprinkle some Parmesan and brown under the grill.
	Eat with spoon and fork.

The Café Royal, The Waldorf and Mr Louis Cipolla

Bernard Shaw, Oscar Wilde, Algernon Swinburne, Ford Madox Ford (Hueffer, if you like), Max Beerbohm: I suppose every worthwhile Edwardian writer dined and had coffee and liqueurs at those marble tables and deep red velvet *banquettes* at the old Café Royal. It has taken perhaps half a century for the ground floor to change from a Bohemian café to a luxury restaurant, but there is one bar where the tables and plush are still to be seen and I always get a mild *frisson* to think, while I am ordering my apéritif, that my fingers may well be drumming on the same spot as were Bernard Shaw's when he was ordering a coffee while mulling over the plot for *St Joan*.

These kitchens have seen my clumsy hands at work too, for over thirty years ago, just after opening my own restaurant, I did a fortnight's stint there – partly to pick up a few tips, but mainly since I could not afford a holiday. It was during one of London's most intense heat waves this century and oh! the dehydration of one's body after a period in the kitchens; on reflection I think I could have paid for a trip to France with what I spent on draught lager at the Slaters and Bodega pub opposite! I worked there under that great Italian chef, Bianchi, who taught me to cook an omelette named after Arnold Bennett which consists of fresh flaked haddock on the inside, topped with really thick cream and then browned under the grill. It might be given a greater intensity of taste if a little Parmesan were to be put in with the cream.

One of the rooms at the Café Royal which has never changed is the small Grill Room. It was there that I met Louis Cipolla, Executive Chef and Food Quality Comptroller. At our first meal together to discuss the projected recipes there occurred a little incident which later caused the Lord Mayor of London to have a new dish served at one of his functions. After a good deal of rather greedy humming and hawing I asked if I could have a bit of plain veal on the bone. 'Yes', said the Maître d'Hôtel, 'We have that very thing'. 'But', I insisted, 'I don't want a piece of Dutch veal with a bit of bone in the middle. I want a real veal chop with the bone running down the outside of the meat, like a giant lamb cutlet'. Cipolla, sitting beside me, was clearly far from annoyed at my insistence and when my chop arrived it was an obvious triumph for his choice of butcher. And so much did I rave about it that I had a letter a few days later, 'For the Lord Mayor's pre-election dinner I served the veal chop – for the first time at the Mansion House – and it was a great success'.

I give one or two of M. Cipolla's recipes, perfected in the kitchens of the Café Royal, the Waldorf and the Festival Hall.

HADDOCK AND CHEESE SOUFFLE (at the Café Royal)

This, I think, is almost my favourite cheese dish and the one I had at the Café Royal was just that much better than those one usually gets. 'The secret', said Louis Cipolla, 'is in the cooking of the haddock, which must – repeat must – be poached in milk first and should only be very lightly cooked. The second secret is to see that the fish should not dominate the soufflé and that the size of the flakes must not be much bigger than a threepenny bit and just about twice as thick; if served for a main course, the flakes should be about twice this size. The final secret is that the fish must be folded into the soufflé mixture very gently and slowly'.

We had the dish as a savoury, but if you should ever have it as a main dish then my own suggestion for an accompanying vegetable is buttered baby carrots, which give a colour contrast, and a flavour which marries with the fish. Asparagus is nice too, but do see that you have (if you use tinned ones) really green tips.

BRAISED CHICORY AND VEAL (at the Waldorf)

This was exceptionally good, but then I have quite a penchant for veal and for chicory, which name seems more and more interchangeable with endive. Anyway, in this instance, I mean the Witloof chicory.

2 pieces of chicory per person
veal escalopes
olive oil
butter
sherry
1 lemon
1 orange
fillet of anchovy
cheese and cream sauce

In the first place do not, on any account, dice or chop up your chicory. Choose the smallest ones you can get – and all of the same size. Braise them lightly in butter and lay in a china dish. Now get some long thick escalopes of veal, 3–4 in. long and 1½–2 in. wide, which have been cooked in a mixture of one-third each of olive oil, butter and sherry. Place these with the juice lovingly and carefully – don't forget the juice in the bottom of the frying pan whatever you do! – over the awaiting chicory and sprinkle on the juice of a fresh lemon and one-third of the juice of an orange. This will prevent the flavour becoming too rich. Now cover the whole with a rich cheese and cream sauce and brown in the oven but, before you do so, lay across the sauce some strips of fillet of anchovy.

Festival Hall

EDAM AND MUSHROOM SPECIAL

1 slice of Edam cheese	Take a large but very thin slice of Edam cheese. Place
1 slice of ham	on top of it an equally thin slice of ham very slightly
purée of 2 oz. mush-	smaller at the top and bottom but not at the sides. Next,
rooms	along the centre lay a portion of purée of mushrooms.
flour	Roll it up. Flour it well and dip it in a mixture of egg
egg	wash (beaten-up egg yolks) and white breadcrumbs
breadcrumbs	and fry. Serve with fried parsley.

The Dorchester and Chef Kaufeler

Solid, spacious yet modern, is a fair description of the Dorchester Hotel, Park Lane, and this is also a fair description of its chef, Eugène Kaufeler, who at the age of 42 became one of the youngest-ever Maître Chefs of one of London's leading hotels. When I approached the Dorchester for recipes I was put in contact with another person who has seen long and continuous service with the hotel, their press officer, Miss Marjorie Lee.

For lunch we started with a cheese and fresh asparagus flan which was so light, so superbly cooked and so well balanced that I boldly asked myself to lunch with the chef the following week. As a professional gastronome this was meant to be a high compliment but even so I had no idea I was going to eat as superbly as I did. First we had a creation of the chef's which was sheer joy. In the first place you hardly ever get real home-made fish *quenelles* these days, for even in France now they all come out of tins, and in the second place they can be a little insipid. We had Dorchester pike *quenelles* which, instead of being poached, were lightly fried and served with a deep rich brown sauce – a marvel. Then we had just the juiciest, tenderest bits of a saddle of hare thinly sliced and covered with a light cream sauce and accompanied by home-made Dorchester ravioli which were rounded and filled with a fabulous stuffing of hazel, hen and ham. 'I thought you would not mind not having potatoes' said the chef – did I imagine a quick look at my *embonpoint*? 'so we are just having braised celery and french beans'. No, I did not mind, for buttons were beginning to take the strain and there was still the cheese soufflé to come and with it – moreover – we had Bollinger.

EVESHAM FLAN DORCHESTER

Ingredients for the
  filling:
½ pint (1¼ cups)
  chopped asparagus
4 whole eggs and
  4 yolks
¼ pint (⅓ pint) milk
5 oz. grated cheese
  salt and pepper to
  taste

Line a flan ring with short paste and bake blind. Beat the eggs and yolks together. Add salt and pepper and pour in the milk. Put the cheese and asparagus in the flan case, pour on the egg mixture and bake in a moderate oven (375°F., 190°C.).

CHEESE SOUFFLÉ DORCHESTER

1 pint (2½ cups) milk
7 egg yolks and
  10 egg whites
2 oz. (½ cup) flour
1½ oz. butter
6 oz. grated Par-
  mesan
salt and pepper

Boil the milk. Mix the butter and flour together and put them into the boiling milk, stirring all the time until it regains boiling point. Take off the fire. Add the cheese, salt and pepper to taste, and the yolks of the eggs. Beat the 10 egg whites until stiff and fold into the mixture. Butter the soufflé case and fill it with the mixture. Sprinkle grated cheese on top. Bake for 20 minutes at (400°F., 210°C.).

Empress Restaurant, Berkeley Street

William James Lacy and John Negri are professionals to their fingertips and have been in the catering profession since their teens. This talented and experienced pair have done much to give the kitchens at the Empress their present fine reputation and I was lucky enough to obtain from them the following recipes:

CHEESE SOUFFLÉ

2 tablespoonfuls
  butter
4 tablespoonfuls flour
⅓ pint (¾ cup) milk
salt
pepper
grated nutmeg
2 oz. grated Gruyère
  or Parmesan
3 egg yolks
4 egg whites

Stir the milk into a white *roux*, composed of 3 tablespoonfuls of butter and 4 tablespoonfuls of flour. Season with salt, pepper and grated nutmeg; stir over a strong heat until boiling. Remove from the heat, add the cheese and the 3 egg yolks and, at the last moment and away from the fire, incorporate 4 egg whites stiffly beaten. Mix quickly, but do not beat. Fill a buttered soufflé dish with this mixture, filling only to within a finger's breadth from the top. Smooth over the surface of the soufflé, cook in a moderate oven for 20–25 minutes. Serve immediately. Season quite strongly to compensate for the weakening effect of adding egg whites.

FRUITS DE MER BIARROTTE AUX FONDS D'ARTICHAUTS DU CHEF

artichokes
1 lemon
6 oz. fish per person
butter
dry white wine
sauce Américaine
Cognac
salt
pepper
sauce Mornay
Gruyère
anchovy butter

Select medium-sized artichokes, clean them of both leaves and chokes, trim them and their bottoms and rub with lemon to prevent blackening, cook in a *blanc velouté*, keeping them somewhat firm. Slice the meat of lobster, fillet sole, turbot, prawns and mushrooms. Cook in a little butter and dry white wine, add salt and pepper. When cooked add sauce Américaine and a few drops of Cognac. Stuff the artichoke hearts with this preparation, arrange them on a buttered dish, coat with Mornay sauce and sprinkle with grated Gruyère. Set to glaze in a fierce oven. Upon withdrawing the dish from the oven, sprinkle the artichokes with a few drops of melted anchovy butter.

The Garden and Geoffrey Sharp

I met a very advanced young caterer through an article I wrote for the magazine *Wine & Food* and its editor, Julian Jeffs. Very little has been written on how much it is good for a person to drink at table and whether, if one attempted to drink rather a lot, there would be any difference if the quality were poor, fair or excellent. I proposed to attempt 3 bottles of mediocre wine from midday to midnight one week and the same amount of fine wine the next, and phoned Geoffrey Sharp and asked him to organize me a suitable meal for such gargantuan potations at his Carosse Restaurant in Elystan Street. To my surprise the quality of the wine made very little difference.

At the age of 34 Sharp decided that he wanted to be his own boss and, quitting the profession of West End stage manager, set about learning the catering trade by getting employment as waiter, wine butler and cook in restaurants belonging to his friends, just as I had done some thirty years earlier. His findings proved invaluable to help him understand the attitudes of those who work in restaurants, but they were disillusioning too; cooking in quantity cannot become an art but is, inevitably, mere routine. So he decided that really careful menu planning was the only thing that could lift restaurant food out of the usual rut. The result was La Carosse, 'which turned out to be much smarter than was originally intended'.

Two years later Sharp opened the sensational Garden Restaurant in Henrietta Street, Covent Garden, and it was here that I tasted braised endives with cheese and tarragon sauce, the recipe for which I give in his own words.

BRAISED ENDIVES WITH CHEESE AND TARRAGON SAUCE

This recipe goes very well as a hot accompaniment to any left-over cold meats, and is excellent with ham.

endives
1 oz. butter
1 oz. flour
½ pint (1¼ cups) cold
  milk
2 squares Demi Sel
tarragon
salt
pepper

Wash endives and remove any sad outside leaves; blanch for 2–3 minutes in boiling water, and then braise in a tin in the oven with a little stock until cooked (about 1 hour at medium heat – 390°F., 200°C.).

Drain well, place in a warm dish and cover with the sauce made as follows. Melt 1 oz. butter in a heavy saucepan, add 1 oz. flour and cook gently until the *roux* is dry and crumbly but not brown. Add ½ pint of cold milk and leave on a very low flame, stirring occasionally with a wire whisk. You will finish up with a thickish Béchamel sauce. Add to this two squares of Demi Sel cheese and a few tarragon leaves and cook on gently for 10 minutes. Adjust seasoning (plenty of salt and pepper) and, if too thick, add some of the braising liquor or some more milk to make a light creamy sauce.

The Mayfair and René Giordano

The Mayfair Hotel has had a curious career. It was opened in the late 1920s under the guidance of Sir Francis Towle and was just in time, in spite of a splendid send-off through being opened by King George V, to do bad business when the big slump came along in the early 1930s. Now it possesses a curious charm: that of being a quite self-sufficient luxury village. Two years ago my friend, René Giordano, took over the general management, and it is now very much to be reckoned with.

When I went to dine with René at the Mayfair we decided, happily, not to have a main course before the cheese soufflé, and so settled for a dozen oysters and a bottle of Corton Charlemagne, 1960 of Louis Latour. We had not finished this admirable wine when the soufflé arrived and so had the chance of trying the two together before we went on to a Clos Vougeot. It was a great experience; so much so that we felt we should ask the chef, M. Rusconi to join us. He had, it transpired, worked under the great Escoffier at the Carlton Hotel in 1927 and remembers the Master reproving him for wearing his carving knife the wrong way round in his belt which he said was very dangerous. Escoffier was growing very old then and did not even wear chef's uniform. His sight may well have deceived him, for Rusconi vividly remembers that his knife was, in fact, anchored blade downwards.

The soufflé should have finished the meal, but a chance remark caused another cheese dish to come to the table. Hardly surprisingly, we were all talking about food, and I chipped in with some remark about my passion for hot pimentos when Giordano said: 'But you should try my wife's pimento Welsh rarebit'. This intrigued not only myself but also Chef Rusconi, who offered there and then to make it. René Giordano described how his wife did the pimentos, down went the chef and in a few moments up came this savoury to round off an excellent meal. The recipes follow:

SOUFFLÉ AU PARMESAN MAYFAIR

4–6 servings

½ pint (1¼ cups) Béchamel sauce

4 egg yolks

6 egg whites

6 oz. grated Parmesan

4 oz. Gruyère

Bring ½ a pint of Béchamel sauce to the boil, stirring all the time, then remove from direct flame and add 4 yolks of eggs gradually, stirring all the time. After incorporating 6 oz. of grated Parmesan cheese let it cool a little and add 4 oz. Gruyère cheese cut in very small dice. Beat 6 whites of eggs to a stiff consistency and fold in gently without too much stirring. Put into a soufflé mould well buttered and sprinkled with grated Parmesan. Cooking time, 30–35 minutes in a medium oven.

PIMENTO WELSH RAREBIT GIORDANO

**thick slice white
  bread**
**⅓ of an unripe
  Camembert**
3 strips red pimento
3 strips green pimento
pepper
celery salt
butter
bacon fat or lard

Fry bread in bacon fat or lard until very crisp. Blend together in saucepan, over heat, the cheese, a knob of butter, pepper and celery salt. Spread mixture smoothly over the fried bread and put under a very hot grill for 2 minutes. Remove, add pimentos in criss-cross fashion and return to grill for another minute. Serve immediately.

The Park Lane Hotel, The Ritz, Paris, The British Hotels and Restaurants Association and Sir Guy Bracewell Smith

A very good turn was done me some years back when Guy Bracewell Smith arranged for me to work incognito in the kitchens at the Ritz in London, of which he is a director. I wanted no privilege but just to be one of the team working under that famous chef, M. Arsène Avignon. It was tough going; but I stuck it and I was rewarded at the end of my stint by being invited to several little lunches in M. Avignon's office, where I ate some classically-cooked French dishes which were superb.

When I asked Guy for a good cheese recipe, it happened that he was going to the Ritz in Paris. He obtained the following recipe by their chef, M. Robert Meyer.

The Tartelettes are a favourite of W. J. Holland, the chef of the Park Lane, and the other two are from the journal of the British Hotels and Restaurants Association.

OEUFS ODETTE, M. ROBERT MEYER

3½ oz. (½ cup) butter
5 oz. (1¼ cups) flour
1 pint (2½ cups) milk
**3 egg yolks and
  4 egg whites**
4 poached eggs
3½ oz. grated cheese
salt
pepper

Mix the butter and flour in a pan and heat for 5 minutes stirring all the time with a whip or a wooden spoon. Add a pint (2½ cups) of milk and boil for 5 minutes still stirring continually. Add 3 egg yolks and 3½ oz. of grated cheese (preferably Parmesan) and salt and pepper. Take the pan away from the stove and let it cool down a little. Add 4 whipped whites of eggs and mix the whole thing together. Spread half of the mixture in a dish (the inside of the dish being covered with butter and grated cheese). Put 4 dry poached eggs on the top and cover with the remainder of the mixture. Cook in a hot oven for 20 minutes.

TARTELETTES DIANE

6 oz. short pastry
2 oz. butter
2 oz. flour
½ pint (1¼ cups) milk
8 oz. grated Cheddar
   cheese
2 yolks of eggs
mustard
Worcester sauce
chicken livers
streaky bacon
pickled walnuts

Line some deep tartelette moulds with the short pastry and cook in a hot oven. Cook the chicken livers and bacon in a little butter, cut into suitably sized pieces and place in bottom of the tartelettes with a slice of pickled walnut. Make the sauce with the butter, flour and milk, cook for 5 minutes, add the grated Cheddar cheese, blend with the sauce, then add the yolks. Pour this mixture into the tartelettes, colour under grill or in a hot oven and serve very hot.

Guy Bracewell Smith comments that these tartelettes can be served with or without pickled walnuts which give them a slightly tart flavour.

HOT CHEESE AND TOMATO QUICHE

for the pastry:
4 fl. oz. (½ cup) corn
   oil
2½ tablespoonfuls
   iced water
8 oz. (2 cups) plain
   flour
½ level teaspoonful
   salt

Put the oil and iced water in a basin and blend well together with a fork. Sieve together the flour and salt. Add gradually to the oil and water mixture to form a rollable dough. (Slightly more or less flour may be required). Roll out between two sheets of greaseproof paper. Line a 9 in. pie plate or flan ring, prick the bottom and sides of the case with a fork and bake blind in a moderately hot oven (425°F., 220°C.) for 10 minutes.

for the filling:
12 spring onions,
   chopped
¾ lb. tomatoes,
   skinned and sliced
¼ oz. cornflour
1 egg
¼ pint (⅓ pint) milk
¼ pint single cream
salt and pepper
2 oz. grated Cheddar
   cheese

Place the chopped spring onions in the pastry case, saving a few for the garnish. Cover with slices of tomato, reserving some for the top of the quiche. Blend together the cornflour, beaten egg and milk. Stir in the cream, add salt and pepper and pour over the tomatoes and spring onions. Sprinkle with half the cheese. Bake for 45 minutes in a moderate oven (370°F., 190°C.). If the pastry becomes too brown, cover the edges with a little aluminium foil. Halfway through cooking, arrange the remaining sliced tomatoes on the top and sprinkle with the remaining cheese. Continue cooking. Garnish with chopped spring onions when cooked. Each quiche serves 8.

HOT CHEESE AND APPLE PIES

25 servings

4 lb. shortcrust pastry
5 pints (12½ cups)
savoury white sauce
3 lb. cored and diced
eating apples
1¼ lb. grated Cheddar
cheese
12 oz. streaky bacon,
sautéed
1 lb. eating apples,
sliced
Salt and pepper
parsley

Line small flan rings or patty tins with pastry. Bake blind in a moderately hot oven (400°F., 200°C.) for 15–20 minutes, or until cooked. Add the diced apples, three-quarters of the grated cheese and the bacon to the sauce. Season to taste. Heat through and turn into the pastry cases. Sprinkle with the remaining grated cheese. Brown under hot grill. Serve hot, garnished with apple slices and parsley.

The Savoy, London

SOUFFLÉ AU FROMAGE

4 servings

¾ pint (2 cups) milk
1 tablespoonful butter
2 tablespoonfuls sifted
flour
4 tablespoonfuls
grated Parmesan
4 egg yolks and 6 egg
whites

Mix the flour and butter together with fingers (*beurre manie*). Bring the milk to the boil. Thicken the milk with the *beurre manie*, taking care that no lumps are formed. Now add the cheese and stir well, follow by adding the yolks individually and continue stirring all the time. Beat the egg whites in a separate bowl until stiff, then fold into the mixture. Season to taste with salt and cayenne pepper. Bake in a soufflé dish, approximately 5–6 in. in diameter which has been previously greased and floured. Baking time, 17–23 minutes in a moderate oven (400°F., 200°C.). Take care to avoid draughts while cooking. Serve piping hot.

6

Classified Cheese Recipes

Hors d'oeuvres

BACON AND CHEESE ROLLS

Cheddar cheese
streaky bacon rashers

Cut the cheese into squares (about 1 in.). Roll the streaky rashers round the cheese and secure with toothpick, cocktail stick or small skewer. Grill the rolls so fast that the bacon is crisp before the cheese melts away. Serve immediately.

THE BULL'S EYE (Denmark)

Butter small, round, unsweetened biscuits or use toasted canapés. Place on each a ring cut from a large olive. In the middle of the olive place a small ball of cheese-butter. Sprinkle with paprika.

(The Danish Food Centre, *Danish Cheese Recipes*)

CHEESE APPETIZER

½ **lb. cheese**
1 **oz. butter**
1 **tin tomato soup**
2 **eggs**
crackers
1 **saltspoonful salt**
½ **saltspoonful pepper**

Cut the cheese into small pieces, then melt in a fire-proof dish, add the butter, seasonings, and tomato soup. When well mixed, add the eggs well beaten. Stir until it begins to thicken, and serve at once on buttered crackers.

(Marion H. Neil, *How to Cook in Casserole Dishes*)

CHEESE CREAMS

2 heaped tablespoon-
   fuls grated cheese
1 cup half-set aspic
   jelly
1 cup whipping cream
1 tablespoonful
   chopped parlsey
salt
pepper
red pepper

Beat up the cream till stiff and stir into it the cheese; add the aspic jelly and the seasonings. Divide into china ramequins; when set, sprinkle over with a little chopped parsley. Serve very cold.

(Marion H. Neil, *How to Cook in Casserole Dishes*)

CHEESE CROQUETTES

4 oz. dry cheese
3 oz. breadcrumbs
1 onion
1 large egg
mustard
salt and cayenne
   pepper
frying fat
batter

Chop the cheese coarsely, and set in a mortar with the sifted dried breadcrumbs, a tablespoonful of minced onion, and a good seasoning of dry mustard, cayenne pepper and salt. Pound these ingredients to a smooth paste, add sufficient beaten egg to moisten thoroughly, then made into balls the size of a walnut. Flatten out slightly, dip in rich frying batter and cook in deep fat. When coloured a delicate brown, drain the croquettes carefully on blotting paper, and pile them up tastefully in a pyramid form. Garnish quickly so as to serve as soon as possible.

CHEESE CROUSTADES

bread
breadcrumbs (about
   1 oz.)
2 oz. grated cheese
1 tablespoonful milk
1 tablespoonful melted
   butter
1 egg yolk
salt
pepper and cayenne

Cut the bread into pieces about 2 in. by $\frac{1}{2}$ in. and hollow out the middle. Mix together cheese, breadcrumbs, milk, melted butter, egg yolk, salt, pepper and cayenne. Fry the croustades in fat or oil until golden, pile the cheese mixture in until you have a cone, put in the oven to brown and serve hot.

CHEESE CROÛTES WITH HORSERADISH

slices of thin bread (no crusts)
1 oz. Gruyère (grated)
1 oz. Parmesan
1 tablespoonful cream
1 dessertspoonful finely grated horse-radish
a few drops tarragon vinegar
paprika
butter (for frying)

Fry the pieces of bread, drain and keep hot. Mix all the other ingredients together and spread on fried bread. Put in a hot oven for about 5 minutes and serve.

CHEESE DELICIEUSES

These are excellent to serve with cocktails, or, if you like, as an accompaniment to a soup or a salad.

egg
salt
pepper
nutmeg
grated Swiss cheese
breadcrumbs
peanut oil

These are delicious and quickly prepared. For each person allow the beaten white of 1 egg. Season with salt, pepper and nutmeg, fold in 3 tablespoonfuls grated Swiss cheese. Using two tablespoons, shape into little sausages and roll in dried breadcrumbs. Drop into deep hot oil and fry at 320°F. (160°C.). As soon as they are golden brown, remove with perforated spoon and serve at once.

(Alice B. Toklas, *Aromas and Flavours*)

CHEESE FEATHERS

¼ pint (½ cup) cold water
½ oz. butter
2 oz. (¼ cup) flour
1½ oz. grated cheese
1 whole egg and half a yolk
pepper

Boil the water and butter together, add flour, stirring all the time, remove from fire and add egg and cheese. Drop with a teaspoon, one by one, into boiling fat till pale brown. Serve with grated cheese.

(J. O. Waller, from Oriana Haynes, *Cooking and Curing*)

CHEESE PUFFS

2 tablespoonfuls butter
4 tablespoonfuls flour
4 tablespoonfuls grated cheese
2 eggs
1 cupful water
½ teaspoonful salt
⅕ teaspoonful pepper

Wet the flour in a little of the water until it forms a smooth paste, and add the cheese, salt and pepper. Place the rest of the water and the butter in a saucepan, and when boiling, add the flour mixture. Cook 3 minutes, stirring all the time; remove the mixture from the fire and set it away to cool. When cold, add the eggs unbeaten, one at a time, and beat the batter at least 10 minutes. Butter a baking tin lightly, and drop the mixture into it, using a heaping teaspoonful for each puff, and leaving considerable space between them, as they increase threefold in size. Bake 20 minutes, and serve hot. Sometimes a plain cream sauce or a brown sauce is served with these puffs.
(*The Pattern Cook-Book*, 1890)

CHEESE ROULETTES

4 oz. St Ivel cheese
3 oz. white bread-crumbs
2 egg yolks
seasoning
fat for frying

Mix the cheese and breadcrumbs (fine and soft) to a smooth paste, until the mixture is heated; spread on a buttered plate. When cool, make into roulettes; dip each in beaten egg or thin frying batter. Fry in hot fat to a delicate brown. Drain, dish and garnish with fried parsley.
(*Isobel's Home Cookery*, 1903–5)

CRAB AND CHEESE TOASTS

1 tin of crab
grated cheese
lemon juice
tarragon vinegar
breadcrumbs
mustard
cayenne pepper
salt and pepper
buttered toast

Make the crab into a pulp. Add a small piece of butter, salt, pepper, mustard, cayenne, and a squeeze of lemon. Wet down with a little tarragon vinegar and add breadcrumbs if too wet. Spread mixture on toast. Sprinkle with lots of grated cheese, add a bit of butter on top, and bake in very hot oven for a few minutes. Serve very quickly. When using very fresh crab, pound the coral with the meat.

CREAM CHEESE, 1741 (Cambridgeshire)

1 pint (2½ cups) of milk
1½ pints (3¾ cups) of cream
rennet

Boil the cream, then put it to the new milk, and when blood warm put in a spoonful of rennet; when it is well come, take a large strainer, lay it in a great cheese fat, put the curd in gently upon the strainer, then lay it on the cheese board with a 1 lb. weight on the top. Let it drain 3 hours, then put the curd in a cheese cloth, smooth it over and put a weight on the top, turn every 2 hours, and next morning salt it and put it in a clean cloth.
(*County Recipes of Old England*)

MOZZARELLA IN CAROZZA

This dish, which means, literally, *mozzarella* in a carriage, is as common south of Rome as eggs and bacon in England. As with eggs and bacon, it is not easy to get it properly cooked.

Remove the crust from thin slices of sandwich bread. They should be about 3 in. long, 2 in. wide and ⅛ in. thick. Put slices of Mozzarella cheese in between each two slices of bread. Beat 2 eggs in a large plate, with a little salt. Put the sandwiches to soak in the beaten egg and leave them for about 30 minutes, turning them over once, so that both sides are impregnated with the egg. Press each side of the sandwiches firmly together so that the cheese is well enclosed. Fry them quickly in hot oil, and drain them on a piece of blotting paper. Serve them at once.

In England the same dish can be made quite well with Bel Paese cheese.
(Elizabeth David, *Italian Food*)

PARMESAN CREAMS

½ pint (1¼ cups) cream
3 oz. Parmesan
½ oz. gelatine

Whip ½ pint of cream, add to it 3 oz. grated Parmesan cheese, a little cayenne pepper, salt and just under ½ oz. gelatine. Put into little moulds and turn out when set.
(J. O. Waller and Oriana Haynes, *Cooking and Curing*)

PRUNEAUX FARCIS AU FROMAGE

stewed prunes
grated cheese
mayonnaise sauce
lettuce

Choose good prunes, stew them until tender (but not broken), drain them and let them cool. Then remove the stones carefully without breaking the prunes in pieces. Take some grated Cheddar or Gruyère cheese, and moisten it with thick mayonnaise sauce. Season the

mixture well and put a little into each prune, giving each its original form. Serve them on small leaves of round lettuce, pouring over a little more mayonnaise if desired. Sprinkle with finely-chopped parsley.
(Florence Jack, *Cookery for Every Household*)

RAMEQUINS SOUFFLÉ

1 oz. butter
1 tablespoonful flour
½ pint (1¼ cups) milk
½ lb. grated Parmesan
  cheese
8 egg yolks
2 egg whites
salt and pepper
little icing sugar

Melt 1 oz. butter; mix into it a spoonful of flour and a little salt; stir for a few minutes over the fire. Have ready boiled ½ pint of milk, and ¼ pint cream. Pour this on the butter and flour by degrees, and work it perfectly smooth. Take the pan off the fire and add ½ lb. grated Parmesan cheese, a little pepper, a very little powdered sugar, the yolks of 8 eggs, and the whites of 2 well beaten. When well mixed, add the other 6 whites, beaten to a froth. It should then be about the consistency of cream. Fill paper cases, but not quite to the top, and bake in a slow oven for 18 minutes.
(Lady Harriett St Clair, *Dainty Dishes*, 1866)

SAMSOE AND BACON SANDWICH (Denmark)

bread
bacon
tomatoes
Samsoe cheese
salt
paprika

Cut bread into slices 1 in. thick, toast lightly, brush with unsalted butter. On each slice lay a strip of broiled bacon. Place a slice of tomato on the bacon, sprinkle generously with grated Samsoe, season with salt and paprika. Put in the oven until the Samsoe has melted. Ham may be used in place of bacon.
(Danish Food Centre, London, *Danish Cheese Recipes*)

SEMOLINA CHEESE

pepper to taste
1½ cups scalded milk
2 cups grated Cheddar
  cheese
1 teaspoonful grated
  Parmesan cheese
4 tablespoonfuls of
  semolina

For a hot first course there is a dish which I never get tired of, as my wife knows only too well.

Boil the milk, and when boiling add semolina. Stir till smooth and thick, add cheese and pepper and cook slowly for 5 minutes. Turn into dish or individual ramequins – sprinkle a little cheese on the top and dot with butter. Brown under grill.
(Eleanor Layton)

SLIPCOAT CHEESE, 1741 (Cambridgeshire)

Take new milk and rennet quite cold, and when it is come, put it into the cheese fat and let it stand and whey for some time, then cover it and put a 2 lb. weight on it. When it holds together keep turning it for 2 or 3 days upon cheese fats till it is dry, then lay it on dock leaves or nettles, shifting the leaves often. In Cambridge the cheese is sold laid on small rushes.

(*County Recipes of England*)

SWEET RED PEPPERS AND CHEESE

1 tin sweet red peppers (pimentos)
Cheddar cheese
salt and pepper
flour
butter for frying
pieces of buttered toast

Drain and dry the peppers. Cut the cheese into pieces smaller than the peppers and season. Wrap the peppers round the cheese and roll in flour. Fry until cheese has melted. Turn once. Serve on the toast.

TIRI MEZEDES

In Greece one eats the most delicious *mezedes* (appetizers) – they are so good and so varied one is often tempted to make a meal of them! One of my favourites is simply made with cheese – usually from fresh white Fetta, but sometimes from Kasavouli.

3 tablespoonfuls un-salted butter
1 lb. Fetta cheese
lemon juice
salt and pepper

Melt about 3 tablespoonfuls of unsalted butter in a fire-proof dish; arrange about 1 lb. Fetta (cut into slices about $\frac{1}{2}$ in. thick) in layers in the dish, seasoning with a little milled pepper. Heat over a low flame until the cheese softens and begins to bubble slightly. Add the juice of a lemon and serve at once, preferably garnishing with coarsely-chopped celery leaves or un-curled parsley.

I sometimes sprinkle some poppy seeds over the dish before serving instead of the parsley. Serve very hot – if this dish is allowed to cool, much of the flavour is lost. (Mrs D. Mangakis)

TVOROG (Russian Curd Cheese)

It is not essential nowadays to make one's own curd cheese, especially if living in or near London, or for that matter any other large town. Not only do the small Continental stores sell vast quantities of curd cheese of good quality, but so do many of the larger stores with grocery counters.

For most of the following recipes, the curd cheese must be dry. If it is not sufficiently dry, wrap it in a piece of fine white cloth, put it between two plates with a weight on top and leave until every drain of liquid has disappeared.

Keep curd cheese as much as possible away from metal containers, as it tends to take on the metallic flavour – although this flavour disappears fairly quickly.

Making curd cheese is a simple operation. Let a quantity of milk go sour (for example, 4 pints will yield up to 2 lb. of curd cheese). When it is thick and the curd well separated from the whey, hang it in a muslin cloth, or jelly bag, from the tap over the sink and leave it all night. By morning it will have dripped quite dry and be ready for use. To make it into cream cheese, mash into it some thick, fresh cream. If the weather is cold and the milk refuses to sour quickly, warm it and add a little lemon juice or rennet. The less rennet used, the more delicate will be the flavour of the cheese. A pinch of salt added just after the milk curdles will help the whey to separate.

Nothing much seems to be done to the whey. In days gone by people considered a glass of whey good when feverish, and in the country, girls used it for washing their faces.

Some people find that highly-pasteurized milk, when sour, is very bitter. To this there is no answer.

(Robin Howe, *Russian Cooking*)

Soups

CHEESE SOUP (Lanarkshire)

a little butter or margarine

1 tablespoonful finely-chopped onion

½ pint (1¼ cups) hot water

1 pint (2½ cups) milk

2 tablespoonfuls flour

seasoning

2 tablespoonfuls finely-grated cheese

Fry the onion, without browning, in the butter or margarine. When soft add the hot water; when the fragments of the onion are fully cooked, add the milk to increase the measure to about a quart, and as soon as it boils stir in the flour mixed smooth with milk. Season to taste, stir and simmer till it thickens. A moment or so before serving, mix in the cheese.

('Farmhouse Fare', *Farmer's Weekly*)

SOUPE À L'OIGNON GRATINÉE (France)

3 or 4 large onions
1 tablespoonful butter
1 tablespoonful flour
1 quart (5 cups) meat stock
French bread
grated cheese

Peel the onions and slice them thinly. Warm the butter in a heavy saucepan, and cook gently until the onions are translucent and golden brown. Stir in the flour, season with salt and pepper, and add the stock. Bring to the boil and simmer for 20 minutes. Slice the bread thinly and dry it in the oven. Have ready and warm an individual bowl for each guest, add a slice or two of the bread to each, pour the soup over the bread, sprinkle a generous layer of grated cheese on top of the bread and brown under a very hot grill before serving immediately.

ZUPPA PAVESE (Italy)

Zuppa Pavese is found all over Italy. It is quick and easy to prepare, and is nourishing and sustaining, being practically a meal in itself.

4 eggs
1 quart (5 cups) chicken, meat or vegetable consommé
French bread
grated cheese

Heat the consommé, and fry the slices of bread in butter; allow two or three thin slices to each bowl of soup. Poach the eggs in the consommé, drain them and slip them into the heated bowls. Pour the consommé over the eggs. Sprinkle a little grated cheese over each slice of bread and arrange round the egg. Serve more cheese separately.

CHEESE BEIGNETS

½ oz. butter
2 oz. (½ cup) flour
4 tablespoonfuls water
1½ oz. grated cheese
2 eggs

Melt butter, add flour, stirring over the fire. Add water gradually, stirring well. Cook until mixture comes away from the pan (at least 10 minutes). When cool, add eggs, one at a time, also cheese, stirring well. Shape into little balls. Cook a golden brown in deep fat. Drain on brown paper. Serve with clear soups.
(Inga Norberg, *Good Food from Sweden*)

CHEESE CROÛTONS

white bread
1¾ oz. butter
1 white of egg
1½ oz. grated cheese

Cut 12 rounds from fairly thin slices of bread. Butter them on one side. Whisk white well, mix with Parmesan or other strong cheese, and spread rounds with mixture. Arrange on buttered tin. Just before serving, bake quickly in hot oven. Serve with clear and thick soups, and purées.

White of an egg can be left out, in which case mix cheese with butter, and spread on rounds.

KÄSESCHNITTEN (Austrian Cheese Slices)

1 tablespoonful butter
1 tablespoonful flour
4 tablespoonfuls milk
1 egg
salt and pepper
2 tablespoonfuls Parmesan or Cheddar cheese
2 tablespoonfuls Dutch cheese
rolls

Warm the butter and stir in the flour to make a soft *roux*. Cook gently, but do not brown. Add the milk, previously warmed, and season. Take the pan away from the heat and stir in the cheese and egg. Cut the rolls into thin slices, and spread with the cheese mixture. Sprinkle more grated cheese on top. Brown in a very hot oven and serve with clear soups.

Sauces

CHEESE SAUCE (Persia and Turkey)

2 tablespoonfuls plain flour
½ pint (1¼ cups) milk
½ teaspoonful paprika
1 tablespoonful butter
1 egg yolk
salt
4 oz. grated cheese

Warm the butter in a saucepan and make a *roux* with the flour. Cook gently before adding the milk gradually, and cook carefully until the sauce thickens. Take off the heat, season, and add the egg, previously beaten well. Finally add the grated cheese.

GARNITURE MILANAISE (France)

A garniture for escalopes. A *julienne* of tongue, mushrooms and truffles or ham, which is added to spaghetti with tomato sauce, a pat of butter and sprinkled with grated cheese.

SAUCE MORNAY (French)

**equal quantities of
  butter and flour
fresh milk
salt and pepper**

Melt the butter, but do not brown it. Add the flour, stirring carefully so that no lumps form. When the mixture begins to bubble add the cold milk very gradually, until all the milk is blended and the sauce is creamy. Keep warm in a double saucepan or in a bowl steaming over a pan of hot water. Add at the last minute grated Parmesan cheese and a little cayenne pepper. For extra richness, stir in a beaten egg yolk just before serving.

Entrées

BAKED CHEESE EGGS

**1 slice of Bel Paese
  cheese per person
a little butter
1 egg per person**

Melt a little butter in the bottom of an individual ramequin dish. Put the slices of cheese in the dishes and break an egg into each. Put the dishes into one baking dish and cover. Bake in the oven until eggs are set.

CHEESE BABA

**2 oz. butter
2 tablespoonfuls flour
¼ pint (full ½ cup) of
  milk
2 tablespoonfuls cream
4 eggs
4 tablespoonfuls grated
  cheese
salt**

Make a sauce with the butter, flour, milk and cream. Cook for a few minutes and then remove from heat and add egg yolks, grated cheese and a pinch of salt. Then fold in the beaten egg whites and turn out on to a fireproof dish. Steam for about 1 hour and turn out on to ovenproof dish. Sprinkle with grated cheese and put in the oven for about 15 minutes to brown top.

CHEESE AND BREADCRUMBS

**1 cup grated cheese
1 cup milk
1 cup breadcrumbs
1 heaped teaspoonful
  butter
3 eggs
salt and red pepper**

Scald the milk and butter; remove from the stove and add the cheese, breadcrumbs, and seasonings. Beat up the eggs and add them lightly. Pour into a buttered fireproof dish and bake for half an hour. Serve at once. (Marion H. Neil, *How to Cook in Casserole Dishes*)

CHEESE CHARLOTTE

bread and butter
breadcrumbs
grated cheese
2 eggs
¾ pint (2½ cups) milk
salt and pepper

Grease the dish and line with breadcrumbs. Put a layer of bread and butter on the bottom. Then a layer of grated cheese (seasoned). Continue in layers until dish is full, finishing with a layer of bread and butter. Beat the eggs into the milk and pour into dish. Leave to soak in for about 10 minutes. Bake in a medium oven for about 20 minutes and turn out on to plate when cooked.

CHEESE CUSTARDS

4 oz. grated cheese
2 eggs
½ pint (1¼ cups) milk
salt and pepper
sprigs of parsley

Mix the eggs and milk in a saucepan over the fire, stir them till they thicken slightly, remove from the fire, and add the cheese, salt and pepper. Divide into small china ramequin cases and bake until brown. Serve with a small sprig of parsley in the centre of each.
(Marion H. Neil, *How to Cook in Casserole Dishes*)

CHEESE PUDDING (North Wales)

slices of thin bread
  and butter
4 oz. grated cheese
2 eggs
1 pint (2½ cups) milk
seasoning

Grease a 1½-pint piedish, cover the bottom with slices of bread and butter, and sprinkle over them a layer of grated cheese. Repeat the layers until the dish is full. Let the upper side of the top layer of bread be the buttered side. Reserve a little cheese for sprinkling over top. Break the eggs into a basin, add salt and pepper, beat well and mix with the milk. Pour this custard over the bread, and leave it to stand for at least half an hour. Bake in a moderate oven for 30–40 minutes, allowing the top to become brown and crisp. Serve very hot.
('Farmhouse Fare', *Farmer's Weekly*)

CHEESE PUDDING

½ pint (1¼ cups) milk
3 oz. grated cheese
3 oz. breadcrumbs
2 eggs
pepper and salt

Boil the milk, and add to it the grated cheese, when all is dissolved pour over the breadcrumbs. Stir all together nicely, pour into a basin, and when cooled a little add the yolks of eggs and seasoning. Whip the whites of eggs till very stiff, stir them lightly into the mixture, pour all into a greased piedish, and bake for 20 minutes in a good steady oven. Serve immediately.
(*Isobel's Home Cookery*, 1903–5)

CHEESE AND OLIVE TART

short-crust pastry
thin slices of Gruyère
stoned olives
4 egg yolks
a little milk
grated cheese
a little butter

Line a baking tin with pastry. Smear with dabs of butter. Arrange in pastry case slices of Gruyère and olives. Cover with custard made from the egg yolks mixed with a little milk. Put some more butter on top and sprinkle with grated cheese. Bake in a quick oven.

CHEESE RICE CAKES

Take 4 oz. rice (wash if you must – and dry), stir into 1 pint of boiling milk, salt, and boil for 20–30 minutes till thick. Add ½ oz. grated cheese. Spread the rice flat, let it cool. Cut into pieces, coat and fry.

MACARONI WITH CHEESE

¼ lb. macaroni
¼ lb. grated cheese
1 oz. butter
1 oz. flour
½ pint (1¼ cups) milk
seasonings

Boil the macaroni in salted water for about 20 minutes, or until tender enough to cut with a fork; drain it; melt butter in a saucepan, stir in the flour, then add milk and stir till well boiled. Remove from heat and stir in half the grated cheese and the macaroni; season with pepper, cayenne pepper, salt and a little mustard if liked. Turn all out on to a buttered dish, sprinkle the remainder of the cheese on top and bake in a quick oven until nicely brown.
(*Isobel's Home Cookery*, 1903–5)

MACARONI, EGGS AND CHEESE

4 hard-boiled eggs
  (chopped)
1 breakfast cup cooked
  short macaroni
1 teacup grated cheese
¾ pint (2½ cups) white
  sauce
onion juice
salt and paprika
breadcrumbs

Mix all the ingredients together lightly and then put into a greased bowl or fireproof dish. Cover the top with buttered crumbs and bake in a medium oven until brown.

OEUFS RAYMOND

1 or 2 eggs per person
1 tablespoonful of
   shrimps (potted or
   frozen)
1 tablespoonful double
   cream
a little grated cheese
salt and pepper

Put a small knob of butter into individual dishes. Scatter in the shrimps, and pour over the cream. On to this break the eggs, and then season. Sprinkle with the grated cheese, and bake in the oven till nearly set, then place under the grill to brown, and serve.
(Jennifer Douglas Webster)

'The Preparation of Omelettes' from *Buckmaster's Cookery*: lectures at the International Exhibition, 1873 and 1874.

Lecture delivered before Her Majesty Queen Victoria at the School of Cookery. May it please your Majesty:

The specimen of cooking which is now to be presented takes only 5 minutes, and is within the reach of almost the poorest of your Majesty's subjects. The materials cost fourpence, and they furnish a savoury and nourishing dish. The omelette is seldom properly cooked even in France, which gives it its name. It is never found in the homes of the poor in this country, and in the houses of the rich it is often very badly prepared. There is no occasion for an omelette pan and spoon. The ordinary frying pan and spoon found in every house will answer perfectly well. And we endeavour to show in this school not only the best and the most economic methods of domestic cooking, but the various uses to which kitchen utensils may be fairly applied without injury.

A CHEESE OMELETTE

If you require a cheese omelette, introduce into the omelette mixture about a dessert-spoonful of grated Parmesan cheese, with a little pepper and salt, and sometimes a few grains of cayenne pepper; sprinkle the omelette when it is turned out with a little grated cheese.
(*Buckmaster's Cookery*, 1874)

CHEESE OMELETTE

5 eggs
2 oz. grated Parmesan
   cheese
pinch of salt
2 pinches pepper

Prepare the eggs as for a plain omelette. Mix with them 2 oz. of finely-grated Parmesan cheese, a small pinch of salt, and two pinches of pepper. Fry the omelette in the usual way, and before folding it over strew an ounce of finely-minced Gruyère cheese upon it. Fold,

and serve immediately. Time, 4 or 5 minutes to fry.
Sufficient for 3 persons
(*Cassell's Shilling Cookery*, 1901)

CHEESE OMELETTE

4 eggs
2 slices white bread
1 tablespoonful grated
   cheese
1 tablespoonful butter
3 tablespoonfuls milk
½ teaspoonful salt
2-3 chives

Soak the bread in the milk, add beaten eggs, mix well
and put through a sieve. Whisk the mixture, add salt
and the grated cheese and fry in hot butter. Serve
sprinkled with chopped chives.

TORTILLA CON QUESO (Spanish Cheese Omelette)

6 eggs
½ teaspoonful salt
pinch pepper
small cup of cream
2 oz. grated cheese

Beat the cream lightly (excessive beating will turn it
into butter) then beat the eggs and fold the cream into
the eggs. Put in the cheese and the seasoning, fry in the
usual way.

(Marina Pereira de Anzar and Nina Froud, *Home Book
of Spanish Cooking*)

PARMESAN BAVAROIS

Essentially this is a Bavarian cream, but it is not sweetened and it is not a dessert, but
rather a cold entrée to be served as a first course at a summer luncheon or dinner or as
a main dish for luncheon or a buffet supper. In France it might be spooned directly
from its own glass bowl or terrine, others may prefer to mould it, in a ring perhaps,
and garnish with hearts of lettuce or cos lettuce.

In Haiti I have tasted such a dish presented as a crown on a platter ringed with
'flowers' that had been cut out of sweet red peppers.

4 servings
1 cup milk
4 eggs
⅓ tablespoon gelatine
1 cup grated Parmesan
   cheese
¾ cup thick cream

Put 1 cup of milk in a saucepan over medium heat.
When it is about to boil pour over the well stirred yolks
of 4 eggs. Replace over low heat and stir until the spoon
is coated. Remove from heat and stir occasionally.
Melt ⅓ tablespoonful of gelatine in ¼ cup of hot milk
and add to milk-and-egg mixture. Stir carefully until
the gelatine is dissolved. Then add ¼ cup of finely-

grated Parmesan cheese. When cold, fold in ¾ cup of whipped cream. Place in refrigerator for 1 hour.
(Alice B. Toklas, *Aromas and Flavours*)

PASTAS

Under this head fall all the vast range of preparations, home-made or bought in a shop, which are in Italy an essential part of the daily diet. They may be served as an entrée or as a main course. With many of them cheese may be served separately or is incorporated in the cooking of the dish. While in France it is rare to dine without having cheese as such as a course on its own; it is equally uncommon to sit down at an Italian table without seeing a generous bowl of freshly grated Parmesan cheese ready to serve with at least one of the courses.

The pastas are far too numerous to mention more than a very few, so from the great varieties of canneloni, anolini, tagliatelle, tortellini, lasagne, gnocchi, ravioli, and spaghetti, here are a few recipes representative of the whole.

CANNELONI

2 eggs
3 oz. breadcrumbs
2 oz. Parmesan cheese
nutmeg
meat stock
minced beef

Fill the cooked canneloni (boiled first in salted water for 5 minutes) with the following stuffing.

Soak the breadcrumbs in the sauce add the other ingredients and season with the nutmeg. Alternatively, simply mix Parmesan, grated Gruyère, milk, egg, herbs, pepper and nutmeg. Lay the filled canneloni on a buttered ovenproof dish. Sprinkle a layer of Parmesan on the top, add a little more butter and a cupful of chicken or meat stock. Cook them in a moderate oven for 10–15 minutes.

GNOCCHI DI RICOTTA (Cream cheese gnocchi)

½ lb. cream cheese
2 eggs
2 oz. butter
4 tablespoonfuls grated
 Parmesan cheese
3 tablespoonfuls flour
salt, pepper, nutmeg

Sieve the cream cheese and stir in the butter, cheese, eggs and flour. Season, and form into gnocchi about the size of a cork, roll them in flour. Poach them in boiling water from 4–5 minutes. Lift them out when they rise to the top of the pan, and drain. Serve them with butter and grated cheese.
(Elizabeth David, *Italian Food*)

TAGLIATELLE BOLOGNESE, or COL PROSCIUTTO

Boil the pasta in salted water, drain well, and serve with *sauce Bolognese*, fresh butter and plenty of grated cheese. For the version with ham, keep the pasta hot while the ham, cut into strips, is warmed in butter. Pour this over the pasta, before serving with the usual helping of grated cheese.

Sauce Bolognese

4 servings

4 oz. minced beef
2 oz. chicken livers
1 oz. bacon
small carrot
1 onion
**tomato purée con-
    centrate**
2 or 3 anchovy fillets
**small glass of white
    wine**
**a little beef or chicken
    stock**
salt, pepper, nutmeg

Brown the bacon, cut in small pieces, in butter; add the vegetables, all finely chopped. Add the mince, and keep stirring and pressing it with a wooden spoon. When it in turn is brown, add the livers, anchovies (both chopped as well), the tomato purée and the wine. Season carefully, add the stock over the pan, and simmer gently for another half hour.

PIROSHKI (Russian Stuffed Pancakes)

½ lb. cream cheese
½ lb. unsalted butter
1 egg
small pancakes
light frying batter
salt and pepper

Work the cream cheese and the softened butter into a smooth paste, add the eggs and season. Divide into lumps of about 2 oz. each, place them in the pancakes, and fold into a rectangle. Dip these pancakes in turn in a light frying batter, and fry in boiling oil.
(Countess Morphy, *Recipes of all Nations*)

QUICHES

Several surprises awaited me as I started working on these dishes. The minor ones were that neither Escoffier, Francatelli nor Soyer had given any recipes for them in their cookery books, and then that none of my four French dictionaries and encyclopedias had any mention of the word. In the *Larousse Gastronomique*, however, I found that an alternative spelling was Kicke, and looking up my *Oxford English Dictionary* I found Kichel, which directed me to Kechel, an old English word for a small cake; I also found that Chaucer talks of a 'Goddes Kechyl or trype of cheese'.

A God's Kechel was a cake given as alms in the name or for the sake of God. On the same page I found the word Kebbeck which, according to Sir Walter Scott, was a cheese made with ewes' milk mixed with cows' milk.

The more important surprise was that a true Quiche Lorraine is *not* supposed to have any cheese in it. Elizabeth in her *French Country Cooking* has not got it, and a very knowledgeable cook, Lucie Marion in her *Be Your Own Chef* (Duckworth, 1948) says 'No cheese or onions or herbs of any kind must be included in this Regional dish. You can use raw ham instead of bacon but always blanch and fry it a little before hand'.

You can, however, have a *Quiche aux Pommes de terre*, and this is how my wife gives it to us over the Easter bank holidays:

3 big potatoes
2 oz. butter
2 rashers bacon
grated English
   Cheddar
2 tablespoonfuls flour
salt
3 oz. (less than ½ cup)
   cream
touch of nutmeg

Cook the potatoes in their skins; peel and mix with the flour. Roll out about ⅓ in. thin and spread in a prepared tin. Fill the tart with the bacon, well cut up, and also the cream. Sprinkle on the nutmeg and cover with the grated cheese. Bake in a moderate oven.

Also very nice cold, but then I like to have plenty of mustard on it.

Here is a non-potato one, which I used to serve in my Cheddar Roast Restaurant in Great Russell Street.

QUICHE AU FROMAGE

short-crust pastry
3 eggs
sliced Gruyère cheese
milk
salt and pepper
nutmeg

First make a fairly short-crust flan 8 in. in diameter, and prick the bottom well. At the bottom place several thin slices of fresh (i.e. not old and dry) Gruyère. Next beat up 3 whole eggs with salt, pepper, nutmeg and milk and pour on top of the Gruyère. First bake it in a brisk oven to let it set, and then in a slower oven to finish it off. It must be served at once.

(For 3 persons as a main dish, for 6 persons as a supper snack).

RAMEQUINS

2 tablespoonfuls grated
  cheese
1 tablespoonful butter
2 tablespoonfuls
  breadcrumbs
4 tablespoonfuls milk
¼ teaspoonful mustard
¼ teaspoonful salt
⅛ teaspoonful pepper
1 egg

Boil the crumbs in the milk until soft, and add the butter, mustard, salt, pepper and cheese and the yolk of the egg. When all are well mixed, stir in the white of the egg, beaten to a stiff froth. Put the mixture in paper cases, filling each case but three-quarters full, and bake 5 or 6 minutes. The *ramequins* should be puffed high above the edge of the paper, and should be served immediately, else they will fall. They will make a pretty cheese course for dinner.

(*The Pattern Cook Book,* 1890)

RAMEQUINS

1 teaspoonful flour
2 oz. grated cheese
2 oz. dissolved butter
2 well-beaten eggs
2 tablespoonfuls
  cream
cayenne and salt

Stir all the ingredients well together, pour into oiled paper cases, and bake in a quick oven. Serve very hot directly they are ready.

RAMEQUINS À LA SEFTON

Make ½ lb. puff pastry (see Pastry); roll it four times, then sprinkle some grated Parmesan cheese all over it; roll it out four times more, repeating the sprinkling of cheese between each rolling; cut the paste with a cutter in any form you please; sprinkle cheese over the top, and bake them a good brown in a moderate oven. Serve very hot on a napkin.

(Lady Harriett St Clair, *Dainty Dishes,* 1866)

SAITOS RETES (Hungarian Cheese Roll)

For the filling blend 4 oz. grated cheese with a little chopped onion and parsley, mix it into a creamy Béchamel and cook slowly until it is rather thick; take off the fire and stir in 3 egg yolks and the stiffly whisked whites of 3 eggs. Spread this mixture on the thin 'retes' pastry, roll very loosely, place on greased baking sheet, brush with melted butter and bake in moderate oven golden brown. To be served warm, cut slantwise into slices, either as an entrée dish or savoury.

(Lilla Deely, *Hungarian Cookery*)

SALE, OR CHEESE FLAN

A very popular dish. While we always served it as a first course, it could make an excellent light main meal with a green salad. It is in fact a variation of the English egg and bacon pie or *Quiche Lorraine*, and is delicious hot or cold. The following recipe will do 4 main or 8 first course helpings.

10 oz. rich short-crust pastry (see apple pie, page 218)
¾ pint (about 2½ cups) Béchamel sauce
3 eggs
¼ pint (about ½ cup) double cream
6 oz. grated Gruyère cheese
salt, pepper and grated nutmeg

Line a 7 in. flan case with the pastry, crimping edges and pricking bottom with fork. Beat and add eggs to white sauce then cream and cheese, mixing thoroughly. Adjust seasoning and flavour with nutmeg. Pour mixture into flan case and bake in a moderate oven at (400°F., 200°C.) for about half an hour.
(Mrs A. Wainman)

SHRIMP, CHEESE AND MUSHROOM PANCAKE

Another delicious main course when combined with salad is shrimp and mushroom pancakes. The following recipe is for 4 main or 8 first course helpings.

½ pint (1¼ cups) pancake batter
¼ pint (about ½ cup) button mushrooms (chopped lengthwise)
½ pint (1¼ cups) Béchamel sauce
5 oz. grated Cheddar cheese
1 oz. butter
3 tablespoonfuls water
salt and pepper
chopped parsley
shrimps

Make the pancakes and keep warm. The amount of batter should produce about 12 medium-sized pancakes or 16 smaller ones. Cook mushrooms for about 15 minutes, in butter and water. Drain and add to white sauce with shrimps, half the cheese and adjust seasoning. Place a little of the mixture in each pancake, fold over, sprinkle with remaining cheese and put under hot grill for a couple of minutes. Dust with parsley before serving.
(Mrs A. Wainman)

TOMATO AND CHEESE PUDDING (Shropshire)

2 lb. tomatoes
2 oz. grated cheese
1 gill (1 cup) bread-
crumbs
2 oz. butter
pepper and salt

Melt half the butter in a saucepan, slice the tomatoes and add to the butter. Cook until soft, then mix in half the breadcrumbs and 1½ oz. of the cheese. Season to taste. Butter a piedish. Sprinkle the bottom with a few breadcrumbs. Pour in the tomato mixture. Cover with grated butter. Bake in a quick oven for 20 minutes. Serve hot.

('Farmhouse Fare', *Farmer's Weekly*)

Cheese and Meat

CHICKEN PARMESAN

An ideal dish for a dinner party which can be prepared in advance is chicken with Parmesan. It is not too expensive to produce, the main cost being the price of the chicken. When I cook this dish for a party I do all the cooking in advance except for the addition of the sauce at the very end and leave it to keep warm. Just before we sit down at table I turn up the oven to hot, add the sauce, and it is just ready by the time the first course is finished. For 4 people you need:

4 servings
2½ lb. roasting chicken
1 tablespoonful olive
oil
¼ pint (full ½ cup)
chicken stock
½ pint (1¼ cups)
Béchamel or white
sauce
3 oz. Parmesan cheese
(finely grated)
2 egg yolks
2 tablespoonfuls
double cream
1 oz. white bread-
crumbs
salt and pepper to
season

Joint the chicken and brown lightly in oil in sauté pan. Season and add stock. Cover pan and cook over gentle heat for about 20 minutes. Meanwhile prepare white sauce and keep warm. Sprinkle ovenproof dish with a little cheese and arrange chicken on this. Add white sauce to juices in sauté pan with all but one tablespoonful of the cheese. Cook until cheese is melted and then thicken with yolks and cream. Pour sauce over chicken, dust with rest of cheese and breadcrumbs and brown in hot oven (440°F., 230°C.) for about 10 minutes.

(Mrs A. Wainman)

OPEN CHICKEN AND CELERY PIE (England)

pastry
1 onion
butter for frying
cooked or tinned celery
chopped cooked chicken
white sauce
grated cheese
seasoning

Cover a 7 in. sandwich tin with pastry and bake blind. Fry slices of onion in butter. Add celery chopped in 1 in. lengths, chopped chicken and a little grated cheese. Immediately pour over ½ pint white sauce (or less according to other quantities). Add seasoning to taste and fill the pastry case with the mixture. Cover with grated cheese and brown under the grill. Serve hot or cold.

(Paul Steinitz, from *Pot Luck*)

ROAST CHICKEN (South of France)

1 large chicken
1 pkt. Demi Sel or any pasteurized soft cheese
5 oz. (full ½ cup) light cream
salt and pepper
grapes

Heat the oven to a moderate temperature. Place the chicken in a baking dish and season with salt and pepper. Place the cheese inside the bird and in course of cooking baste with cream. When the chicken is almost cooked, toss in some peeled and stoned grapes just to warm them.

(Mrs Witting, from *Pot Luck*)

CHEESE CHOPS

4 oz. cooked or soaked beans
1 oz. grated cheese
onion or leek
relish or sauce
some butter or margarine
flour or oatmeal for coating
fat for frying

Chop up the onion or leek (cooked first for preference), mash together, season with a bought relish or sauce, add butter or margarine. Then stir into a thick sauce. Amuse yourself if you like by shaping them like chops. Then grill or give 10 minutes in the oven, or coat with flour or oatmeal and fry.

(Wilson Midgley, *Cookery for Men Only*)

CHEESE AND SAUSAGE (Flintshire)

½ lb. grated cheese
½ lb. (2 cups) bread-
   crumbs
2 oz. boiled rice
2 eggs
2 tomatoes
1 large onion
½ lb. sausages
1 lb. mashed potatoes
2 oz. (¼ cup) butter
1 dessertspoonful meat
   extract

Mince the onion; and with the sausage and skinned and sliced tomatoes, fry in butter. Mix the cheese, potatoes and breadcrumbs together, add the meat extract, and then the beaten eggs and rice. Put the sausages, tomatoes and onions into a buttered piedish, spread over the cheese mixture, cover with some thick gravy, and bake in a moderate oven until a golden brown. ('Farmhouse Fare', *Farmer's Weekly*)

FRICADELLES OF CHICKEN, FISH, OR VEAL, WITH RICE AND CHEESE SAUCE

cooked chicken, white
   fish, or uncooked
   minced veal
egg
flour
breadcrumbs
white sauce

Cook the rice and keep hot. Mix the meat, chicken or veal with beaten egg and breadcrumbs to make light, firm mixture. Season with salt and black pepper. Form into tiny balls, roll in flour, and poach in boiling chicken stock. Drain the balls and keep warm. Heat the white sauce, and stir in a generous measure of grated Parmesan cheese.

Place the rice in a ring on the serving dish; heap the *fricadelles* in the middle and pour the sauce over them.

Instead of the *fricadelles*, shrimps or prawns warmed in the sauce with a little white wine make a very quickly prepared luncheon or supper dish.

BOLOGNESE VEAL CUTLETS (Italy)

4 servings
4 escalopes of veal
2 oz. grated Parmesan
   cheese
butter
stock
Marsala

The escalopes should be about 3–4 oz. in weight, and ¼ in. thick. Flour and season, and brown them quickly: take off from the fire, add a wineglassful of Marsala. Now spread a good layer of Parmesan on each escalope, moisten with a little stock, and add about 2 fl. oz. of stock to the sauce. Simmer for another 5 minutes, with the lid on, and pour over the cutlets.

VEAL À LA CREOLE (France)

4 servings

1 green pepper
(4–5 oz.)
1 onion peeled
(3–4 oz.)
1 large clove garlic
1 lb. tomatoes
3½ oz. can pimentos
1 oz. butter
1 tablespoonful oil
1 chicken cube
¾ teaspoonful oregano
or marjoram
½ teaspoonful sugar
salt and pepper
4 scallops of veal
(1¼ lb.)
4 thin slices Gruyère

Discard the seeds and stalk from the pepper, and cut the flesh into ½ in. pieces. Chop the onion coarsely and the garlic finely and crush it. Skin the tomatoes and chop roughly. Slice the pimentos thickly. Fry the pepper, onion and oregano in the butter and the oil until tender, 5–7 minutes. Add the tomatoes, garlic, crumbled cube and sugar and continue frying gently until the vegetables are cooked, 8–10 minutes. Stir in the pimentos and season with salt and freshly-milled black pepper. Dip the scallops in seasoned flour and fry quickly in butter until lightly browned both sides. Place in a heatproof dish and pour over the sauce. Cover with foil, and heat through in the oven when required. Then lay a slice of Gruyère on each scallop and slip under the grill until bubbling.
(Mrs R. Bennett, from *Pot Luck*)

GRENADINS DE VEAU CHASSEUR (France)

3–4 servings

¾ lb. fillet of veal
1 small onion
4 tomatoes
½ lb. mushrooms
¼ lb. (½ cup) margarine
juice of ½ lemon
a little grated cheese
flour
salt and pepper

Cut fillet of veal into four slices, dip in seasoned flour and fry quickly in pan with half the margarine until nicely browned on both sides. Put into fireproof dish. Now lightly fry chopped onion and add peeled and sliced mushrooms with chopped tomatoes. (First skin tomatoes by putting them into boiling water for 20 seconds). Add salt and pepper to taste. Cook for 3 minutes, add a little water and 2 oz. margarine, and then pour over veal and cook for 15 minutes in a moderate oven. Add lemon juice and chopped parsley before serving. As an alternative to parsley, sprinkle grated cheese before cooking in oven.
(Mrs Henderson, from *Pot Luck*)

TERNERA CON QUESO (Veal and Cheese Fritters)

4 servings

½ lb. veal
3 oz. grated cheese
2 oz. (½ cup) grated
 breadcrumbs
2 cups white sauce
2 beaten eggs

Cut the veal and fry. Coat the veal with the white sauce and roll in grated cheese and breadcrumbs and beaten eggs. Fry in olive oil.

VEAL LUCULLUS

A main course using veal, which is simple to prepare but quite expensive, is Veal Lucullus. While it is a good dinner-party dish – it can be cooked while the first course is being eaten – it really is only suitable for small numbers unless you have innumerable frying pans and lots of cooking space. My pan manages enough for 4 quite comfortably, after that it becomes rather complicated as it entails too much juggling when I should be busy arranging the first course.

4 servings

4 escalopes of veal (if
 these are cut fairly
 thin by your butcher
 they should need
 little or no batting
 out)
2 oz. (½ cup) flour
4 oz. (1 cup) white
 breadcrumbs
1 egg
a little olive oil
1 tablespoonful milk
4 slices ham
4 oz. roughly-grated
 Gruyère cheese
2 oz. butter
salt and pepper to
 season

Whip the eggs with the milk and oil. Season one side of each escalope, then dip in flour, egg mixture and breadcrumbs. Place cheese (1 oz. each) on other side of each escalope and cover with ham. Cook (breadcrumbed side down) in butter over a low fire for about 15 minutes.
(Mrs A. Wainman)

VEAL WITH MOZZARELLA CHEESE AND WINE SAUCE

4 escalopes of veal
4 slices of Mozzarella
   or Bel Paese cheese
red wine
fresh-chopped herbs
   and parsley

Place a slice of cheese in each escalope and roll it up carefully. Lay in a flat casserole, add butter and a good glass of red wine. Season well and cook gently in a moderate oven till the meat is tender. Remove the meat to a serving dish and keep warm. Thicken the sauce with flour, add a little chicken stock if it has reduced too much, stir in the herbs liberally and pour the sauce over the meat before serving.

Vegetables

AUBERGINES AND CHEESE (Middle East)

4 servings
2 large aubergines
2 eggs
4 oz. (1 cup) toasted
   brown breadcrumbs
4 oz. fresh cream or
   cottage cheese
2 teaspoonfuls finely
   chopped chives
2 tablespoonfuls
   chopped parsley
1 dessertspoonful
   minced dill
a little garlic salt and
   cayenne pepper

Cut off the tops of the aubergines, and peel the skin lengthwise. Sprinkle with salt and leave to absorb for half an hour. Wash, drain and fry in hot oil till golden brown. Leave to cool. Beat eggs, add the herbs and seasoning. Work this mixture into the cheese using a fork. Fill one half of each aubergine with the mixture and cover with the other half. Egg and crumb the aubergines with the other egg and brown crumbs, and fry very quickly in smoking hot oil.

ASPARAGUS MILANESE

asparagus
grated Parmesan
   cheese
melted butter

Cook the asparagus in boiling salted water. When tender, drain well and arrange in a flat oval dish. Sprinkle the tips with the cheese, then pour the melted butter over them and brown under the grill just before serving.

ASPARAGUS MORNAY

Cook and drain the asparagus as above. Cover the tips with *Béchamel* sauce, sprinkle grated cheese over them, and brown under the grill at the last moment before serving.

CHEESE AND CORN

¼ lb. grated cheese

1 tin corn

4 crackers

1 egg

½ cup milk

salt and paprika

1 teaspoonful butter

Roll the crackers, add the egg well beaten, butter cheese, seasonings, milk and corn. Mix well and turn into a buttered fireproof dish. Bake for 30 minutes in a hot oven.

(Marion H. Neil, *How to Cook in Casserole Dishes*)

BAKED POTATOES AND CHEESE SHAVINGS (Northumberland)

Wash and scrub the number of potatoes required. Dry in clean cloth. Slip a knife lightly round each potato, then with a piece of lard rub well over the skins, place on rack or shelf in a good oven and bake 1 hour. Then the skin will peel off like a leaf without wasting any of the potato. To serve, surround each potato with a ring of fine shavings of cheese, sprinkled with cayenne.

(*County Recipes of Old England*)

CELERY CHEESE

Cold cooked celery in sticks, or celery boiled in salted water (twenty minutes to half an hour) and drained. Cover with grated cheese and put under grill to cook the cheese. If you have any cold sauce left, mix in grated cheese, warm up, and pour over the warm celery.

(Wilson Midgley, *Cookery for Men Only*)

CHEESE EGGS FLORENTINE

Purée of spinach

1 egg per person

grated cheese

white sauce

Put the spinach into the bottom of individual soufflé dishes. Sprinkle with grated cheese and break an egg on top. Cover the egg with white sauce and sprinkle grated cheese on top. Bake until tops are brown.

CREAM CHEESE AND POTATO FRITTERS

2 large potatoes

1 lb. cream cheese

2 eggs

4 oz. flour

2 tablespoons milk

2 tablespoons butter

½ cup sour cream

salt and pepper

water

Peel the potatoes, boil in salted water, strain and mash with the milk. Add the cream cheese, eggs, ½ cup flour, ½ teaspoon salt and a dash of pepper and mix well. Put on a floured board, flatten out to about one inch thick and roll up into a sausage shape. Cut into 1 in. slices, dip in flour and fry in butter on both sides, until golden brown. Serve with melted butter and smetana.

(Musia Soper, *Cooking the Russian Way*)

EGG, ONION AND POTATO WITH CHEESE AND CHIVE SAUCE

4 servings

5 or 6 hard-boiled eggs
6 potatoes
4 oz. grated cheese
2 tablespoonfuls of chives
sour cream
salt and black pepper
1 large onion
2 oz. (¼ cup) butter
flour

Peel and cut the potatoes in slices roughly an inch thick, and cut the onion into rings. Cook these together in salted water, until the potatoes are tender and the water cloudy. Drain the potatoes, but return the potato water to the pan. Add the butter and stir in the flour, making sure there are no lumps. Cook for about five minutes or so; add the potatoes, eggs cut in halves or quartered, the chives previously chopped very finely, the grated cheese and finally sour cream to give piquancy. If chives are out of season, parsley can be substituted.

HAM AND CHEESE ENDIVES

A winter dish, both cheap and easy to prepare. The cheese used can either be Cheddar or Gruyère, which goes particularly well with ham.

4 servings

12 large-sized heads of endive or chicory (about 2 lb.)
12 small or six large slices of ham
5 oz. grated Cheddar cheese
2 oz. (¼ cup) butter
juice of 1 lemon
salt and pepper to season
chopped parsley

Wash chicory and boil in salted water for about twenty minutes. To prevent discoloration add some of the lemon juice to the water and also make sure that the chicory is completely covered by the water. (Unfortunately it tends to float so weigh it down with something heavy.) When cooked let the chicory drain for several minutes but keep warm. Meanwhile butter an oven-proof dish. Wrap each head of chicory in a slice – or half if large – of ham and place in dish. Season with salt, pepper and rest of lemon juice, cover with grated cheese and knobs of butter and bake in a hot oven (440°F., 230°C.) for about fifteen minutes. Sprinkle with parsley and serve.

(Mrs A. Wainman)

PAN HAGGERTY (Northumberland)

1 lb. potatoes
½ lb. onions
¼ lb. of cheese
pepper and salt
a little dripping

Wash and peel the potatoes and cut in very thin slices, dry in a cloth. Peel the onions and also cut these in thin slices and shred the cheese. Then make a little dripping hot in a frying pan, spread over it first a layer of potatoes, then of onions, then cheese, and a final layer of

potatoes at the top, seasoning each layer with pepper and salt. Fry gently until nearly cooked through, then either turn in the pan to brown the top or brown the haggerty before the fire.
(*Country Recipes of Old England*)

PATATAS AU GRATIN (Spain)

2 lb. potatoes
2 oz. ham
2 tablespoonful butter
1 cup white sauce
1 oz. grated cheese
1 beaten egg
seasoning

Boil the potatoes in their skins, peel, cut in half long ways and scoop out the centre. Chop 2 oz. ham, add to it bits of the potato which have been scooped out, 1 oz. butter, seasoning and a beaten egg. Fill the scooped out potatoes with this mixture heaping it on top. Place in a buttered dish, pour in a cup of white sauce, sprinkle with grated cheese, put into a hot oven for a short time to brown and serve.
(Marina Pereira de Aznar and Nina Froud, *Home Book of Spanish Cookery*)

PATATAS CON QUESO (Spain)

Take small round potatoes; boil and peel. Hollow out a part of the centre and fill with grated cheese. Dip in beaten egg, roll in flour and fry.

POTATOES AU GRATIN

1 lb. peeled raw
   potatoes
1 teaspoonful salt
¼ teaspoonful white
   pepper
(a very little grated
   nutmeg)
1 egg
1–1½ cups boiling milk
1 oz. grated fresh
   Gruyère cheese
1 slice onion
3 tablespoonfuls butter
2 tablespoonfuls grated
   Gruyère cheese

Peel potatoes, rinse and dry, and cut into thin slices. Mix well with beaten egg, boiled milk, seasoning and cheese. Rub omelette dish with onion slice, then with half of the butter. Arrange potato slices, sprinkle with cheese and dot with the rest of the butter. Bake in hot oven until potatoes are soft, or for about forty-five minutes. Serve with the hors d'oeuvres or with fried or boiled sausages.

RISO A QUATTRO FORMAGGI (Rice with four cheeses)

1½ oz. each of Provolone, Bel Paese, Gruyère cheese
3 oz. grated Parmesan
½ lb. Patna rice
2 oz. tongue or ham

Cook the rice. Cut the cheeses and the ham or tongue into small pieces, and add half the Parmesan. Put a layer of the rice in a buttered dish, then some of the cheese and ham mixture and some butter. Fill up the dish with layers of alternate rice and cheese and meat with the last layer being of rice. Sprinkle the rest of the Parmesan on top with a few dots of butter. Bake or steam in a hot oven.

RAKOTT BURGONYA (Hungarian Potato Pie)

There are several Hungarian recipes for this dish. Here follows the most popular variety:

10–12 King Edward potatoes
2 oz. (¼ cup) butter
3 eggs
½ pint (1¼ cups) milk or cream
salt and pepper
5 oz. chopped smoked sausage

Cook potatoes in their jackets, then peel, mash and mix with butter, eggs, milk, salt and pepper and smoked sausage. Brush a fireproof dish with melted butter, sprinkle with fine breadcrumbs and fold in half of the potato mixture; place on it a layer of sliced hard-boiled eggs (3 eggs) and finish with the rest of the potatoes. Sprinkle top with grated cheese, breadcrumbs and a few spoonfuls of melted butter. Place in a warm oven for 20 minutes.
(Lilla Deely, *Hungarian Cookery*)

SOMERSET POTATOES

4 potatoes baked in jackets
2–3 oz. Ilchester cheese, according to size of potatoes
1 beaten egg
1 oz. butter
salt and pepper
1 tablespoonful cream (optional)
parsley and paprika to garnish

Halve baked potatoes lengthwise and scoop out. Beat all ingredients (except cream) with potato until mixture is smooth and fluffy. Stir in cream and fill jackets. Brush with beaten egg and grill until brown. Sprinkle with parsley and paprika.

STUFFED MARROWS, COURGETTES, TOMATOES AND PEPPERS

All these vegetables can be stuffed with a mixture of rice, eggs, flavourings, fish or meat and cheese; with the exception of the marrows, these make an excellent hors d'oeuvres; or serve as a main luncheon or supper dish, either hot or cold.

Cut the vegetables in half, and spoon out the centre. If tomatoes are used, keep the extract and add it to the mixture.

STUFFING

cooked long rice
eggs
cooked chicken liver or tunny fish
smoked haddock or fresh white fish
cooked minced beef, lamb, or veal
cooked chicken
grated cheese, Cheddar and Parmesan

Add enough beaten egg to the cooked rice to moisten. Season well, and add the chosen fish, meat or poultry, all cut up into small pieces or flaked with a fork. Stir in some of the cheese, and fill the vegetable cases with the mixture. Sprinkle a generous covering of Parmesan on top, dust with white breadcrumbs, and cook in a moderate oven until cooked. Replace the tomato caps if desired and serve either piping hot or cold.

Salads

CHEESE CRAB (cold)

1 oz. good flavoured cheese
1 oz. fresh butter
pinch of cayenne pepper
a saltspoonful dry mustard
a teaspoonful of vinegar or Prince Alfred's sauce
a few drops of anchovy essence
salt to taste

Rub the cheese and butter together until well mixed, add the other ingredients gradually and work the whole into a smooth paste. Serve with crisp dry toast.
(Mary Hooper, *Little Dinners*, 1878)

CHEESE SALAD

6 servings

11 firm lettuce
1 cup cooked peas
1 cup sliced celery
½ lb. of Cheddar
½ cup sweet pickle relish
¼ cup chopped green onions
½ cup mayonnaise
2 tablespoonfuls chili sauce
¾ teaspoonful salt
2 tomatoes quartered

Cut the cheese into ¼ in. cubes. Trim lettuce and wash, remove outside leaves for garnish. Break remaining lettuce into bite-size chunks in a bowl. Add remaining ingredients and toss lightly. Garnish with the whole lettuce leaves.

(Mrs Jack Moore)

CREAM CHEESE MIMIZAN

1 large cream cheese
¼ pint (½ cup) cream
¼ teaspoonful salt
¼ teaspoonful Tarragon vinegar
4 teaspoonfuls milk
3 teaspoonfuls gelatine
1 teaspoonful chopped almonds
1 gill (full ½ cup) cream

1 large cream cheese dissolved in 1 gill of single cream, add to this: 1 teaspoon chopped almonds, ¼ teaspoonful salt, ¼ teaspoonful of Tarragon vinegar, 4 teaspoonfuls of milk. Soak 3 teaspoonfuls of gelatine, dissolve, and strain into the mixture. Stir over ice till setting, then add 1 gill of stiffly whisked cream. Put into a mould which has been wetted. When set, garnish with orange quarters and lettuce.

(Jennifer Douglas Webster)

DANISH BLUE AND SAMSOE SALAD (Denmark)

2 oz. of Samsoe cheese
1 oz. of Danish Blue cheese
1 red pimento
1 green pimento
French dressing
1 onion

Cut the pimentos lengthways, remove the grains, and put the pimentos into boiling salted water for a moment. Allow them to drip and cool. Cut them into small pieces and let them soak in a dressing. Cut the Samsoe into small strips, chop the onion. Cut the Danish Blue into small pieces and mix everything into a dressing, seasoned with mustard, paprika, salt and pepper. Eat with cheese straws.

(Danish Food Centre, London, *Danish Cheese Recipes*)

HORIATIKI (Greece)

To me this immediately conjures up memories of delicious meals eaten under clear Greek skies, often served at the water's edge with yachts and small boats riding lazily at anchor nearby. I think it is the subtle flavour of the Fetta in *Horiatiki* (it means 'village style') which gives it distinction. Fetta is a smooth white Greek cheese, made from goats' or ewes' milk – and it can be bought in Greek shops and delicatessens here. This is how I make *Horiatiki*.

5 oz. Fetta cheese
1 cos lettuce (or endive)
½ lb. tomatoes, firm and ripe (unpeeled)
⅓ cucumber (unpeeled)
1 small green pepper, cored and seeded
1 small onion, sliced very thinly
1½ tablespoonfuls capers
14 large black olives
French dressing

Wash and dry a cos lettuce and break the leaves into large pieces; cut the tomatoes into wedges and season with salt and milled pepper; cut cucumber into 1 in. sections, then cut into thin wedges lengthwise, and season very lightly.

Dice the Fetta on a plate and add a little milled pepper; if the cheese is dry, add a dessertspoonful of olive oil so that the dice glisten slightly. Combine all ingredients and serve at once. Garnish with a few of the olives and tomato wedges. If available some coarsely chopped coriander leaves or uncurled parsley add a pleasant tang. I use Greek capers, which are larger than French ones, and olives from Kalamata or Amphissa (near Delphi). These are absolutely luscious and have a superb flavour. In Greece, the dressing is usually olive oil and lemon juice, but in England a well-flavoured French dressing is sometimes preferred.
(Mrs D. Mangakis)

GIPSY SALAD

mayonnaise, seasoned with mustard and Worcester sauce
salt and paprika
small boiled green peas
boiled potatoes
slices of salami
slices of gherkin
Samsoe cheese

Cut the salami and the cheese into small squares. Mix all the above-mentioned ingredients into the mayonnaise, seasoned with the various spices. Serve with toast.
(Danish Food Centre, London, *Danish Cheese Recipes*)

MOCK CRAB

**This really needs
  tomato**
½ lb. grated cheese
½ lb. chopped tomatoes
egg
**a little butter and
  breadcrumbs may
  also be added**

Cook the tomatoes in a saucepan in butter till soft, add the rest mashing up to a paste. When cold this is a splendid savoury paste to be eaten with bread, with potatoes, or with salad.
(Wilson Midgley, *Cookery for Men Only*)

ROQUEFORT SALAD RING

6 servings

**2 teaspoonfuls un-
  flavoured gelatine**
**3 tablespoonfuls cold
  water**
¼ lb. Roquefort cheese
**2 cups cottage cheese
  – (cream cheese)**
**1 teaspoonful
  Worcestershire
  sauce**
dash Tabasco sauce
salt to taste
½ cup mayonnaise
**½ cup heavy cream,
  whipped**

Combine gelatine and cold water, leave to set for 5 minutes. Dissolve over hot water. Mash the cheese, stir in cottage cheese and blend well. Add the seasoning and melted gelatine. Fold in the mayonnaise and cream. Pour in to 6 in. ring mould and chill. Unmould on lettuce cups and garnish with tomatoes and ripe olives. Serve with French dressing.
(Mrs Jack Moore)

SAMSOE CHEESE SALAD (Denmark)

½ cup French dressing
**1 teaspoonful prepared
  mustard**
**1 small onion,
  chopped**
salt, pepper to taste
**3 oz. Samsoe cheese,
  finely cut or diced**

Mix dressing, mustard, onion and seasoning in a salad bowl. Cut the Samsoe into small pieces, mix well with the dressing. Let stand for an hour at least before serving on a bed of crisp lettuce leaves.
(Danish Food Centre, London, *Danish Cheese Recipes*)

SPRING SALAD WITH CHEESE DRESSING

6 servings

1 head of lettuce
½ head of chicory
2 tomatoes
1 small bunch of
   watercress
1 green pepper cut
1 onion sliced thin
1 small can of
   anchovy fillets
½ cucumber sliced
¼ cup mayonnaise
1 cup French dressing
¼ cup of white Stilton
   cheese crumbled
   fine

Cut the pepper into rings, after removing the seeds. Prepare the salad in a bowl mixing all the ingredients well with the seasoning and anchovies. Combine the mayonnaise and French dressing and blend in the cheese. Mix well and pour over the salad – and serve at once.

(Mrs Jack Moore)

ITALIAN PIZZAS

If you have been up at crack of dawn on the Mediterranean coast; if you have only had the lightest of Continental breakfasts; if by eleven you are feeling famished because you have been for a big swim and are going yet again for another before a very late lunch; then this is the moment when a pizza (it is merely the word for pie) comes into its own.

For me personally, though I adore the taste, though I love individually every ingredient that goes into it, this is the only sort of occasion when I can use the pizza, for the good reason that it is far too filling to have as a first course and far too stodgy and fattening to have as a main course.

The following recipe is a family one, and one I used for many years at my wine restaurant facing the British Museum. If you follow the ensuing recipe reasonably faithfully you can imagine you are actually on the Bay of Naples.

PIZZA ALLA NAPOLITANA

Get some ordinary baker's dough (not a fancy short-pastry crust full of fat), and when it has risen, put the dough in a baking tin which has been well moistened with olive oil. Get some large tomatoes, skin them and chop them coarsely (not into silly little thin slices) and spread over the bottom of the tin. Take some black olives, stone them and dot around, also some anchovy fillets and finally some small slices of Gruyère.

Don't be too generous with the last three things in proportion to the tomato or you will make the pizza too strong. Sprinkle on the top a generous amount of basil or thyme or marjoram and bake in an oven. You must eat this particular type of pizza as soon as it is done.

If you want a variation try *Francican Pizza*. For this make as the Napolitana, but add sliced mushrooms.

CALZONE

½ lb. (2 cups) flour
½ oz. yeast
salt
water
cooked ham
Bel Paese cheese
    slices

Prepare the dough as described in the recipe for *Pizza alla Casalinga* (*see* page 209). Roll is very thin, after proving. Cut into rounds about 2–3 in. across. Lay a slice of ham and one of Bel Paese on half of each round. Season with salt, pepper and a little oil. Fold the pizza in half, and cook in a fairly hot oven for 20 minutes.

PIZZA BEL PAESE

Pizza Bel Paese is a fairly filling dish. This is to be expected as its basic ingredient is a rich bread dough which is coated with a mixture of tomatoes, cheese and anchovies. While perhaps not the dish for a smart dinner it is ideal for say an informal gathering as it can be prepared well in advance and heated up when needed. (NB. If preferred black olives can be substituted for the anchovies).

12 oz. rich bread
    dough
1 lb. peeled and
    seeded tomatoes
10 anchovy fillets
1 tablespoonful olive
    oil
1 tablespoonful
    chopped onion
½ clove garlic
1 dessertspoonful
    chopped basil
4 oz. Bel Paese cheese
salt and pepper to
    season

Divide dough into four and pat out into round shapes about ¾ in. thick. Split the anchovy fillets in two. Chop the garlic finely, and shred the cheese. Chop tomatoes into fairly large bits and sauté with onions and basil in oil over fairly high heat for a few minutes. Pour off excess liquid and place on dough. Sprinkle over cheese and anchovy strips. Bake in hot oven (440 °F. or 230 °C.) for about 20 minutes.
(Mrs A. Wainman)

PIZZA ALLA CASALINGA (Italy)

6 oz. (¾ cup) flour
2 oz. (¼ cup) butter
1 egg
¼ oz. yeast dissolved
    in water
salt and water
12 anchovy fillets
10 tomatoes
oregano or basil
6 oz. grated Bel Paese
    or Gruyère cheese

Make a pastry dough with the flour, butter, egg and yeast dissolved in a little water, salt and enough extra water to form a medium stiff dough. Let it rise for 2 hours. Roll out the pastry, cut it into two rounds and garnish with basil or *oregano* and cheese. Cook the pizza in oiled tins or fireproof dishes in a fairly hot oven for 25 minutes adding the cheese only during the last 5 minutes.
(Elizabeth David, *Italian Food*)

RUSTIC PIZZA

5 oz. (1 cup) flour
4 oz. (½ cup) lard
1 cup of sugar
pinch of baking
    powder
1 pint Béchamel sauce
2 eggs
3 oz., each grated
    Parmesan and
    cream cheese
4 oz. Pel Paese
3 oz., each cooked ham
    and salami
2 hard-boiled eggs
handful of sultanas
salt, pepper, nutmeg

A pizza made from pastry.

Make the pastry from the flour, lard, sugar and baking powder to produce a soft paste.

For the filling, make a pint of Béchamel sauce, stir in the yolks of the eggs, the grated cheese, the Bel Paese cut into dice; the ham, salami, and hard-boiled eggs, all cut into slices. Season with salt, pepper and nutmeg, and fold in the beaten whites of egg. Line a tart tin with the pastry, fill with the prepared mixture, cover with a lid of pastry, and bake in a moderate oven for 30 minutes.
(Elizabeth David, *Italian Food*)

Fondues

Cheese has been used over the centuries as an adjunct to cooking. Most so-called cheese dishes incorporate cheese rather than depend upon it as their main ingredient. The exception, perhaps, is *fondue*, a dish invented by the Swiss in the Alpine regions, to use their most famous native cheeses, Emmenthal and Gruyère.

Though now mainly eaten in Switzerland and Savoy at *après ski* parties as a consolation for the cold weather outside, *fondue* needless to say is a dish with a world-wide reputation, and is universal in all the French regions where Gruyère cheese is produced.

The recipes for *fondue* are so many and various that it would be difficult to contain them within a simple formula. All the traditional recipes have one thing in common – they vary from one bank of the river or from one side of the street to the other.

As soon as one enters the Jura, and the whole region centred on this French Department, one is aware of the respect which is due to French Gruyère cheese. Public opinion has long remained wrongfully ignorant of what the French Gruyère cheeses really are.

CAQUELON

The traditional *fondue* is basically a mixture of white wine and cheese given the added flavour of kirsch and garlic, eaten on chunks of bread dipped directly into the *caquelon* or casserole, which in turn is kept gently bubbling over a small methylated spirit lamp. Otherwise the whole dish, if allowed to grow cold, separates and congeals into a sticky mass of cheese and alcohol. It is no use attempting the *fondue* without the proper equipment which is readily available at all purveyors of such material, who will also sell you the special long forks for dipping the bread. I learnt this to my cost, as I had been under the impression that one could eat it at table off a plate. When I tried, it was disastrous.

The other thing about *fondue* (which I had not previously realized) is that it is a very rich dish. A little goes a long way, so that after a few dips into the simmering pan one realizes that it is more suitable as a cold-weather dish.

The classic Swiss and Savoyard recipe, however, is a simple one:

bread cut up into squares
½ lb. Gruyère
½ lb. Emmenthal
⅓ pint of dry white wine
1 teaspoonful potato flour
3 liquid oz. Kirsch
Season with black pepper and nutmeg

Rub the *caquelon* or casserole thoroughly with garlic. Grate the cheese. Stir the Kirsch into the potato flour until smooth and thin. Heat the wine in the *caquelon* and as it comes to the boil add the cheese piecemeal and stir to a smooth consistency. Add the seasoning and the Kirsch and flour mixture. Remove from the stove and bring at once to table where it should remain bubbling very gently over the modest flame of a methylated spirit lamp. As the last of the *fondue* is forked up on the squares of bread a very tasty crust will be found on the bottom of the *caquelon* and should be divided evenly among the guests.

A variation which produces even better results in the opinion of many Swiss gastronomies, and of the editor of this book, is to replace the Emmenthal cheese, which has a certain sweetness, by its equivalent weight of the strongest possible English or Canadian Cheddar. This gives the dish more bite.

One can of course perform many variations and, for instance, make coloured *fondue* (or, more correctly, mock *fondue*) by using vegetables. An example of a mock *fondue* follows:

1 lb. spinach
1 oz. plain flour
1 oz. butter
½ pint (1¼ cups) milk
2 oz. grated Gruyère cheese
salt and pepper to season

Cook spinach and purée it through a mouli or sieve. Melt butter in saucepan, add flour and cook for a couple of minutes. Take off heat, add milk, stirring all the while with a wire whisk. Replace over low heat, add the cheese and the spinach, stirring constantly. When mixture thickens to the right consistency, remove and serve.

An example of an older form of *fondue*, using eggs and milk, and much more resembling a soufflé, is to be found in Francatelli's recipe on page 146.

FONDUE AU BEAUFORT*

Cut the cheese into small cubes. Put it into a basin or small salad bowl. Spread it out suitably and cover it amply with dry white wine. Put the enamelled cast-iron *caquelon* to heat and pour in the white wine which covered the cheese. It does not matter if some of this white wine still moistens the pieces remaining in the salad bowl. Pierce a very slightly crushed clove of garlic with a silver fork (or a fork of metal which does not give a nickel-silver-copper taste) and stir the wine until it reaches just below boiling point. *This operation must be carried out slowly.* Take out the garlic and the fork. Add the cheese and stir to perfect smoothness. Thicken with cornflour and Kirsch in the proportion of a ½ coffeespoonful of cornflour to 4 oz. of cheese and 2 dessertspoonfuls of Kirsch.

The quantity of cheese cannot be stated with absolute precision, it depends upon the

---

*This Gruyère is made in the high Alpine mountains, the paste is soft and supple, like butter.

appetite of the guests. However, generally one can reckon on about 7 oz. of cheese per person. The proportions automatically balance themselves out, and are determined by the procedure rather than by weight or volume.

FONDUE AU COMTÉ

Cut the cheese into small cubes. Put it into the enamelled cast-iron *caquelon*, and cover it with very good quality dry white wine. Gently crush a clove of garlic and put it into the mixture. Heat gently, stirring all the time. Take out the clove of garlic as soon as the mixture commences to melt. Then add a pinch of cayenne pepper. Stir, while increasing the intensity of heating if possible, until the *fondue* is smooth. Then remove from heat, thicken with a pinch of cornflour mixed with Kirsch. Serve on the chafing dish.

FONDUE À L'EMMENTHAL

Grate the cheese and spread it on a board or on a sheet of paper, so that no small heaps are formed. Take the enamelled cast-iron *caquelon* and rub in a clove of garlic. Pour dry French white wine of your choice into the *caquelon*, and heat. Before the wine starts to boil, add the grated cheese. If necessary, add a little wine so that the wine covers the cheese to a depth of about ¼ in. Stir with a wooden spoon until the cheese starts to melt. Remove from the heat and continue stirring to obtain a homogeneous *fondue*. You may need to heat afresh, but do so only if absolutely necessary. Mix up a ½ coffeespoonful of cornflour (per 4 oz. of cheese) with 3–4 times its volume of Kirsch. Thicken and serve the *fondue* on the chafing dish.

CHEESE FONDUE
½ **pint (1¼ cups) milk**
4 oz. grated cheese
2 egg yolks
4 egg whites

Pour ½ pint of boiling milk on the crumbs of a French roll, beat it up with a ¼ lb. of good cheese grated, and the yolks of 2 eggs well beaten. Just as it is ready for the oven, stir in the whites of 4 eggs beaten to a solid froth. Bake in a quick oven, either in a silver or tart dish, with a high band of paper round. It will take about 20 minutes and must be served as quickly as possible.
(Mary Hooper, 1878, *Little Dinners*)

CHEESE FONDUE

1 oz. butter
3 oz. grated Parmesan
   cheese
1½ oz. breadcrumbs
2 eggs
a little made mustard
1 gill milk
pepper and salt
a pinch of cayenne

Put the breadcrumbs and butter into a basin, boil the milk and pour it over them. Add the cheese (keeping back about 1 dessertspoonful), yolks of eggs, and seasonings. Mix well. Beat up the whites of eggs into a stiff froth and mix them in lightly at the last. Pour the mixture into a greased piedish or fireproof dish, sprinkle the rest of the cheese on top. Bake in a good oven about 20 minutes or until nicely browned and well risen.

(Florence Jack, *Cookery for Every Household*)

CHEESE FONDUE WITH ONE EGG

3 oz. (¾ cup) bread-
   crumbs
1 egg
3 oz. grated cheese
1 oz. butter
½ pint (1¼ cups) milk
salt and pepper

Heat the milk and pour it over the mixed breadcrumbs, cheese and seasoning. Beat the yolk of the egg and stir by degrees into the mixture. Beat the white very stiff with a knife and stir in lightly. Put into a soufflé dish, sprinkle the top with grated cheese, and bake.

(J. O. Waller, from Oriana Haynes; *Cooking and Curing*)

PIEDMONTESE FONDUTA

4 servings
4 eggs
3 oz. Fontina cheese
   (Gruyère will be an
   adequate substitute)
milk
butter

One of the most famous dishes from Piedmont (not to be confused with Swiss fondue). Cut the cheese into small dices and cover with the milk. Leave to soak for at least 4 hours.

Put the cheese, the beaten eggs, and a nut of butter in a double saucepan, adding salt and pepper. Cook gently, stirring all the time. The minute the cheese and eggs have amalgamated into a thick cream pour it into an earthenware or porcelain dish and cover it with very fine slices of raw white truffles. The combination of the cheese and the truffles is so remarkably right that there is really no substitute.

(Elizabeth David, *Italian Food*)

Fish

COQUILLES ST JACQUES MORNAY

1 large scallop to each person
salt
pepper
lemon juice
sauce Mornay
grated Parmesan

Rinse the scallops well and drain them. Cut off the strip of dark muscle and skin outside the white part. Cover each scallop cover completely with a coating of a good thick sauce Mornay, season, and sprinkle with a dusting of Parmesan. Bake in a medium oven for 20–30 minutes according to size.

HADDOCK ROLL

Haddock roll is a particularly good main course. It is basically a soufflé in the form of a Swiss roll made with smoked haddock and Parmesan cheese. Its greatest drawback is that it must be served immediately after being cooked and so is not suitable as a dinner party dish unless the hostess is prepared to sacrifice most of her evening in the kitchen.

4 servings
½ lb. cooked, boned, smoked haddock
4 eggs
¼ pint (full ½ cup) double cream
4 oz. finely grated Parmesan cheese
½ pint (1¼ cups) Béchamel or white sauce
4 hard boiled eggs (chopped)
salt and pepper to season
chopped parsley

First prepare the filling. Add hard boiled chopped eggs with teaspoonful chopped parsley to white sauce. Keep warm.

Separate eggs and add yolks, double cream and half the cheese to haddock. Work into a smooth paste. Adjust seasoning. Spread a rectangular shaped baking tin with buttered greaseproof paper making sure that the paper is sticking up at least a couple of inches round the side to allow the soufflé plenty of room to rise. Whip whites till stiff and fold into haddock mixture. Turn into baking tin, smooth and sprinkle with half of remaining cheese. Bake in moderate oven (400°F. or 210°C.) for about 15 minutes. Turn out into greaseproof paper sprinkled with rest of cheese and peel off baking paper. Spread soufflé with filling and roll up. Dust with parsley and serve immediately.
(Mrs A. Wainman)

HOMARD AU GRATIN À LA NORMANDE

1 lobster
1 pint (2 cups) Bécha-
    mel sauce
½ cup grated Gruyère
    cheese
2 tablespoonfuls
    double cream
butter
fish stock

Put the live lobster in the cold stock and very slowly and gently bring it to the boil. Then boil fast until it is tender, and leave in the pan until quite cold. Drain well, and remove the flesh from the body, tail and claws. Cut into cubes. Meantime heat the sauce, add the lobster meat and stir in the cream and cheese. Put the shell in an ovenproof dish, and fill it with the mixture. Sprinkle some more cheese over this, and cut the butter in small pieces. Brown in a hot oven and serve immediately.

HOMARD THERMIDOR

2 small lobsters
2 tablespoonfuls butter
½ teaspoonful chopped
    onions
½ lb. mushrooms
1 tablespoonful tomato
    purée
½ glass dry white wine
1 cup white sauce
grated Parmesan
    cheese

Boil the lobsters in the manner described above. Remove all the meat from the body and claws and cut it into cubes. This includes the coral if it is a hen lobster. Heat the butter, add the onions, lobster, white wine and cayenne pepper. Simmer gently for 5 minutes, stirring the while, then add the mushrooms, previously sliced or chopped finely, the tomato purée and season to taste. Simmer for a further 5 minutes. Now return the mixture to the shells, cover with the white sauce, and cover that in turn with a layer of grated Parmesan. Heat thoroughly in a hot oven, take out and serve immediately it is browned.

SOLE MORNAY

fillets of sole
butter
fish stock
Parmesan cheese
    grated, or Gruyère
    and Cheshire cheese
    in equal quantities
sauce Mornay

Cook the fillets in the butter and a little stock. It is easiest to cook them in a heavy flat pan on top of the cooker. The liquid should be just simmering and no more. When cooked, add the sauce to the reduced stock, season, sprinkle with the grated cheese and brown in a very hot oven.

TURBOT OR HALIBUT WITH MUSHROOM PURÉE AND CHEESE SAUCE

4 servings

1 turbot or halibut steak not less than 2 in. thick
1½ lb. mushrooms
2 eggs
2 tablespoonfuls double cream
6–8 oz. grated cheese, Cheddar or Gruyère
lemon juice
salt, freshly ground black pepper
6–8 oz. (1 cup) butter
small glass of dry white wine
fresh herbs

Place the fish on a flat ovenproof casserole suitable for serving at table. Pour in the wine and put in the butter. Season well with lemon juice, salt and pepper. Cover with foil and bake in a moderate oven till the flesh is just beginning to come away from the bone. While this is cooking, cut the mushrooms into small cubes and set cooking gently in a mixture of oil and butter. Season lightly, and add just a suspicion of finely chopped fresh herbs. When the mushrooms are cooked stir in 3–4 oz. of flour, and bring the mixture to boiling point. Cook until the liquid is absorbed by the flour and the mixture is firm. Beat the eggs with the cream, add the cheese and seasoning, and keep this separate. Take the fish from the oven, remove the foil, spread in a thick layer the mushroom mixture. Now run the egg and cheese sauce over the mushrooms and brown under the grill or in a hot oven.

Soufflés

BACON AND CHEESE SOUFFLÉS

streaky bacon
1 lb. Gruyère cheese (grated)
1 large cup cream
1 egg

Mix the cheese with two crisply fried rashers cut into small pieces and a breakfast cup of cream with the egg beaten into it. Fill individual soufflé dishes, already greased, two-thirds full and bake in medium oven for about fifteen minutes or until risen and set.

CHEESE SOUFFLÉ

Do not heed feminine warnings about this. They are couched in terms of steamed soufflés which have to be blown up with white of egg, and, under the least provocation or no provocation at all, flop, and in any case must be eaten at once, almost before you get them out of the oven. But most men are not interested in eating air.

Instead make what is more correctly called cheese pudding:

4 oz. grated cheese
1 oz. breadcrumbs
½ pint milk
2 eggs
**mustard, salt and
cayenne (optional)**

Beat the eggs slightly; add the solids. Boil the milk and add, pour into a greased baking-dish and bake for about twenty minutes in a brisk oven.
(Wilson Midgley, *Cookery for Men only*)

CHEESE SOUFFLÉ

2 servings

This is a very nice way of serving up stale pieces of cheese. Grate the cheese, say, till you get a couple of tablespoonfuls. Mix this with a quarter of a pint of milk. Take 2 eggs and beat the white to a stiff froth, adding the yolks to the mixture, put in a little pepper and salt, and mix in the beaten white. Pour it into a buttered tin – a round cake tin is best – and place it in a brisk oven. It will rise to four times the height it was when put in the tin. Serve as quickly as possible, as it commences to go down again directly it is taken out of the oven. Time to bake the above quantity, about twenty minutes. Wrap a dinner napkin folded, or a piece of ornamental paper, round the tin. It is best to have the napkin or paper ready, so that the hot tin can be dropped in it quickly.

POTATO SOUFFLÉ

6 potatoes (large)
4 eggs (separated)
3 oz. sweet butter
4 oz. grated cheese
pepper and salt

Boil six large potatoes and mash them with 3 oz. of sweet butter, a little pepper and salt, and 4 oz. grated cheese (half Parmesan and half Gruyère is the best mixture), add the yolks of 4 eggs and the whites, previously whisked to a rather stiff paste. Mix these thoroughly and put into a piedish and bake. When the top is nicely browned in the oven it is ready. Precautions – the ingredients should be thoroughly mixed before baking and the whites well whisked before mixing.

Sweets

APPLE PIE AND CHEESE
4 servings

8 oz. (2 cups) flour
4 oz. (1 cup) vegetable fat and margarine mixed
1½ lb. cooking apples
sugar
lemon juice
2 oz. (¼ cup) butter

Peel and cut up the apples. Place a layer in the piedish, cover with sugar, dot with small pieces of butter, add a little lemon juice. Continue with another layer until all the apples are used up. Some people add a few cloves. Add a very little water. If a deep oval piedish is used, place an upturned egg cup or similar support in the centre to keep the pastry from sagging. Cover with the pastry and decorate with pastry leaves and flowers. Press the back of a fork round the border and trim. Bake in a hot oven until the pastry is golden brown. Dust with sugar and serve with the cheese freshly cut in wedges or slices, handed separately.

To make the pastry. Sieve the flour, add a little salt but no sugar. Rub in the fat with the tips of the fingers; be as quick and light as you can. Add enough ice cold water to bind the paste, using a knife. Turn out on a floured board, and roll out about quarter of an inch thick. Cut it about an inch bigger all round than your piedish, and trim it just a little bigger than the rim, to allow for shrinking. Never stretch your pastry to fit your pie.

BUDINO TOSCANO (Tuscan Pudding) (Italy)

¾ lb. Ricotta or un-salted home-made cheese
2 oz. ground almonds
1½ oz. candied orange peel
4 oz. (½ cup) sugar
1 oz. each of raisins and sultanas
4 yolks of eggs
vanilla sugar
grated peel of a lemon

Put the cream cheese through a foodmill. Stir in the beaten yolks of eggs and all the other ingredients. This pudding should be cooked in a buttered mould in the oven for 30 minutes, but as a matter of fact it is very much better in its natural state, as a kind of thick cream. When it is cooked it is more like a cake. In either case sprinkle the top with vanilla sugar.

(Elizabeth David, *Italian Food*)

BUDINO DI RICOTTA (Italian Cream Cheese Pudding)

6 or 7 servings

10 oz. Ricotta or un-salted cream cheese
3 oz. (under ½ cup) sugar
3 oz. ground almonds
2 or 3 crushed bitter almonds
5 eggs
lemon peel
breadcrumbs

Sieve the cream cheese, add the sugar, the almonds, the beaten whites of eggs and the grated peel of the lemon. Pour into a buttered mould. Spread with breadcrumbs, and cook for 30 minutes in a moderate oven. Serve cold. (Elizabeth David, *Italian Food*)

CREMA DI MASCHERPONE (Italian Sweet Cream Cheese)

Mascherpone is an unsalted cream cheese made from thick cream, chiefly in Lombardy. It is used for many sweet dishes, although it is also eaten with salt, or quite plain with strawberries. Home-made cream cheese, very fresh unsalted, can be made into a very delicious sweet on the same lines as *Crema di Mascherpone*.

Allow about 2 oz. cream cheese per person
(4 pints (10 cups) of milk will give about 1 lb. of cream cheese)
for 1 lb. of cream cheese allow 4 oz. (full ½ cup) sugar
4 yolks of egg
2 or 3 teaspoonfuls of brandy, rum, or best of all, kirsch

Put the cream cheese through a sieve and stir it until it is quite smooth. In another basin beat up the eggs and sugar, then add the liqueur. Add this mixture gradually to the cream cheese until it is a thick cream. Put it on the ice for 2 or 3 hours.

When cream is available, a pint, left to go thick and slightly sour, drained in a muslin, and then beaten up with sugar and liqueur, produces something very like the original *Crema di Mascherpone*.
(Elizabeth David, *Italian Food*)

FROMAGE DE FONTAINEBLEAU (France)

4 servings

½ pint (1¼ cups) **double cream**
2 oz. (¼ cup) **fresh milk**
1 **dessertspoonful caster sugar**
strawberries, raspberries

Leave the fresh cream to stand in a covered bowl for 3 or 4 days. It should stand in a cool place but not in the refrigerator. Sprinkle the sugar over the cream and begin to whip it. As it gets stiffer, add the milk little by little. When it is light and keeps its shape pile it in individual glasses or in one bowl. Serve it at once simply with sugar or with the fresh red fruits of midsummer.

LITTTLE CREAM CHEESES

1 **quart (6 cups) milk**
2 **teaspoonfuls rennet**
1 **teacupful fresh cream**

Put the milk in a warm place overnight, when it will set like junket. Pour it into a piece of butter muslin and leave it to drip till it is nearly solid. Put it in a basin, add 1 teacup of fresh cream, mix well. Put into a mould in a cool place. Turn out, and serve with caster sugar.

NOODLES AND CREAM CHEESE PUDDING (Russia)

8 oz. noodles
1 egg
4 oz. cream cheese
1 tablespoonful sugar
1 tablespoonful sour cream
1 tablespoonful breadcrumbs
1 tablespoonful butter
water
salt

Put the noodles into plenty of boiling, salted water and cook until tender. Strain off the water and mix the noodles with the cream cheese, beaten egg, sugar and a pinch of salt. Put into a buttered piedish, sprinkle with breadcrumbs, brush with smetana and bake in a moderate oven for 20 minutes.

(Musia Soper, *Cooking the Russian Way*)

PANCAKES WITH SOUR CREAM STUFFING (Austria)

Pancake mixture:

½ **lb. (2 cups) flour**
2 **eggs**
1 **pint (2½ cups) milk**
pinch of salt
dessertspoonful of oil

Mix the flour and salt; drop the eggs in a well in the centre with a third of the milk, mixing well to avoid any lumps. Add the rest of the milk beating well to a smooth creamy consistency. Beat in the oil and leave to stand in a cool place or in the refrigerator for an hour before using.

Filling:

½ lb. cream cheese

1½ oz. butter

2 eggs

3 tablespoonfuls sugar

salt

flour

Cream the butter, add the yolks, and beat till they are worked in thoroughly. Mix in the cream cheese and the sugar. Beat the whites stiffly, and add to the mixture. Add enough flour to make the paste firm enough to roll into small balls. Poach in boiling water for 5 minutes.

Cook the pancakes in the usual way using a minimum of oil. Fill each one with a ball of the poached mixture, roll up, dust with sugar and serve immediately.

PRINCESS CHEESE

This is a delightful cinnamon-and-coriander-flavoured dessert cheese to serve with fresh fruit, or, in the Italian manner, with thinly sliced panettone or coffee cake.

½ lb. cream cheese

salt

lemon peel

⅛ teaspoonful each of powdered or pounded coriander seed, cinnamon, sugar

Mix in a bowl ½ lb. cream cheese with ⅛ teaspoonful of salt, 1 grated lemon peel, ⅛ teaspoonful of powdered or pounded coriander seed, ⅛ teaspoonful of cinnamon and ⅛ teaspoonful of sugar. Place in a mould lined with waxed paper. Chill in refrigerator for 4 or 5 hours, but remove from refrigerator ½ hour before serving.
(Alice B. Toklas, *Aromas and Flavours*)

PURPLE CHEESE

This moulded dessert cheese takes on a more definite purple hue if it is made with grape instead of currant jelly. Generally the extra tablespoonful of sugar is not needed. The jelly makes it sweet enough to suit most tastes.

1 cup cream cheese

½ cup currant jelly

1 tablespoonful sugar

Mix 1 cup of cream cheese, ½ cup of currant jelly and 1 tablespoonful of sugar in electric beater at low speed until perfectly smooth. Then place in a small mould lined with waxed paper and in the refrigerator for 1 hour before serving.
(Alice B. Toklas, *Aromas and Flavours*)

RICOTTA AL CAFFE (Cream Cheese with Coffee)

Again, home-made milk cheese can be used for this sweet. If Ricotta, the ewe's milk white cheese very widely used in Italian cooking, cannot be used for this sweet.
4 servings

8–10 oz. cream cheese
4–6 oz. ($\frac{3}{4}$ cup) caster
   sugar
4 dessertspoonfuls of
   freshly roasted, very
   finely ground coffee
2 oz. rum

Put the cream cheese through a sieve, add the sugar, the coffee and the rum, and stir it until it is smooth and thick. Make the cream at least 2 hours before serving so that the coffee flavour has time to develop. Keep it in a cold place. Serve it with fresh cream and thin wafer biscuits.

(Elizabeth David, *Italian Food*)

Pastries

CHEESE CAKE

1 lb. (4 cups) flour
1 lb. pot cheese
2 teaspoonfuls baking
   powder
juice of $\frac{1}{2}$ lemon
6 oz. ($\frac{3}{4}$ cup) sugar
6 oz. ($\frac{3}{4}$ cup) butter
$\frac{1}{2}$ cup milk
1 egg
$\frac{1}{2}$ cup cleaned currants

Rub $\frac{1}{2}$ cupful of the butter into the flour, add $\frac{1}{2}$ cupful of the sugar, baking powder, egg well beaten, milk and strained lemon juice. Line a buttered baking earthenware dish with this paste. Mix the cheese smoothly with the rest of the sugar and butter. Spread this filling into the prepared casserole. Sprinkle the currants on the top and bake in a hot oven for $\frac{1}{2}$ hour.

(Marion H. Neil, *How to Cook in Casserole Dishes*)

CHEESE TARTLETS

2 oz. cheese
1 oz. butter
salt and dry mustard
2 yolks of egg and
   1 white
$\frac{1}{4}$ lb. short-crust pastry
cayenne pepper

Cut up the cheese into small pieces and pound in a mortar with salt and dry mustard and cayenne pepper to taste. Add 1 oz. of butter. Pound these ingredients till they form a smooth paste, then stir in the yolks of eggs and part of the white beaten to a stiff froth. Line some patty-tins with thin pastry, half fill them with the cheese mixture; bake for 15 minutes in a brisk oven, then serve very hot, arranged on a folded napkin.

(*Isobel's Home Cookery*, 1903–5)

CHEESE TARTLETS

pastry
**1 oz. grated Parmesan
  cheese**
1 large egg
**4 tablespoonfuls white
  sauce**
chopped parsley
pepper and salt

Beat the yolk of an egg, add it to the white sauce with the grated cheese, salt and pepper. Line some patty pans with pastry. Beat the white of the egg to a stiff froth, stir it lightly into the mixture; then fill the patty pans. Bake about quarter of an hour. Sprinkle a little grated cheese and chopped parsley over. Serve hot or cold.

(*Isobel's Home Cookery*, 1903–5)

CHEESE BISCUITS

short-crust pastry
7 oz. butter
1 egg yolk
1 oz. sugar
bare 9 oz. flour
cheese mixture
3½ oz. butter
**good 2½ oz. fairly
  strong grated cheese**

Wash butter, remove all water, and stir for 5 minutes. Stir yolk and sugar for 10 minutes, add butter and flour and work into smooth and elastic consistency. Stand in cold place for 2 hours. Roll out into about one sixteenth inch thickness. Shape with round pastry cutter, and bake a nice golden brown in hot oven. To make cheese mixture, stir butter and cheese until light and creamy. Spread on one biscuit, and put another one on top. Two drops of green colouring, added to the mixture, will make it look nice. Serve with clear soup.

(Inga Norberg, *Good Food from Sweden*)

KENTISH CHEESE PASTIES (Kent)

1 lb. flour
¼ lb. butter
¼ lb. lard
cayenne and salt
**¾ lb. cheese cut in very
  thin flakes and
  mixed with little
  pieces of butter**
1 egg

Make some flaky pastry with the flour, butter and lard. Roll out ⅛ in. thick, cut into rounds the size of a saucer. Place a tablespoonful of the flaked cheese and butter in the centre, and sprinkle over some cayenne and salt. Moisten the edges of the pastry and form into little pasties. Brush over with beaten egg. These should be served quite hot.

(*County Recipes of Old England*)

PASTEL DE QUESO (Spain)

3 tablespoonfuls plain flour
8 oz. cream cheese
2 small lemons (rind only)
2 eggs
large pinch cinnamon
¾ lb. sugar
3 tablespoonfuls self-raising flour
1 tablespoonful butter

Mix the cheese, sugar and butter in a bowl. Stir, don't beat; add the raw eggs folded in and the ground cinnamon and lemon rind. Now add the flour and put all in a greased baking dish and bake in a moderate oven for ½ hour.

RAIFF OF CHEESE

20 sheets of pastry
9 oz. semolina
1 egg
7 oz. sheep cheese
almost ½ pint olive oil

Pound the cheese in a mortar. Fold ½ tablespoonful of cheese in a sheet of pastry, making a pastry 4 in. broad. Seal the edges of the pastry with a whipped raw egg. Put at once into a plate of boiling oil about half an inch deep and brown slightly on both sides. This will make about twelve pasties.

PASTRY

A successful result can scarcely be expected without a great deal of practice.

Take 3 lb. 6 oz. of coarse semolina and one handful of flour.

Knead the semolina with water into a dough.

Knead four handfuls of this dough with the flour, throwing in a little flour from time to time while working the dough.

Continue kneading for three quarters of an hour or more, until the dough becomes exceedingly elastic.

Take a handful of this dough and flap it quickly on a hot plate – a flat metal tray over the fire – so as to leave on the hot plate a transparent patch of flour of some 3 in. in size.

Each dab must be done so quickly that the dough never entirely leaves the hand nor rests for any time on the hot plate. This process is performed, by those who are expert, by jerking the dough over the thumb without allowing the whole of it to leave the hand, while the back of the hand is downwards towards the hot plate. The dough thus jerked over the thumb will strike the hot plate, but, owing to its elasticity, will immediately recoil back to the hand.

Continue making dabs, one beside and touching the other until there is a round patch of flour on the hot plate some 12 or 14 in. in diameter.

Lift this off the hot plate immediately. It should come off in one transparent sheet. Put it aside to cool. This is the pastry.

This amount of dough is enough to make some fifty sheets.

(John, Marquis of Bute, *Moorish Recipes*)

RICHMOND MAIDS OF HONOUR (Surrey)

½ lb. cottage cheese

6 oz. (¾ cup) butter

4 egg yolks

glass of brandy

6 oz. (approx. 1 cup) caster sugar

1 oz. sweet almonds, pounded

1 oz. bitter almonds, pounded

grated rind of 3 lemons

juice of 1 lemon

½ nutmeg, grated

1 very floury baked potato

Sift the cottage cheese and mix it with the butter. Break the yolks of 4 eggs into another basin and add a glass of brandy. Add to it the caster sugar and beat well together with the cold potato, the almonds, lemon rind and lemon juice. Mix these together well and add to the cottage cheese and butter, stir together well. Line some tartlet tins with short-crust pastry and bake quickly.

(*County Recipes of Old England*)

TOASTED CHEESE ROLLS

Ingredient amounts are somewhat misleading as it really depends on how many Toasted Cheese Rolls one can eat so I shall only say that the following recipe should produce about twenty-five rolls.

1 gill (½ cup) milk

8 oz. grated Cheddar cheese

1 medium onion

salt and dash of cayenne pepper to season

1 loaf white bread

3 oz. butter

Cut the crusts from the bread and slice. Grate the onions or chop finely. Mix cheese, milk, onions and season. The consistency of the resulting liquid should be stiff enough so as not to soak into the bread on which it is to be placed. Butter slices of bread, spread with cheese mixture and form into rolls. Place on baking tray and cook in hot oven (440°F., 230°C.) for about ten minutes or until golden brown.

(Mrs A. Wainman)

Savouries

CAMEMBERT SAVOURY
A delicious savoury to begin or end a meal can be made with Camembert.

4 servings

1 medium ripe Camembert
½ pint (1¼ cups) Béchamel or white sauce
1 egg yolk
2 tablespoonfuls flour
1 egg
1 tablespoonful milk
1 dessertspoonful olive oil
2 oz (½ cup) white breadcrumbs
enough fat for deep frying
2 oz. Parmesan cheese (finely grated)
salt, pepper and dash of Tabasco sauce

Remove rind from cheese and put through mouli or fine sieve. Make white sauce, season and cool. Blend Camembert and yolk into sauce with dash of Tabasco until smooth. Shape into little balls about the size of a small plum on a floured board. Beat other egg with milk and oil, dip cheese balls into this mixture, roll in breadcrumbs and fry in deep fat until golden brown. Dust with Parmesan cheese and serve hot.

(Mrs A. Wainman)

CHEESE AND ALMOND FINGERS

3 tablespoonfuls blanched almonds (chopped)
3 tablespoonfuls butter
3 tablespoonfuls thick cream
6 tablespoonfuls grated cheese
salt and pepper

Fry the almonds until golden brown. Mix all the other ingredients together and spread on fingers of toast. Sprinkle with the chopped almonds and put in a hot oven to heat well through. Serve immediately.

CHEESE BARS (Derbyshire)

flaky pastry
4 oz. grated cheese
1 tomato
1 egg
cayenne or mustard to
  season

Line a flat tin with flaky pastry. Mix all the other ingredients together (leaving a little white of egg), spread the mixture on the pastry. Brush over with the white of egg and cook for about twenty minutes in a fairly hot oven. Cut into finger lengths and serve hot.
(Farmhouse Fare, *Farmers Weekly*)

CHEESE STRAWS

6 oz. (1½ cups) flour
3 oz. (under ½ cup)
  butter
6 oz. grated Parmesan
  and fresh Cheddar
salt
pepper
cayenne pepper

Sieve the flour, add seasoning. Rub in the butter with quick, cool hands, and add the grated cheese, and enough egg yolk to make a stiff paste. Flour the board well and roll out to about quarter of an inch thick. The finished pastry will be very breakable and fragile so do not make the straws too thin. Cut into straws, and if liked some rings as well. Bake in a moderate oven (320–370°F., 160–190°C.). As a savoury, slip straws through the rings and serve very hot with plenty of English mustard. Or leave to cool and serve with drinks before dinner.

CHEESE TOASTS WITH CHICKEN'S LIVER

2 chicken livers
1 anchovy fillet
stock
grated cheese
breadcrumbs
salt and paprika

Fry livers in a little butter with salt and paprika. Chop up and mix with anchovy in oil. Put a spoonful of stock in a saucepan and cook liver mixture until it becomes like a spread. Spread mixture on to pieces of buttered toast and top with grated cheese and breadcrumbs mixed. Top with butter and place in oven to colour.

CROÛTES À LA ST IVEL

St Ivel cheese
2 tablespoonfuls cream
1 teaspoonful grated
  horseradish
seasonings
croûtes

Mix half a St Ivel cheese with the cream and horseradish, season with a saltspoonful of paprika pepper and a few drops of tarragon vinegar. Cut some thin slices from a stale tin loaf of bread, stamp a sufficient number of rounds, 1½ in. in diameter, fry in butter and drain. Spread them rather thickly, on one side only, with the above cheese mixture, place them on a baking sheet in a hot oven for about five minutes. Dish. Garnish with sprigs of parsley and lemon slices. Serve hot.
(*Isobel's Home Cookery*, 1903–5)

CHEESE WAFERS

2 oz. grated cheese
¼ lb. short crust
cayenne and salt

Make some nice short crust, and into it mix as much dry grated cheese as it will take up, adding if necessary, a very little cold water. Season with a dash of cayenne pepper and salt. Prick each wafer closely with a fork and then bake.

(*Isobel's Home Cookery*, 1903–5)

DEVILLED CHEESE

2 oz cheese
1 teaspoonful mixed pickle
1 teaspoonful curry powder

Grate the cheese and chop the pickle, mix them with the curry powder. Butter some toast and spread the mixture on each side of it. Bake 4 minutes on a buttered tin.

(Oriana Haynes, *Cooking and Curing*)

GLOUCESTER CHEESE AND ALE

Cut some good Gloucester cheese into thin flakes, removing first any rind. Put these in a fireproof dish, spread some mustard over and cover with strong ale. Cook until quite tender and the cheese is dissolved. Have ready some slices of thick brown toast. Pour hot ale over them sufficiently to moisten it, then the cheese, and serve very hot.
(*County Recipes of Old England*)

LIPTOI (Hungarian Savoury Cheese)

Liptoi is a goats' milk cream cheese; Liptoi is sold in Hungary packed in small bladders and owes its name to the county of Lipto (now in Czechoslovakia). It has a peculiar acid flavour and is always served as *Korozott Liptoi*, or garnished cheese.

½ lb. sour cream cheese (curd)
½ lb. butter
½ teaspoonful paprika
½ teaspoonful caraway seed (chopped)
¼ teaspoonful mustard
a few chopped capers
½ teaspoonful chives
a little ale or beer
radishes for garnishing

Chop the chives, or spring onions if preferred. Take ½ lb. of good, sour cream cheese (curd) and cream it with the butter; season with remaining ingredients. When all is well blended and the mixture has a reddish-pink colour, pile high on a dish, garnish with radishes and serve with thin slices of brown bread. The German name of this cheese, *Liptauer*, is often used in shops and restaurants both in Hungary and abroad, and it is sold under this name in England.

MUSHROOMS AND CHEESE ON TOAST

olive oil or butter
1½ lb. mushrooms
tomato paste
3 tablespoonfuls grated cheese
salt and pepper

Peel mushrooms and slice thinly. Fry slowly in oil or butter for about 15 minutes with salt and pepper. Then add 1 tablespoonful tomato paste which has been dissolved in 2 tablespoonfuls of stock or boiling water. Cook slowly for 5 minutes. Add grated cheese and continue to cook slowly for 10 minutes.

ANCHOVY RAREBIT

Surely good bottled anchovy sauce is one of the most neglected of all culinary condiments in north Europe today. And it may be the sign of a jaded palate, though I don't think so, to state that cooks seem to be exaggeratedly frightened of using too much. A weak anchovy sauce is horrible.

Try then making an ordinary Welsh Rarebit mixture and stir in a goodly dollop of anchovy sauce. Then as a refinement put anchovy fillets criss cross wise on your rarebit, and brown under the grill. Use the mildest cheese you can get and *don't* add that pinch of salt.

DERVISHES DELIGHT

1 glass Red Algerian wine
1 cup Mulligatawny soup
1 tablespoonful flour
½ teaspoonful salt
2 eggs (beaten)
1 small shredded onion
¼ teaspoonful dry mustard
2 tablespoonfuls butter
3 cups grated Cheddar cheese

Put the butter in a frying pan and cook the onion until it begins to turn, then put in the flour, the wine, the soup and the mustard. Next stir in the cheese and cook again. Finally add the eggs and continue stirring until the mixture gets lovely and unctuous. Serve on soft buttered toast.

PERUVIAN RAREBIT

**1 fresh green pimento
finely chopped
(don't forget to take
out the pips)
2 tablespoonfuls butter
¼ cup tomato purée
2 eggs (beaten)
pinch pepper
pinch salt
cup of sweet corn
small chopped onion
3 cups grated cheese**

Fry the pimento and the onion in the butter; add tomato purée and stir. Next add the cheese and later add the corn. Finally the eggs. Do not cook too long. Pour over plain hot toast.

PORTUGUESE SARDINE RAREBIT

First make a very simple Welsh rarebit but with a little purée of tomato added. Then on the top put sardines which have been boned and cut in half. Grill.

PUNJAB CURRY RAREBIT

**1 tablespoonful mango
chutney
3 cups grated
Leicester cheese
½ teaspoonful curry
powder
1 tablespoonful corn-
flour
2 cups milk
2 finely shredded
onions
1 tablespoonful
tomato purée**

Melt the cornflour in the milk until it is well cooked and begins to thicken. When it does, pour in the cheese, curry powder and onions and stir well with a wooden spoon until a first-rate blending has taken place. Then stir in the tomato purée, stir again rather more vigorously this time and serve on thick hot buttered toast.

WAY DOWN SOUTH RAREBIT

2 eggs (lightly beaten)
3 cups cooked
   tomatoes
1½ tablespoonfuls
   sugar
4 cups grated cheese
1½ tablespoonfuls
   butter
1 shredded onion
big pinch salt
good shake pepper

Get a good thick frying pan and fry the onion in your butter and then add the tomatoes and the sugar. Never let this mixture boil, and then keep on adding the cheese and stirring it so that it melts. Then stir in the eggs. Serve piping hot on fried bread.

WELSH RAREBIT

¼ lb. rich cream
   cheese
¼ cup cream or milk
1 teaspoonful mustard
½ teaspoonful salt
a few grains cayenne
1 egg
1 teaspoonful butter
4 slices toast

Break the cheese in small pieces, or if hard grate it. Put it with the milk in a double boiler. Toast the bread, and keep it hot. Mix the mustard, salt and pepper; add the egg and beat well. When the cheese is melted, stir in the egg and butter, and cook 2 minutes, or until it thickens a little, but do not let it curdle. Pour it over the toast. Many use ale instead of cream.
(*Mrs Lincoln's Boston Cook Book*, 1900)

WELSH RAREBIT

This is a favourite dish for gentlemen's suppers and for luncheons. Cut bread into thin slices, shape these into diamonds or squares, toast them, and while hot, butter lightly. With a teaspoon dip boiling water on to the toast to moisten slightly, wetting only the unbuttered side. Place each slice on a separate hot plate, allowing one for each person at table; sprinkle with a little salt, pour over the toast enough melted cheese to cover, and serve the moment this is done, since otherwise the cheese will harden, the toast will cool, and the dish will be altogether spoiled. Rich new cheese should be chosen for this purpose, as it melts more easily. The cheese should be put in a cup to be melted. If the rarebit is stringy and tough, the cheese has not been sufficiently rich.
(*The Pattern Cook-Book*, 1890)

WELSH RAREBIT WITH EGGS

1 cupful grated cheese
1 egg (yolk only)
¼ cup milk
salt and pepper

Prepare the toast the same as in the preceding recipe. Place the milk in a stewpan, and when hot, put in the cheese, and stir continually until the latter is melted. Add the salt, pepper and the beaten yolk, stir but a moment, and pour the liquid over the toast.

WELSH RAREBIT (Old Sarah)

Put the cheese in a small teacup of milk and warm it till it melts. Beat up 1 egg and add it to the milk, boil while stirring. Add a little beer.
(Oriana Haynes, *Cooking and Curing*)

SARDINE AND CHEESE TOASTS

1 tin sardines
cayenne pepper
grated cheese
2 tablespoonfuls meat glaze
2 teaspoonfuls capers
fingers of toast

Cut sardines in half. Remove back bone and lay each half on a finger of toast. Dust with cayenne and sprinkle with lots of grated cheese. Cover with greased paper and heat in oven so that cheese melts but does not brown. Melt the meat glaze in saucepan and add capers. Pour the sauce over the toasts and serve hot.

SAITOS RETES (Cheese Rolls) see under Entrées.

STEWED CHEESE

½ lb. cheese
2 eggs
ale or Chablis
mustard
bread
cayenne

Cut into thin slices ½ lb. of good Gloucester or Cheddar cheese. Take a clean quart stewpan and put in the cheese with a little old ale or Chablis, and stir over the fire till it is melted, beat up the yolks only of 2 eggs and a small teaspoonful of dry mustard and a very little cayenne; stir for 2 minutes over the fire, and serve very hot with toasted or fried snippets of bread. The top may be browned with a hot iron or grill, or in front of a brisk fire. Sometimes the cheese is spread over toast and served.

Precautions: Do not let it burn, and if the cheese is not very rich add a little butter or salad oil; serve hot; and be careful with the cayenne.
(*Buckmaster's Cookery*, 1874)

TOASTED BLUE CHEESE

**any kind of blue
  cheese**
tomato chutney
Worcestershire sauce
a little onion juice
**crisply grilled rashers
  (optional)**

Make a paste with the cheese, tomato chutney, Worcestershire sauce and onion juice. Spread paste thickly on pieces of bread and bake in a very hot oven. Serve immediately garnished with grilled bacon if desired.

TOMATO AND CHEESE SAVOURY

½ lb. tomatoes
1 oz. butter
**½ oz. grated Parmesan
  cheese**
2 eggs
rounds of toast

First slice the tomatoes thinly and fry the onions gently in the butter until cooked. Then add the Parmesan and seasonings of pepper and salt. Beat 2 eggs thoroughly, pour into the tomato, etc., and stir gently till all is quite the consistency of a smooth paste. Pile on hot buttered toast, and serve very hot.

(*Isobel's Home Cookery,* 1903–5)

THE WAR OFFICE MANUAL OF MILITARY COOKING
AND DIETARY
PART I – GENERAL 1940
Notified in A.C.Is. 4 March 1942

NOT TO BE PUBLISHED

The information given in this document is not to be communicated, either directly or indirectly, to the Press or to any person not holding an official position in His Majesty's Service.

CHEESE – ONION SAVOURY

12 lb. cheese	1 qt. thick white sauce
1 lb. finely chopped onions	1 oz. mustard
4 oz. margarine	12 lb. sliced bread

Method. Stew onions in margarine until tender. Add chopped cheese, and melt slowly. Add white sauce, mustard, and spread on fried or toasted bread.

CHEESE - POTATO PIE

25 lb. potatoes	3 lb. dripping
6 lb. cheese	4 oz. baking powder
2 lb. onions	salt, pepper
8 lb. flour	4 qts. milk

Boil and mash potatoes. Grate cheese. Make short paste. Chop onions finely. Stew without taking colour. Layer with mashed potatoes, cheese, onions, and cover with short paste. Bake in moderate oven for 1 hour.

Another method. Slice potatoes and onions. Season with salt and pepper. Arrange in alternate layers with grated cheese. Three parts fill the pie dish or baking dish with milk or stock, cover with a short crust and bake for approximately 1 hour.

CHEESE - SCRAMBLED EGGS

150 eggs	pepper
2 lb. grated cheese	2 qts. white bread sauce
salt	

Scrambled eggs. Sprinkle with grated cheese. Grated cheese may be added and mixed with the eggs.

FRIED CHEESE PASTIE

6 lb. cheese	3 eggs
8 lb. flour	4 lb. breadcrumbs
3 lb. margarine	2 qts. thick white sauce
2 oz. baking powder	salt, pepper, nutmeg
water for paste	

Method. Make short paste of flour, margarine, water and baking powder. Chop cheese, and melt slowly. Add thick white sauce and seasoning. Cut out paste in 4 in. circles, place 2 oz. Welsh rarebit in centre, egg wash sides, fold over, egg and breadcrumb, and fry in hot deep fat. Drain well and serve hot with tomato, piquante, lyonnaise, or curry sauce.

MACARONI AND CHEESE FRITTERS

8 lb. macaroni	2 lb. flour
4 lb. cheese	6 eggs
3 qts. thick white sauce	8 lb. breadcrumbs
4 eggs	$\frac{3}{4}$ gal. tomato sauce

Method. Break macaroni into 1–2-in. lengths. Boil in salt water for 20 minutes. Well drain. Add white sauce, grated cheese, 4 eggs and stir on stove until mixture leaves sides of pan. Spread out on flat tray, cover with greased paper and allow to get cold. Make paste of eggs and a little water. Cut mixture into squares. Pass through flour, egg and breadcrumbs and fry in hot deep fat to golden brown. Drain and serve hot, with tomato sauce separate.

TOMATO AND CHEESE CROQUETTES

8 lb. cheese	8 lb. breadcrumbs
3 qt. thick tomato sauce	3 lb. flour
8 eggs	

Method. Reduce the tomato sauce till it leaves the sides of the pan, add sliced cheese. Allow to melt; add yolks of eggs one by one; well mix and cook. Spread out on tray, cover with greased paper and allow to get cold. Mould cork shape, pass through batter made of flour, egg and water, breadcrumb and fry in deep fat to golden brown. Well drain and serve hot. (A dish considered impracticable for large messes).

Comparative Cookery Terms
and Measures

BRITISH MEASURES	AMERICAN MEASURES	APPROXIMATE METRIC MEASURES
Liquid Measures		
1 teaspoon	1$\frac{1}{4}$ teaspoons	6 c.c.
1 tablespoon	1$\frac{1}{4}$ tablespoons	17 c.c.
1 fluid ounce	1 fluid ounce	30 c.c.
16 fluid ounces	1 pint	·480 litre
20 fluid ounces, or 1 pint	1$\frac{1}{4}$ pints	·568 litre
1$\frac{3}{4}$ pints	2 pints	1 litre
1 quart	2$\frac{1}{2}$ pints	1·136 litres
1 gallon	10 pints	4·544 litres

British Standard Measuring Cup is equivalent to 10 fluid ounces
American Standard Measuring Cup is equivalent to 8 fluid ounces

BRITISH MEASURES	AMERICAN MEASURES	APPROXIMATE METRIC MEASURES
Solid Measures		
1 ounce	1 ounce	30 grammes
16 ounces or 1 lb.	16 ounces or 1 lb.	500 grammes
2 lb., 3 ounces	2 lb., 3 ounces	1 kilogram

British and American Equivalent Ingredients

BRITISH	AMERICAN
Icing sugar	Confectioners sugar
Cornflour	Cornstarch
Sultanas	Raisins
Rusk crumbs	Zwiebach
Single cream	Light cream
Double cream	Heavy cream
Bicarbonate of Soda	Baking Soda
Scone	Biscuit
Soft brown sugar	Brown sugar
100 per cent wholemeal flour	Graham flour
Digestive biscuits	Graham crackers
Trex or Spry	Soft shortening
Butter or margarine	Shortening
1 oz. cooking chocolate	1 square chocolate
$\frac{2}{3}$ oz. bakers yeast, or	
3 level teaspoonfuls dried yeast	1 cake yeast
Okra	Gumbo
$\frac{1}{3}$ oz. powdered gelatine, or 1 level tablespoonful	1 envelope gelatine
Caster sugar	Granulated sugar
Biscuit	Cookie or Cracker
Minced Meat	Ground Meat

Throughout this book, English measures are given first; the American equivalent follows in brackets.

Vintage Chart

CHAMPAGNE	WHITE BURGUNDY	SAUTERNES	RHINE	RHONE	BURGUNDY	CLARET	PORT	YEAR
5	4	3	3	5	4	4	6	1965
7	6	3	6	7	6	6	4	1964
4	5	2	4	5	4	4	6	1963
6	5	6	6	6	5	6	5	1962
6	6	5	5	5	6	6	4	1961
4	3	4	5	5	5	4	7	1960
7	7	7	7	6	6	7	3	1959
5	4	5	5	6	4	5	5	1958
2	5	3	5	4	5	5	5	1957
4	3	4	3	5	2	3	2	1956
7	6	6	5	7	6	6	7	1955
3	4	3	3	5	4	4	5	1954
7	7	7	7	6	6	7	5	1953
7	6	6	6	7	7	6	4	1952
2	3	3	2	4	3	3	3	1951
3	6	4	5	6	4	6	6	1950
6	6	5	7	6	6	7	4	1949
4	5	4	5	4	5	6	7	1948
7	7	7	6	7	7	7	7	1947
3	5	3	4	4	4	3	5	1946

CHAMPAGNE	WHITE BURGUNDY	SAUTERNES	RHINE	RHONE	BURGUNDY	CLARET	PORT	YEAR
6	6	7	6	6	7	6	7	1945
3	2	4	3	3	2	4	4	1944
5	6	6	5	6	5	5	5	1943
5	4	4	5	5	3	3	6	1942
4	1	0	2	3	1	1	4	1941
3	1	3	3	2	2	3	5	1940
2	2	2	3	3	2	2	3	1939
4	4	3	4	5	3	4	5	1938
5	7	7	6	6	5	5	4	1937
2	4	3	1	5	2	3	3	1936
3	5	2	5	3	4	2	7	1935
6	6	5	7	5	6	6	6	1934
5	5	2	6	6	6	4	4	1933
2	2	0	3	2	2	0	1	1932
2	1	2	2	0	0	2	6	1931
1	3	0	3	1	1	1	2	1930
7	7	7	5	7	6	7	3	1929
7	6	6	1	5	5	6	1	1928
1	2	2	4	6	1	1	7	1927
6	6	5	3	4	6	5	3	1926

Fresh Food in its Best Season

	JANUARY	FEBRUARY	MARCH	APRIL	MAY	JUNE	JULY	AUGUST	SEPTEMBER	OCTOBER	NOVEMBER	DECEMBER
MEAT												
Beef	x	x	x	x	x	x	x	x	x	x	x	x
Veal		x	x	x	x	x						
Spring lamb					x	x	x	x	x			
Fed lamb	x	x	x	x						x	x	x
Pork	x	x	x	x	x	x				x	x	x
POULTRY												
Chicken	x	x	x	x	x	x	x	x	x	x	x	x
Duck	x	x	x	x	x	x	x	x	x	x	x	x
Turkey	x	x	x	x	x	x	x	x	x	x	x	x
FISH												
Bass	x	x	x	x	x	x	x	x	x	x	x	x
Carp	x	x	x	x	x	x	x	x	x	x	x	x
Cod	x	x	x	x	x	x	x	x	x	x	x	x
Dab	x	x	x	x	x	x	x	x	x	x	x	x
Eel	x	x	x	x	x	x	x	x	x	x	x	x
Flounder	x	x	x	x	x	x	x	x	x	x	x	x
(Grey) mullet	x	x	x	x	x	x	x	x	x	x	x	x
Haddock	x	x	x	x	x	x	x	x	x	x	x	x
Hake	x	x	x	x	x	x	x	x	x	x	x	x
Halibut	x	x	x	x	x	x	x	x	x	x	x	x
Herring	x	x	x	x	x	x	x	x	x	x	x	x
Lemon-sole	x	x	x	x	x	x	x	x	x	x	x	x
Mackerel		x	x	x	x	x	x	x	x	x	x	x
Pilchard	x	x	x	x	x	x	x	x	x	x	x	x
Salmon	x	x	x	x	x	x	x	x	x	x	x	x
Sardine		x	x	x	x	x	x	x	x	x	x	x
Sole	x	x	x	x	x	x	x	x	x	x	x	x
Trout	x	x	x	x	x	x	x	x	x	x	x	x
Whiting				x	x	x	x	x	x	x	x	

	JANUARY	FEBRUARY	MARCH	APRIL	MAY	JUNE	JULY	AUGUST	SEPTEMBER	OCTOBER	NOVEMBER	DECEMBER
CRUSTACEANS												
Crab	x	x	x	x	x	x	x	x	x	x	x	x
Lobster	x	x	x	x	x	x	x	x	x	x	x	x
Prawns – Shrimp	x	x	x	x	x	x	x	x	x	x	x	x
MOLLUSCS												
Mussel	x	x	x	x	x	x	x	x	x	x	x	x
Oyster	x	x	x	x					x	x	x	x
Scallop	x	x	x	x	x	x	x	x	x	x	x	x
Clams	x	x	x	x	x	x	x	x	x	x	x	x
FRUIT AND VEGETABLES												
Anise	x									x	x	x
Apples									x	x	x	
Apricots						x	x					
Artichokes	x	x	x	x	x						x	x
Asparagus			x	x	x							
Avocados	x	x	x	x	x	x	x	x	x	x	x	x
Beans, Lima						x	x	x	x			
Beans, Green			x	x	x	x	x	x				
Beets					x	x	x	x	x	x		
Blackberries						x						
Dewberries						x						
Loganberries						x						
Blueberries						x	x	x				
Huckleberries						x	x	x				
Broccoli	x	x	x							x	x	x
Brussels Sprouts	x									x	x	x
Cabbage	x	x	x	x	x					x	x	x
Cantaloupes						x	x	x	x			
Carrots (home-grown)								x	x	x	x	
Cauliflower (home-grown)									x	x	x	x
Celery	x	x	x	x	x						x	x
Cherries					x	x	x					
Collards	x	x	x								x	x
Corn						x	x	x				
Cranberries										x	x	x
Cucumbers					x	x	x	x				
Currants						x						

FRUIT AND VEGETABLES (*continued*)

	JANUARY	FEBRUARY	MARCH	APRIL	MAY	JUNE	JULY	AUGUST	SEPTEMBER	OCTOBER	NOVEMBER	DECEMBER
Eggplant							x	x	x	x		
Endive and Escarole								x	x	x		
Grapefruit (imported)	x	x	x	x						x	x	x
Grapes (home-grown)								x	x	x		
Kale					x	x			x	x		
Lettuce					x	x	x					
Melon (Cantaloupe)						x	x	x				
Mushrooms	x	x	x	x					x	x	x	x
Mustard Greens	x	x	x									
Okra							x	x	x	x		
Onions, Dry	x	x	x						x	x	x	x
Onions, Green					x	x	x	x				
Oranges	x	x	x	x	x							
Parsley	x	x	x	x	x	x	x	x	x	x	x	x
Parsnips	x	x	x							x	x	x
Peaches						x	x	x	x			
Pears								x	x	x	x	
Peas, Green				x	x	x	x					
Peppers								x	x	x		
Persians									x	x	x	
Plums						x	x	x	x			
Potatoes	x	x	x	x	x	x	x	x	x	x	x	x
Sweet Potatoes	x								x	x	x	x
Pumpkins										x		
Radishes			x	x	x	x	x					
Raspberries						x	x	x				
Rhubarb			x	x	x	x						
Shallots	x	x	x	x								x
Spinach			x	x	x	x						
Squash									x	x	x	x
Strawberries				x	x	x	x					
Tangerines	x										x	x
Tomatoes						x	x	x	x	x		
Turnips and Rutabagas	x	x	x							x	x	x
Watermelons						x	x	x				

Indexes

Index of Cheeses of the World

(by countries of origin)

Index of Recipes

General Index